LEAD!

BOOK TWO

LEAD!

BOOK TWO

Developing Your Leadership Style

GREGORY H. GARRISON

PEAKPOINT
PRESS

Peakpoint Press books may be purchased in bulk at special discounts for sales promotion, corporate gifts, fund-raising, or educational purposes. Special editions can also be created to specifications. For details, contact the Special Sales Department, Skyhorse Publishing, 307 West 36th Street, 11th Floor, New York, NY 10018 or info@skyhorsepublishing.com.

Peakpoint® and Peakpoint Press® are registered trademarks of Skyhorse Publishing, Inc.®, a Delaware corporation.

Visit our website at www.skyhorsepublishing.com.

10 9 8 7 6 5 4 3 2 1

Library of Congress Cataloging-in-Publication Data is available on file.

Cover design by Tom Lau and David Ter-Avanesyan

ISBN: 978-1-5107-8010-1
Ebook ISBN: 978-1-5107-8025-5

Printed in the United States of America

Dedicated to my sons Matthew and Christopher

Contents

Introduction

Enlightened and accomplished leadership are rare and valuable commodities in business today.

At this point, many of you will have already read *LEAD! Book 1: Finding Your Leadership Identity*. This extensive examination of the leadership field will have helped you learn and understand the successful underpinnings of leadership philosophy, theory, and principles, plus a review of current thought leadership. We then constructed a consummate model of the twenty essential characteristics of leadership through which you could assess, evolve, and find your own unique leadership identity.

While exceptional leadership is a lifelong journey, from that comprehensive foundation of knowledge and learning, we will now complete the second leg of our journey, that of learning and applying leadership best practices, skill development, methods, and tools through tried-and-true examples and robust case studies enabling us to develop our own distinctive leadership style.

Developing Your Leadership Style provides deep insight and expertise on effective "extrinsic operational behaviors," actions, and processes. This comprises cutting-edge and best-practice management techniques, tips, and the latest research into a vast array of leadership strategies and management methodologies. In addition, we impart extensive on-the-ground, real-world experience and detailed case studies on the practice and performance of leadership.

In addition to the comprehensive review of management methods and research, we provide an in-depth and imaginative study of creativity and innovation based on my experience running three innovation labs and initiatives. Further, extensive case studies derived from experience in multiple CIO/CTO roles and senior positions at two of the world's largest consultancies, PricewaterhouseCoopers (PwC) and Accenture, provide insightful, applicable, and proven approaches, techniques, and tools for outsourcing, managing external teams, virtual teaming, and remote working. Finally, we look at leadership strategies and cutting-edge organizational design methodologies.

With your leadership identity defined, and enhanced by this array of proven, practical skills, methods, technologies, and tools, you will be exceptionally well prepared to develop and apply your own unique leadership style in virtually any leadership role in the future.

Developing, refining, and mastering your leadership style will help you be more successful and result in more rewarding and worthwhile relationships with colleagues throughout your leadership career. Life and work are challenging but exciting journeys in which we all must strive to live to the fullest and finest we can. Let's continue our journey.

CHAPTER 1

Awakening the Muse—Conjuring Creativity and Catalyzing Innovation

Creativity

> *From a management standpoint, it is very important to know how to unleash people's inborn creativity . . . Anybody has creative ability, but very few people know how to use it.*
>
> —*Akio Morita, founder of Sony*[1]

Creativity is, of course, a profoundly important capability for any leader and the organization as a whole. Therefore, I included creativity as one of the prominent personal leadership characteristics in Book 1. Critically, however, in addition to the leader's own capabilities, here we provide guidance and a road map for developing and optimizing creativity throughout your staff and teams.

Creativity as the forerunner and catalyst to innovation is crucial in every business and, ideally, should be a core competence throughout the organization. However, that does not categorically mean that creativity must exist exclusively or even primarily in the leadership as it often does in new media and technology start-up businesses. Creativity must also exist within the team, and often with the leader taking on the additional role of enabler, champion, and supporter of creativity and innovation initiatives.

Whether you are the primary creative leader and catalyst, a creativity champion, or a creativity contributor, we would doubtless agree on the importance of strongly emphasizing and cultivating creativity and innovation in any organization. The primary rationale is that having a healthy pipeline of new products and services is vital for the organization's current and future success and for its evolution and transformation over time. Finally, it is a major contributor to your staff's motivation, satisfaction, and self-actualization.

As an innovation lab director, naturally, I was expected to possess some of these skills. Consequently, I've studied creativity extensively, particularly how to instill creativity and innovation in the team and organization, including the vital process of identifying, hiring, and developing many exceptionally creative staff. Without these outstanding individuals, we could never have achieved what we did. Thus, this chapter explores how you, as a leader, can build a creative culture and how to catalyze, develop, and manage creativity throughout your teams and across the extended organization.

Everyone contains attributes of creativity, initially perhaps some more and some less; however, I'm also convinced that creativity can be learned and undoubtedly developed further over time. Therefore, let's dissect creativity, how it occurs, and how to stimulate and support it within your team. Let's start by exploring creativity from a slightly analytical perspective, and then we can weave in examples and discussions relative to the imaginative, inventive, and innovative aspects of creativity.

The Creative Process

We are all familiar with "flashes of inspiration," "spontaneous insights," an "aha moment," or an "epiphany." Perhaps they've happened when you were shaving, cooking, driving, or when you wake in the middle of the night. Suddenly, the fog clears on a seemingly unresolvable predicament, and you see clearly how to solve a problem, do something immensely better or easier, or make an obscure connection between situations.

Those marvelous moments like Isaac Newton's legendary gravity insight from a falling apple are precious and invaluable, and we will discuss a number of those. However, we don't have to sit back and wait for the apple to fall, the Oracle of Delphi to prophesize, or the muse to speak to stimulate creativity and gain insight.

We can train ourselves and improve our ability to instinctively and consistently make those creative connections to generate insights. The more we develop and practice our creative skills and techniques, you will discover that spontaneous insights will increase in frequency as we learn to associate, correlate, extrapolate, deconstruct, and reconstruct new thoughts, ideas, models, products, and solutions.

Let's examine the science or analytics of creativity and how it can stimulate and inspire our imaginative and inventive thinking. My innovation teams and I developed the following "steps to creativity" along with the "innovation tool kits" in the next section to catalyze and stimulate creativity and foster ideation across the organization.

Challenge Statement—Crystallize and Frame the Issue

To start our creativity generation processes: Whether you encounter an intractable problem, have a specific "challenge" opportunity identified by the business, or desire an open-ended ideation workshop, start by breaking the issues down to their basics to understand and identify the root cause or challenge. This will help eliminate extraneous issues and distractions, allowing you to concentrate on the problem or opportunity without obfuscating the situation with irrelevant factors.

Next, simplify and constrain the issue down to its essence with as short and concise a statement as possible to frame and communicate it to the team or workshop participants. All this aids in crystallizing and focusing creative thinking and ideation onto the crux of the matter.

Gather Information and Identify Commonalities

With the precise challenge statement in hand, your next ideation task is to gather all relevant related information. Again, be careful not to add irrelevant or extraneous details that distract you and divert your thinking. During this process, attempt to log applicable or analogous commonalities while remembering and being cautious that "correlation is not causation"! Just because things look initially similar or related does not necessarily mean a causal connection exists.

Further, be careful not to digress into "analysis paralysis" or start leaping to conclusions at this point. We are still generating 360 degrees of information (remember holistic, system-thinking) for the next step of creativity, that of incubating the topic thoroughly. We are not yet ready to begin solutioning, as we could miss something important, novel, or unique if we leap to conclusions prematurely. Nothing is worse than taking a knee-jerk, snap decision to embark on a lengthy and costly, partial or faulty solution to a problem.

Incubation / Gestation

Here is where things get interesting. Once you have a focused agenda or campaign and have generated enough information and correlations to understand the issue at a high level, then the marvelous ingenuity of the mind takes over to ponder, compare, synthesize, and extrapolate the nuances of the matter. The issue drops into a sea of tens of billions of neurons in the brain, where it begins to glow and hum with the synthesizing interactions of conscious cognition, memory, and creative connections. While it is not our task to deconstruct consciousness, I'm sure you all appreciate this process and recognize that one must allow the mind time to disconnect from distractions, rest, and relax. Then, it can freely gestate on the issues, reduce information overload, and begin to crystallize, conceptualize, and work its creative correlations.

During this process, take your time, and make sure you honor your inner thoughts and follow your intuition, hunches, and insights. This is where the associative alchemy of the mind sparks those marvelous "flashes of inspiration," "aha moments," "spontaneous insights," and sometimes "epiphanies." Next, we'll come on to brainstorming, "free association," and other techniques for workshop groups to generate rich sets of scenarios and hypotheses on problem root causes, enabling or inhibiting activities and realizing potential solutions or new opportunities.

Generate multiple, diverse ideas

With all the background data in mind and having spent time in contemplative pondering and permitting the challenge to gestate subconsciously, it's time to collaborate creatively with your team, meeting, or workshop participants. In these lively and collaborative sessions, you can actively and playfully generate as many correlations and ideas as time permits about causality, influencing factors, conceptual gaps, missing elements, and early hypotheses relative to solutions.

There are hosts of approaches and methodologies for brainstorming and lateral thinking. You will find an extensive list of these techniques, tools, and alternatives in the Ideation section of the upcoming innovation chapter. Whichever method or device you use, they all encourage an imaginative, "playful" and nonjudgmental atmosphere of "thinking outside of the box" for ideation. For further information, Edward de Bono is a legendary pioneer in creative thinking, and his book *Six Thinking Hats*[2] is a good starting place.

During brainstorming, ensure that you provide a safe, lively, and lighthearted environment that allows participants to shift from their typical routine, analytical "left-brain" work modes to their more creative, associative, artistic, and social "right brain." The group can "free associate" in this setting using rich visual imagery and verbal analogy. Thoughts will float up from the subconscious incubation sessions and even surface wild and crazy ideas that morph and evolve through brainstorming to catalyze new and original concepts. Of course, many of these ideas will be throwaways, which is fine and to be expected. Still, the creative brainstorming process will also likely identify a novel, innovative approach, product, or solution that might not have been discovered through endless emails, tedious meetings, and traditional business strategy sessions.

Association / Compare and Combine Ideas

Eventually, you will discover the creative but mentally taxing brainstorming session's energy, creativity, and enthusiasm will begin to exhaust itself. People will tire mentally, and the volume and quality of idea generation will trail off. Being aware of this allows you to anticipate it and shift mental gears and energy from the lively idea generation to a more analytical and tactical mode. This is when you can begin to systematically compare and combine ideas to reduce the total number of ideas into a few richly elaborated concepts. Again, a caution that you may need to validate the linkage between situations as "correlation does not always imply causation." To vividly drive this point home, have a look at the hilarious book *Spurious Correlations*[3] and the website of the same name by Tyler Vigen.[4]

Diverge /Converge and Deconstruct/Reconstruct

With a rich list of elaborated concepts, you can now embellish and mature your ideas through some tried and proven analysis methods. Building on the previous exercise of combining and enriching the proposed ideas, you can elaborate, extend, and challenge these ideas through the concepts of convergence and divergence. Ask what and how you might combine and converge these ideas, products, or solutions with other ideas or solutions, and further, how they might be different and diverge to create something entirely new. Likewise, by consciously deconstructing these ideas or solutions into their constituent parts, you may see novel approaches to issues that might not be apparent when looking at them holistically or at a high level. In this manner, you may have a new insight or identify a suboptimal system element that can be redesigned or replaced to improve the overall solution.

Once you have deconstructed the issue into its constituent parts, consider how it can be reconstructed in new ways, potentially in conjunction with other solutions or ideas. This appears simplistic at first glance; however, by robustly applying these techniques of convergence and divergence, deconstruction, and reconstruction, my innovation labs were able to identify numerous new value-creating products and features. I share a couple of interesting examples at the end of this chapter.

Narrow the Options/Final Selection

With a rich dataset of ideas, inspirations, solutions, or new product suggestions, the next thing to do is document all the ideas carefully. This will ensure you don't lose anything in your rush to make a final selection or recommendation. It also assures you capture any other related ideas that might be appropriate and worthwhile in the future.

You'll be surprised how often during the brainstorming, someone will say, "Ah yes, we talked about that same thing a few years ago!" Well, that may be, but did they do anything about it? Therefore, documenting each idea, even if premature at the moment or unrelated to the issue at hand, is vital to capturing the full value from the rich pool of ideas generated through brainstorming.

Now, you need to narrow the options and make a final selection. There are many ways of achieving this, from polling the workshop participants, voting on the solutions, or widening the decision-making beyond the workshop participants to involve business partners and stakeholders. This will ensure that your final decision is representative of the business and the requirements at large.

My favorite tool for analyzing and informing the selection, voting, and decision process is the "Efficient Frontier" matrix and graph (see below and the end of this chapter for more detail). It is a simple but powerful visualization and analysis tool for mapping your ideas and products on a grid. In this approach, benefit and value are plotted on the x-axis, and complexity and cost are plotted on the y-axis. This will allow you to rapidly identify quick wins as well as strategic or game-changing opportunities. In addition, plotting each idea's cost/benefit is extremely helpful for informing participants of the viability and value in the prioritization, voting, and final selection process. Furthermore, the Efficient Frontier tool can facilitate decision-making in a workshop mode. Finally, you can create a highly sophisticated, quantitatively reinforced version for a formal presentation and to create a persuasive business case.

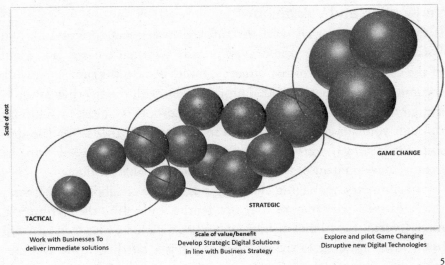

Scale of cost

GAME CHANGE

STRATEGIC

TACTICAL

Work with Businesses To
deliver immediate solutions

Scale of value/benefit
Develop Strategic Digital Solutions
in line with Business Strategy

Explore and pilot Game Changing
Disruptive new Digital Technologies

This powerful but easy-to-use concept and diagram, derived from economist Dr. Harry Markowitz's Nobel Prize–winning "Efficient Frontier" investment theory,[6] can be applied rapidly in most decision-making and investment business case situations.

Observation/Experimentation

We now arrive at the stage where all the brainstorming, creative thinking, and analysis have provided you with rich and innovative ideas and recommendations that look viable and valuable based on the initial assessment measures. Expanding the exposure and alignment of your proposals to a broader, cross-functional group of stakeholders, including the business, business processes, operations, finance, and IT, will give a crucial 360-degree evaluation of the solution's feasibility.

Now is the time to bring in other resources and diverse skills to observe, analyze, and prove the solution through a "low-fidelity" (cheap and cheerful) assessment, including potentially a proof of concept (PoC). If the PoC is successful and agreed upon with stakeholders, you can move on to prototype, internal alpha tests, and then externally with beta trials. Remember to use fleet-of-foot agile methodologies to focus on a minimum viable product (MVP) rather than machinating endlessly or prematurely on an overdesigned industrial-strength solution.

Verification and Validation

If everything goes well with the internal assessment, prototypes, and PoCs, you can package the results, prepare a formal business case, and in the case of a large formal project submit them to the project steering committee for evaluation and approval. Then, with the steering committee, go ahead; you are ready to present the products, ideas, or solutions through your governance processes to the business owners and leadership. Or ideally, if your culture and processes permit, proceed with the iterative development of your initial minimum viable product.

In summary, managing creativity is an active collaboration between the "creatives" who may or may not be the leadership, the champions, management, functional operations, and stakeholders who own and will implement and operate the product or service. Further, it involves creative ideation processes to generate new and unique ideas, plus analytic and systematic techniques to assess the product or solution's viability. Finally, you will need the input, buy-in, and alignment of the internal operational and execution teams to take the idea from a creative concept through to a viable launch.

Following is a practical personal case study that is an example of some of the aforementioned creativity techniques and tools demonstrating:

- A flash of inspiration
- Association and comparison
- Convergence and divergence
- Synthesis and extrapolation
- Elaboration and execution
- Team collaboration

We then transition from catalyzing creativity to inspiring and instilling innovation processes in an organization.

Takeaway: Creativity as the forerunner and catalyst for innovation is crucial for every business. Ensure you build a creative culture and catalyze creativity across your entire team. Practice the skills of association, correlation, extrapolation, deconstruction, and reconstruction until they become habitual.

A Crisis Catalyzing a Creative Idea

During the spring and summer of 1994, the catastrophic Rwandan genocide occurred. The Rwandan Hutu majority slaughtered an estimated 800,000 Tutsi Rwandans. In my experience, this was the first international political/humanitarian crisis that tragically unfolded with live television coverage, minute by minute, day by day, right before our eyes.

One late night, I sat in front of my television, transfixed by the tragedy, overwhelmed by the senseless slaughter and the ineffectiveness, impotence, and inadequacy of the international aid response. I questioned how it was possible, in that day and age, that I could sit in the comfort of my home in London and watch the massacre and suffering on live TV half a world away. What kind of world do we live in? How can the journalists stand there and film the tragedy? At the time, I worked for Reuters and understood the journalistic code. Journalists were to be objective and impartial and not to interject themselves directly into the events they cover. However, I had to ask myself, if I was there, could I (should I) stand by dispassionately? This is a perennial debate and challenge for journalists as they risk their lives and limbs to bring us honest and unbiased information on pressing events.

One poignant moment triggered a flood of emotion and anger. A journalist (not Reuters) was doing a voice-over of the evacuation of a group of refugees. An overcrowded, decrepit bus was pulling away from a mob of people. Hanging half out of the bus, a young woman was reaching desperately for a child of perhaps five or six who was running for her life, trying to grasp the outstretched arms. The bus accelerated, and the child stumbled, sealing her fate. The mother screamed, and the journalist fatefully zoomed in on the inconsolable child. She commented this was only one of the thousands of daily occurrences where the parent and child were separated. She continued; the probable consequence was that they were unlikely ever to see each other again. I fumed, I ranted, I wept. "How in the name of God can you film that? Drop the goddamn camera, grab the child, race alongside the bus, and hand her to the mother!" I could not accept this detached, objective attitude. Code or no code, we had a moral responsibility that superseded any commercial or professional practice.

I was working for Reuters at the time, yet I could not accept what had happened, what was happening. If you are not part of the solution, you are part of the problem![7] Full stop. While not a journalist, I knew many in London and from my years in Hong Kong and Singapore, where I belonged to the Foreign Correspondents Club. To be fair, there are countless amazing, committed, and concerned journalists, people with heart and conscience. And many have lost their lives and limbs in the process.

But what could we do? What should we do? In my mind's eye, as a technologist, I immediately envisioned us outfitting our journalists with satellite phones, tape recorders, video cameras, and every technology and mobile convenience to be packed off to places like Biafra and Rwanda to chronicle the pathos and tragedies unfolding daily. I also simultaneously envisioned the idealistic, struggling charity workers rushing to the aid, ill-equipped to struggle against overwhelming odds to make a small dent in the cataclysmic suffering. Why couldn't we work together as actors or protagonists in the same crises? My passionate but obviously flawed image was of frantic aid workers desperately searching for a phone, fax, or telex with quarters in their hands to make an urgent call and plea for help. All of which would undoubtedly arrive far too late for whatever circumstance they were dealing with at that moment. All the while, the exhausted journalists, after a grueling day, are perhaps sitting in a bar anesthetizing their distress or flat out in bed in stunned despondency with all their gear, including the satellite phone, sitting idly by.

My rant continued: journalists don't file stories twenty-four hours a day! Why can't we work with NGOs and charities to let them use our state-of-the-art telecommunications to uplink these urgent relief requests instantly, in real time, to anyone, everyone, anywhere in the world? It would be a small payback for the fact that the news agencies make money reporting the news, even for catastrophes like this!

"That could work! That should work!" Now, my non-journalistic technologist background shifted into high gear. There are always problems all over the place and all the time. "Why do we just sit around and wait for them to happen?" Whether in business or global relief, preparation, logistics, and readiness are the key to a rapid response to any eventuality. "We could set up a network of aid and news agencies and, in a nonpolitical way, organize ourselves to be prepared in advance and ready to respond whenever a crisis hits. If we had the communications network, operational system, and organization, we could share requirements and information with the communications tools already at our disposal. If we shared vital, urgent information, then we could create a database of critical necessities and instantly spread the word among the relief community and news agencies to see who could help!" The ideas poured out of me over a couple of hours, and I sketched out a cross-functional, joined-up international aid and journalistic organization. Once a database existed and we logged and shared information, we could instantly flash the emergency needs out to the rest of the world.

Further, we could tap into the moral conscience of not just the journalist community but the corporate community. Virtually every major corporation has its own philanthropic charities. Why couldn't we connect with them, too, contacting them directly, alerting them to the crisis and any specific need they might be uniquely placed to address? For example, why couldn't Macy's in Chicago respond to a need for hundreds of blankets from their overstock or unsold seasonal sales? Walmart has over two thousand stores; couldn't they provide excess unsold food that was ready to go stale? What about GlaxoSmithKline, which might have thousands of units of antibiotics about to stale-date? They would likely be willing to donate them and even write them off on their taxes,

Anticipation, planning, preparation, and logistics are the keys to the puzzle. For example, the United States moved half of a million people into the middle of the Saudi desert in preparation for Desert Storm, with food, lodging, materials, and even video theaters, for goodness' sake. Therefore, it should certainly be possible to marshal the resources to save half a million poor souls, including children, from starvation or worse. I recalled that Caterpillar Corporation, the manufacturer of huge earth-moving machinery, could supply machine parts virtually anywhere in the world within twenty-four hours and guaranteed delivery within forty-eight hours. If they could move a huge piece of machinery anywhere within twenty-four hours, why is it taking weeks or months to supply food and medicine to starving children? With our telecommunications, databases, network of protagonists, and commodity suppliers, we could use the same technology Reuters used for instantaneous global commodities trading to bring it all together with partners to reengineer the charities' entire worldwide supply chain overnight.

"We could then ask the transportation suppliers and airlines to provide logistics and shipment." My idea was to go to British Airways, which had the most extensive aviation network globally, and ask them for urgent spare cargo space. We could ship the blankets from Chicago, food from California, and medicine from London to Rwanda, the Middle East, or Asia whenever and wherever needed. If BA wasn't interested, we could go to Richard Branson, who certainly would like the idea, and then other airlines' consciences would be piqued to participate as well!"

The crisis ensued, the idea germinated, and a concept took form. AlertNet had its origin during that late-night flurry of frustration to make some attempt to eradicate the monstrous carnage and to reengineer the unnecessary fragmentation of the relief community to optimize it for hyperefficiency.

I then had the idea and while I fervently believed in the concept, I didn't know how to proceed with such an ambitious venture. Various impassioned conversations with Reuters' staff ultimately led to Stephen Somerville, director of the Reuters Foundation. Stephen was a person of vision and a very enterprising and well-connected individual who immediately bought into the vision and took on the role of championing and catalyzing the idea.

The extraordinary synchronicity of this meeting was that Stephen instantly saw the concept's potential and that it could also be highly beneficial for Reuters, whose news business thrived on geopolitical, environmental, and climatic events. While Reuters makes a great deal of money reporting on the news, it could also be part of the solution through its vast communication network and technical systems support for the global aid and NGO communities' efforts. The idea took off, and AlertNet was presented and accepted by Reuters' board of directors.

While slightly different, somewhat scaled-down, but more immediately pragmatic than I had envisioned, the solution blossomed. It rapidly exploded into a nonpolitical NGO community where aid agencies could communicate, share information and resources, and publicize

major humanitarian events globally through the AlertNet website. Over
the next few years, under Stephen's and the dedicated staff's guidance,
AlertNet grew to be the world's largest NGO community at that time.
It created a collaborative relief community communications hub to
respond immediately to aid humanitarian crises worldwide. After the
Reuters acquisition by Thomson, the name was changed to trust.org.
http://www.trust.org.[8]

The British government subsequently recognized AlertNet through
a Millennium Award in 2000.[9] I can't take the credit for the tremendous, follow-on work that Stephen and the AlertNet team achieved
over the next ten years. Nevertheless, it was my idea and concept, and
I know in my heart that although it may not have aided that original
mother and child, I am certain that some family and some child somewhere has been touched by the creation of this concept and through
this program.

This important footnote in my life has taught me that a single person
with an idea and a vision can absolutely make a difference in the world
despite feelings of stunned impotence in the face of enormous global
challenges. But, further, critically, beyond the initial inspiration and
idea, it takes a committed team to turn that dream into a reality.

I trust these ideas have demonstrated how one's creative juices can be
stirred and inspired by an urgent need. Further, dare to believe in yourself and think BIG! I remind you of a reference I made in Book 1, where
Terry Leahy in *Management in Ten Words*[10] provides a terrific quote from
Architect Daniel Burnham, "Make no little plans. They have no magic
to stir men's blood."[11] You may not always be successful, but, if you continue to go to bat and keep swinging, you may just hit a home run, as in
the case of AlertNet.

Picking up on the difference between simply having a good creative
idea and delivering a successful solution. First, your nascent creative ideas
must be incubated and gestated into an innovative concept or invention,
which can be developed, refined, and delivered into a formal executable
plan or innovation. Next, let's examine innovation in detail, which represents the critical catalyst and processes for taking creative ideas and
inventions and transforming them into viable operational or commercial
successes.

Imagination is more important than knowledge. For knowledge is limited, whereas imagination embraces the entire world.
                                                              —*Albert Einstein*[12]

Takeaway: The fundamental difference between having a creative idea and creating successful innovation is effective execution.

Innovation—the Successful Exploitation of Ideas

Innovation has nothing to do with how many R&D dollars you have. It's not about money. It's about the people you have, how you're led, and how much you get it.

—*Steve Jobs, Apple*[13]

The classic distinction between invention and innovation is that invention is the creation of a new idea or concept, while innovation is the commercialization of the new idea into a commercial or operational success. Therefore, innovation is not just a blinding flash of inspiration by a creative genius; any idea must be consciously catalyzed, and moreover, it must also be carefully cultivated, developed, and implemented.

No business leadership discussion can be complete without an in-depth exploration of innovation as a core principle and requirement for an effective leader. Innovation has been a lifelong journey for me, beginning with my father's frequent inventions around the house, striving to improve things in line management roles, and creating and running three separate corporate innovation initiatives and labs.

My first innovation lab was at Reuters Group in the 1990s, which I referred to previously and provide a detailed case study of later on. The second was an Innovation Lab Initiative for PricewaterhouseCoopers in London in 2007–2008. The third was creating the TUI Group Innovation Labs in 2013–2016. Thus, innovation is an integral part of my leadership journey, as well as being part of my management tool kit. Consequently, with that orientation and background, let's examine the topic extensively here.

Innovation has been an increasing topic of interest and discussion for decades. Attention to innovation has dramatically intensified over the past twenty years with the explosion of the high tech and new media industries and the increased emphasis on technology within professional services firms. Regardless of the industry, virtually every company is now a digital technology company that demands a continuous stream of innovation to compete and thrive. In Steve Jobs's words: "Innovation differentiates a leader from a follower." Therefore, my assumption is that no reader would doubt that innovation is essential for any organization, and further, to be a highly effective leader, one must actively and competently foster innovation. Thus, our challenge is how to do effective innovation, as well as how to set up and run an innovation initiative and avoid the many pitfalls of creating and running innovation programs in corporations.

Following is a detailed discussion of the topic, with examples from my innovation lab experiences, including successes, failures, and lessons learned from both.

Sparking Innovation

As discussed in the previous chapter, creativity and innovation are inextricably connected. Creativity is the inventive process, and innovation is the implementation and commercialization of that invention.

Having explored the theme of creativity extensively, we will now focus on catalyzing and transforming that creativity into a commercial success. The creative process is both an art and a science; therefore, you will benefit significantly from developing and mastering your creativity techniques and employing an ideation tool kit for catalyzing innovation.

As we delve into innovation, I encourage you to refer frequently to the creativity section as a vital link and corollary to the innovation processes. Key topics and associated techniques to review are:

> The Creative Process
> Challenge Statement—Crystallize and Frame Issues
> Gather Information and Identify Commonalities
> Incubation/Gestation
> Generate Multiple Diverse Ideas
> Association/Compare and Combine Ideas
> Diverge/Converge and Deconstruct/Reconstruct
> Narrow the Options/Final Selection
> Observation/Experimentation
> Verification and Validation

As a powerful introduction to the topic, the following discussion of the Medici Effect vividly details the process of creativity and how to successfully catalyze innovation.

The Medici Effect

The Medici Effect is an innovation classic that explores why the most powerful innovation happens at the Intersection, where ideas and concepts from diverse industries, cultures, and disciplines collide. Innovation today is less about expertise and more about how you can rapidly combine insights and ideas, often widely disparate, to create surprising and unique breakthroughs.

—*Frans Johansson*[14]

The Medici Effect: Breakthrough Insights at the Intersection of Ideas, Concepts, and Cultures *is a 2004 book by Swedish entrepreneur Frans Johansson.*[15]

16

If you've not read *The Medici Effect*, I highly recommend it. I found it exceptionally insightful and applicable to my innovation roles and responsibilities. *The Medici Effect* concept and techniques further influenced my strategies and methods for instilling creativity and variety into teams and innovation activities. I'll briefly lay out the initial context and summarize the fundamental principles, which should not obviate the value of reading this outstanding book.

The Medici family was an Italian banking and textile dynasty from Florence, Italy, in the fourteenth century. A fortuitous coincidence was that at the same time, Johannes Gutenberg in Germany invented moveable type, which fueled an explosion of mechanical book publication, essentially replacing hand-copied books. This then stimulated a growth in literacy, dramatically increasing the demand for rag paper used for printing in those days. As the dominant supplier of textiles and rag, the

Medicis were among the principal financial beneficiaries of this immense increased demand.

As a result, the Medicis became one of Europe's wealthiest families and became extensive patrons of the arts. The Medicis sponsored artists, painters, sculptors, writers, poets, scientists, architects, physicians, and philosophers and also provided housing, studios, and supplies for many of them. Among the many artists, scientists, and thinkers the Medici sponsored were Leonardo da Vinci, Raphael, Donatello, Michelangelo, Machiavelli, and Galileo.

This was an exceptionally diverse collection of artists and thinkers cast together, creating an extraordinary boiling cauldron of creativity through the cross-fertilization of ideas and talents. Each discipline advanced dramatically in its own right but also became a catalyst for spurring the creativity of the others. Each individual shared, compared, and inspired the others to new heights and in new directions.

One vividly documented example is how Michelangelo, through his interactions with physicians, studied science, medicine, and surgery, which included human autopsies to profoundly understand the physical structure of the bodies he so graphically depicted in his sculptures and paintings. Undoubtedly, Leonardo da Vinci would have also interacted with scientists, artists, and architects, providing rich stimulus to enhance his prodigious artistic, scientific, and creative talents.

Each of these fields was remarkably enriched, and eventually, new ideas and even new disciplines began to blend and merge at the "intersection" of the boundaries between the diverse specialties. This melding and fusion of ideas spawned entirely new concepts, techniques, and original approaches to art, techniques, and tools. This creative explosion and subsequent flourishing of the arts and ideas contributed significantly to and was perhaps even the initial spark that ignited the Renaissance. This blossoming of ideas and talent helped wrestle Europe out of the clutches of the Dark Ages/Middle Ages as a vital stimulus for the transition to the modern world.[17]

These concepts have dramatic implications for us as leaders. Whether you are an aspiring leader or c-suite executive, we are all expected to contribute to the continuous improvement of our products and services, as well as being innovators and positive agents of change. Ensuring we have sufficient creative talent and diversity in our organizations is the primary condition for establishing a creative work culture. Then, actively training and leading the teams with the tools and techniques described in *The Medici Effect* and will ensure you have an active and robust innovation modus operandi.

As we dissect these dramatic macro-level transformations, we can distill down what transpired into the underlying or causative factors. These "synergies," as Frans describes them, using "associative thinking" at the "intersection" between the disciplines, encouraged the enhancement and extrapolation of ideas and concepts to extend into adjacent and entirely new areas.

Associative thinking and the simultaneous breaking down of the barriers (i.e., low associative barriers) between domain boundaries can result in expansively creating new ideas and products at the intersection of disciplines. Further, it is a powerful tool for converging different perspectives, ideas, and activities to develop new solutions and resolve specific problems. The employment of diverse tools and technologies, as well as cultural, racial, ethnic, and gender diversity, enhances perspectives for creative problem-solving and can significantly inspire new product design.

Specifically, this means looking at a problem or potential opportunity and considering how other situations, products, or services are similar, dissimilar, or could relate to it. Then, how can you apply and combine successful concepts or solutions from another area or domain to solve the problem or create a new product or service?

Association, intersection, convergence, and extrapolation tools and skills are some of the simple but powerful innovation techniques presented in *The Medici Effect*. Over the years, I have had considerable success using these same tools to advance my innovation endeavors.

Fred Smith cites an excellent example of associative thinking regarding the founding of Federal Express:

> *My innovation involved taking an idea from the telecommunications and banking industries and applying that idea to the transportation business.*
> —*Frederick W. Smith, founder and chairman of FedEx*[18]

Another outstanding example of intersection and association is how Mick Pearce, a Zimbabwean architect, became intrigued by how termites built their mounds. Termites construct an optimal structure to cool themselves naturally through atriums, chimneys, and cooling vents. He studied and employed these concepts as a metaphoric model for designing a major retail and office building in Harare, Zimbabwe. These approaches provided natural cooling for the building complex in the blazing African heat while simultaneously cutting air-conditioning costs.[19]

Clayton Jacobson is another brilliant example of product innovation at the intersection of different domains. His family moved from Norway to Minnesota in the early twentieth century and later to Oregon and Southern California. As a thrill-seeking young man, Clayton liked anything that went fast, from street racing and snowmobiling in winter to motorcycle racing in summer. Eventually, his fascination with speed and engines took him to the US Marine Corps Aviation, where he worked on airplane jet engines.

After the Marines, he became an avid motorcycle racer. One day, after a motorcycle spill on the gravel in the Mojave desert, he lamented the falls and mused it would be great if you could have the thrill of motorcycle racing without the danger. As the story goes, that night, with his knowledge and experience of motorcycles, snowmobiles, and airplanes, he conceived of a converged jet-powered snowmobile/motorcycle that would race across the water. It promised the thrill of the race without the peril of the falls. Thus, the Sea-Doo and, subsequently, the Jet Ski were born. It is fascinating to consider how the Jet Ski was conceived by an associative idea in the white space at the intersection of the orthogonally related snowmobile, motorcycle, airplane, and kayak. His innovation created an entirely new class of sports vehicle, the PWC—personal watercraft.[20] This idea and the resulting product creations made Clayton a multimillionaire by following his vision, passion, and creativity.

Finally, a recent 2020 example of the Medici Effect association and convergence is a major artificial intelligence breakthrough in three-dimensional DNA "protein folding," which has puzzled scientists for fifty years. Demis Hassabis, the cofounder of Google DeepMind, was inspired by digital gaming technologies to apply novel approaches to artificial intelligence to solve this challenge.[21]

The bottom line is that we all have diverse experiences, backgrounds, and perspectives, regardless of our title or seniority. We can draw on those distinct differences and expertise to examine each problem or opportunity uniquely. We can consciously create the habit of thinking radically and expansively about each situation, recognizing its unique characteristics, and then trying to compare, contrast, or associate it with other things within our experience. You can then combine and extrapolate these ideas into new concepts, solutions, or products.

In retrospect, in analyzing my career's twists and turns, I can see how the Medici Effect of associative thinking at the intersection of diverse subjects distinctly influenced my career development. For example, my early medical, neurology, and cognitive sciences studies later influenced my thinking as a training director, running technology usability, and then as a psychometric testing company COO. Further, my training and usability roles became a critical foundation for designing new products in my responsibility as a CTO. Finally, all this contributed to my roles as an innovation director and enhanced my insights and value as a strategy and technology consultant.

As I look back on the learnings, associations, and synergies from one role to another, I couldn't have imagined or anticipated how each of these highly diverse jobs and experiences would positively and directly influence and enhance the subsequent ones. We all have personal and career journeys that create our experience and build our capabilities. Take a moment to consciously map the treads of your experiences through your successive roles and how this foreshadows potential future career opportunities.

I'll share two concrete personal examples of associative thinking and the intersection of adjacent domains, as in the Medici Effect, in my own life relating to my time at Reuters Group. The first was the AlterNet.Org solution discussed. I'll briefly mention the second, as we will revisit this in a more detailed case study later. When I was the training director for Reuters in Asia, I began developing computer-based training and e-learning to cope with the explosion of new products across the vastness of the Asian market. This led me to recommend building support systems into products to improve our products' usability and avoid training entirely. I was subsequently reassigned to the London home office to reengineer our product range. Applying my training and cognitive sciences experience in analyzing the problem led to the conception and creation of a global usability lab network to understand customer workflows and design improved product usability. It sounds basic today, but remember, this was the 1990s.

Subsequently, one day, when flying back from Hong Kong to London, I was on the upper deck of a 747 in an aisle seat with a good viewpoint of the pilot's cockpit and flight controls. As a technologist and usability specialist, it was evident that the instruments were rigorously optimized for pilot control. I'd also recently read about "heads up" controls for fighter pilots where the instrument displays were projected on the pilot's visor or potentially the windscreen. As I reflected on recent usability tests, it struck me that the financial traders' workstations, with their vast amount of data, analytics, and graphs, were overly complicated and operationally suboptimal for their complex split-second trading tasks. The idea struck me: we should learn from the fighter pilot environment to see what lessons we could adopt to redesign our Reuters trading system to emulate a fighter pilot's navigation environment.

When I shared this idea at the office, one of my directors, Peter, had coincidentally been playing with a fighter pilot game simulation. We then used pilot navigation systems as an analogy and model to design and prototype a highly optimized new financial trading workstation. The "intersection" and convergence of financial trading systems, usability labs, pilot navigation systems, and computer gaming all contributed to the concept and design of an innovative new banking financial trading system.

I subsequently shared this story with colleagues at What*IF*!, a specialist innovation firm that featured the idea in the following feature on innovation in their book *Sticky Wisdom*.

Takeaway: Remember the Medici Effect technique of associative thinking at the intersection of products and services to explore, extend, and expand your products and services into adjacent markets.

Greg Garrison's flight of fancy

In 1993, Greg Garrison was put in charge of a key initiative at the financial services and information giant, Reuters. Garrison was given the task of improving the usability of the computer trading systems the company supplies to the dealing rooms of banks in over 130 countries.

A key aim of new product development was to ensure that computer systems—especially the graphical interface that the customer sees—can be mastered quickly, so that dealers minimize their down-time. In a business where millions of dollars can be made and lost at the stroke of a keyboard, users of the Reuters systems were understandably reluctant to spend time retraining. Usability was vital. They said they didn't have time to read instruction manuals, but were adept at feeling their way.

What was needed, the Reuters team realized, was a graphical interface that was easy to learn, and could master updated features. With the launch of the company's new product range approaching, the team sought inspiration. But in the pressure cooker atmosphere of the company's London base, the creative juices didn't seem to be flowing. Even the cool-headed Garrison was starting to worry. A breakthrough was needed. But it wasn't going to happen in the office.

Garrison set off on one of his frequent fact-finding missions, travelling to the Far East to talk to customers in other markets. Away from the hustle and bustle of the Fleet Street office, he relaxed. His curiosity returned. He began to search out fresh stimulus to jolt his thinking around the task.

On his return flight he asked to see the flight deck of the 747 he was travelling on. Surrounded by a wall of sophisticated instrumentation, he was amazed at how pilots could move from one aircraft to another in the same class with such ease—and without retraining. When he asked them, the pilots explained that instruments were arranged in a logical and consistent way across the 747 class, which made flying one aircraft much the same as any other.

Garrison made a new connection. What if the graphical interface on the next generation of Reuters systems was modeled on a pilot's cockpit? It would mean that switching from one system to an updated system would be relatively straightforward. Back in London, he reported this idea to the rest of the team. The idea took off.

Team members built on the original insight, adding a range of features that included autopilots and navigators, which would help the dealers find their way around the new system. Like a pilot's instrument panel, the idea was to place technical support and training at the customer's fingertips. At the touch of a button, traders would be able to move from the realtime market environment into on-screen simulations, calling up features such as autopilot tools to steer them through products—without having to call Reuters for support. In the end, the system was not implemented in full as it was superseded by adherence to the new Microsoft Office style desktop environment. Nevertheless, many of the tools the aviation metaphor gave rise to were included in the next generation of Reuters products, providing trading and operating support for end-users.

The Innovator's Dilemma

Motivation is the catalyzing ingredient for every successful innovation.
—Clayton Christensen[23]

As we have stressed, creativity and innovation are the lifeblood and future of any organization. However, catalyzing new creativity into innovation and commercializing new ideas into successful products is notoriously challenging. Further, for established companies and products, new innovations and disruptive technologies present significant risks to companies that are unable to adapt and evolve rapidly enough to keep pace with new technologies and market developments. Dr. Clayton Christensen from Harvard, who coined the term "disruptive technologies," has articulated this problem perhaps better than anyone in his book *The Innovator's Dilemma.*

Dr. Clayton Christensen—Harvard Business School

24

The Innovator's Dilemma—Why Good Management Can Lead to Failure— Sustaining versus Disruptive Technologies[25]

This brilliant and still renowned book written in the late 1990s was inspiring and formative for me just as I jumped ship from Reuters Group to catch the internet wave. I'll share my takeaways from Clayton's book, including my own successes and failures relating to the principles he discusses. These innovation experiences will add color and personal credence to the Innovator's Dilemma; however, I still encourage you to read this trailblazing book on innovation and disruptive technology.

One of Clayton's central ideas is that successful organizations self-reinforce, entrench, and perpetuate their tried and proven product research and development behaviors that have been historically successful in creating the existing company's products and services. However, these same capabilities and learned behaviors that were successful and appropriate for the current products and services may be insufficient or entirely inappropriate for new emerging and "disruptive" products in new markets. As a result, this traditional approach may ultimately result in a product death spiral, leading to their demise. Remember, sometimes prior skills, tactics, and tools are inadequate for new challenges, especially in evolving and emerging markets.

This is particularly perilous for successful and mature multinationals that embark into new hyper-growth industries where change is no longer incremental but radical, exponential, and disruptive. In these cases, the pace of technological progress will often outstrip what the markets need over time. While the traditional company is diligently occupied with improving and incrementing its entrenched product range, a vacuum may be created at the lower end of the market.

Thus, new entrants can gain entry into the lower, cheaper, entry-level end of the market and begin to consolidate their beachhead. These new entrants with disruptive new technologies initially functionally underperform in the marketplace, with simpler and often easier-to-use products compared to the market leaders. Consequently, they start encroaching on and capturing the lower end of the traditional leaders' market share.

All the while, under the radar of the market leaders, the disruptive players with cheap and cheerful products, initially making market entry via low price, begin to develop new modern features that touch just the right customer nerves and gain traction.

Eventually, they develop just enough and more modern features and at a much more attractive price point. He then points out the next element of failure in the traditional company's relentless drive to maximize market share and product revenues. The traditional player eventually detects the encroachment and loss of market share and often responds with even more exclusive products and features at higher prices to defend their existing revenue levels.

Meanwhile, with its single-minded focus on perfecting its current products for its existing clients, the traditional company often overdesigns and frequently overshoots the market's needs. The company's overdesign often results in bloated products with a plethora of features that are well in excess of the client's basic needs. This results in heavyweight or luxury products that provide customers with more functionality than they need and at a higher price point than they are comfortable with, especially when compared with the appeal of the streamlined new entrants.

Further, given the traditional company's established models for product design and revenue expectations, their investment assessment for the lower end of the market does not stand up financially against their current business metrics. So, in denial, they refuse to invest in the simpler, lighter, and cheaper end of the market until it's too late.

Finally, they embark on defensive trench warfare with extraneous bells and whistles and discounts to protect the existing product and revenues and cede more and more market share and territory over time. Thus, the vicious cycle of decline begins with the disruptive player taking over more and more of the incumbent's territory and market share.[26]

We have all witnessed similar excessive and misguided product developments in the past twenty years with the growth of software product suites, desktop operating systems, ERP suites, financial products, consumer electronics, and even luxury cars. Particularly vivid examples are the modern TV and entertainment systems' remote controls with thirty to forty buttons, which defy logic and usable operation for many who repeatedly lament or even curse their complexity. Then compare this with the elegant simplicity and function of the Apple TV remote control with a grand total of three buttons! Exquisitely usable!

Dr. Christensen models the sustainable versus disruptive product trajectory through the following diagram:

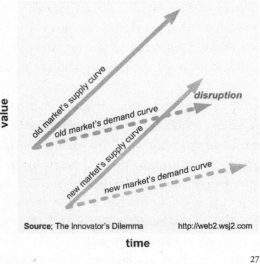

Disruptive Innovation

27

Dr. Christensen goes on to crystallize the Disruptive Technologies and Innovation Dilemma and provides guidance on recognizing and dealing with this challenge.

Harnessing the Principles of Disruptive Innovation

Principle 1: Resource Dependence. Companies rely not only upon their organization for resources but on Customers and Investors as well

As we've described, successful companies are very effective at defending their business model and current ways of operating. Consequently, they effectively kill off new disruptive ideas, including innovations and especially disruptive technologies that realize lower margins. That is, until it is too late. Further, it is extremely difficult to reinvent within the existing structures and strictures of the traditional organization.

He cites examples of organizations that have successfully combatted the competition and adopted new technologies. However, historically, this has been almost exclusively by setting up new independent and autonomous organizations (often referred to as "skunk works") and through adopting and deploying new modern disruptive technologies alongside or outside the existing organization.

An example I am familiar with is Accenture, the world's largest systems integrator with major offerings in the ERP and supply chain areas. Over recent years, it's made a significant move and investment in digital transformation and new, more modern, and flexible technologies. Had they overconfidently and sluggishly languished as the market leader in traditional technologies, they would have ceded significant ground to new entrants. Instead, they have embraced and, in many cases, snapped up these new competitors. This is an excellent example of a massive multinational that has brought about its own transformation, thus securing its future.

Principle 2: Disruptive technologies are a precursor to the creation of new emerging markets.

Dr. Christensen further stresses the criticality of the first-mover advantage, which needs to be recognized and adopted or overcome by the traditional company. However, if one does not enjoy a first-mover advantage or become a fast follower, then the organization must think carefully about the market and its product range to determine how to address this emerging disconnect, often with an adjacent or orthogonal offering or even potentially exiting that part of the market.

The current artificial intelligence (AI) business and technology transformation represents this generation's greatest opportunity and, conversely, risk. The sluggishness of many companies in embracing digital transformation in the past should be a stinging lesson relative to the take-up of AI. If you are not currently on the AI runway, you are involuntarily on a journey toward obsolescence.

Principle 3: Nonexisting markets can't be assessed by traditional research and Financial Methodologies.

Another challenging dilemma for the mature organization is that it is particularly tricky to build a strong business case for a significant investment in a nascent or emerging market with traditional metrics, financial planning, and business case development. The situation is even more challenging for a product or market that either does not exist or does not have a sufficient track history to build financial models and business cases according to existing tools and metrics currently used in the traditional company.

Over the years, these situations have been the bane of my existence in promoting innovation within multinationals. I struggled for a decade and a half from 2000 to 2015 in virtually every company I worked for or consulted with to try to open their eyes to the new, then nonexistent, or nascent mobile internet market and mobile content applications and services. It seems incredible from the current vantage point, but it was an enormous challenge to get entrenched management to look over the parapet to see the light. These stakeholders would occasionally see the opportunity. However, because of the existing market and financial projection methodologies, they would not take the bold leap of faith necessary to invest in the new technology and market to seize the high ground through a first-mover advantage strategy. In particular, when it meant possibly sunsetting or jettisoning an existing product or service.

Again, as mentioned previously, the current AI revolution is one such tectonic, disruptive transformation that one hesitates on at their own peril.

Principle 4: A company's capabilities automatically dictate their disabilities

By definition, an organization's capabilities conversely dictate its disabilities. In other words, your capabilities drive self-fulfilling actions but also delineate those you do not possess. An organization has values, people, and processes, each of which can operate in concert or independently. This is critical relative to emerging markets and technology evolution. New business models and technologies require new skills that may or may not be able to be retrained or repurposed from within your organization's skill sets.

A company should assess these assets and capabilities against future business requirements to leverage and maximize its strengths and compensate for disabilities or liabilities, particularly relative to the competition. Identifying and understanding one's limitations or potential future gaps over time is vital to mitigating risk and developing emerging capabilities. With that clear, objective perspective, one must then have the courage to make the necessary decisions to address these capability gaps. Again, having been a part of Accenture's digital transformation, it was impressive and reassuring to see how they strategized, invested in, and embarked on the wholesale digital transformation of a company with 738,000 staff. Flexibility and adaptability at such a colossal scale are no mean feats.

Principle 5: Organizational capabilities or technical abilities do not define market demand

Again, the current metrics of the incumbent enterprise do not typically justify investment in emerging markets. At least until it becomes clear that the existing products exceed the marketplace's demands and considerable market share leakage has passed over to the new entrant. By then, it will often be too late to reengineer and retool to recapture ground lost to the disruptor, who has now built an almost unassailable marketplace beachhead. Moreover, the new entrant will often build an attractive brand presence as a more modern and customer-responsive company.

In summary, traditional companies must recognize that in fast-moving emerging markets, existing metrics and methods, as well as legacy customers and products, can be a "ball and chain" drag on innovation. Conversely, new disruptive companies can recognize this opportunity when they can identify a tired traditional company whose product range is overly mature, overbuilt, and unnecessarily expensive relative to the customer base's emerging or evolving core needs.[28]

The principles of Christensen's landmark book are still crisp and relevant and, therefore, invaluable in identifying and confronting disruptive technology challenges and opportunities in any era and arena.

Takeaway: Disruptive technologies are a precursor to the creation of emerging markets.

- Traditional research and development methods don't apply to nascent markets.
- New entrants can enter at the cheaper, entry-level end of the market.
- Don't respond to new entrants by overdesigning existing products.
- Current tools and capabilities don't apply to emerging markets.

An Innovator's Dilemma Case Study

I will cite a pertinent personal example of precisely the same Innovator's Dilemma conundrum. In the mid-1990s, at the Reuters Financial Services usability and design labs in London, we conceived and prototyped a cutting-edge, internet-based investment bank trading system. Unfortunately, this system was not implemented due to several of the same challenges Dr. Christensen discusses above. Had we not been overwhelmed by these extraneous obstacles, this system might have resulted in a successful competitive response to the Bloomberg Trading System tsunami, which was breaking on our shores and eventually besieged Reuters.

By the spring of 1996, in the Reuters Innovation Labs, we had a fully functional internet-based financial service trading system proof of concept on the table. Our objective was to create the "Bloomberg killer," as Bloomberg was winning the hearts and minds of Wall Street traders across the pond in the United States. Each time we ran usability lab tests with our New York clients, they always mentioned how user-friendly the Bloomberg system was and cited a plethora of personalized features that endeared the product to them.

We code-named our new system Enterprise for the scope and size of the product and the venture and to engage with the Trekkies (Star Trek aficionados) among the "Techies" in the development labs. This new system was fully internet-based and benefited from the standard Windows-style interfaces we had been codeveloping with Microsoft in those early days of Microsoft Windows.

Despite the previously discussed competitive initiative within our labs to emulate the type of heads-up displays used by fighter pilots to create a series of highly efficient "wizard style" navigation techniques, we settled on the Microsoft Interface standards. This was because of our assessment of Microsoft's market lock-in and the benefits of customers learning rapidly from emerging consumer PC standards.

In the summer of 1996, we presented the Enterprise at the Reuters global technology conference and walked away with the conference innovation award. Consequently, we were invited to present the Enterprise system at a Group Board in the autumn of 1996. As we hurried the preparation for the board presentation, we rehearsed our storyline for the

"Bloomberg killer" pitch. We wanted to deal a competitive killer blow to Bloomberg and simultaneously to the entrenched and stagnant thinking within Reuters' product and development groups.

The day came, and I was "on." I charged through the presentation like an evangelizing preacher, explaining how the internet-based Enterprise system would transform the financial trading arena. I felt I had the board on the edge of their seats and in the palm of my hand. Then, in my enthusiasm, I delivered what I hoped was the killer blow and the deal clincher. Not only would we kill off Bloomberg, but also the old stagnant Reuters itself! I began an impassioned discussion of the promise of the Enterprise and the internet and how we would revolutionize the old way of doing things.

In retrospect, I now realize this was too much and appreciate that I was delivering this message to the very barons of industry who had created the Reuters Financial Services business in the first place. Suddenly, a booming voice called out, "What in the hell are you talking about!?" "Kill off Reuters?" "We have the most powerful system in the market, and you are talking about replacing it with an internet-based system." "First, the internet is too slow; second, even worse, it has no proper security. This is completely wrong and off track!"

A cacophony of me-too protests then jumped in for the kill. They drowned out my protestations of the future of the internet, competitive threats, market development, and coming security. The board objector continued, "The internet may be good for email, but it has no place in international investment bank trading. The project is rejected and furthermore is to be immediately canceled."

In one overly enthusiastic and insensitive moment, I not only derailed our pet project but, at the same time, also sunk a genuine opportunity for Reuters to become the market leader in the internet trading space with the future evolution of this promising initiative. Not long after, I gave notice and jumped ship from Reuters to AOL and a series of dot-coms to catch the internet wave.

A postscript to this story was bittersweet for me two years later when I ran into the CTO of Reuters, and he said: "Ah, Greg, remember your Enterprise system? We have been trying to reverse engineer it, as we now think it is the way forward! You don't have the source code anywhere, do you?" I replied yes, I did, and so did he, as I had provided the team with the relevant documentation and source code on a hard disk when I departed.

But I cautioned, "Unfortunately, no, I did not think it was the way forward anymore." "Why?" he responded in dismay. As I explained, "It is now over two years old, and the internet is moving so fast that what we developed three years ago is no longer likely to be state-of-the-art given the extraordinary pace of change in the industry." I felt somewhat vindicated but disappointed all over again for the missed opportunity and what might have transpired had I been less provocative in that fateful board meeting.

This was a classic Innovator's Dilemma problem mapping almost exactly the obstacles identified by Clayton Christensen above. Unfortunately, he published the book nearly a year after this incident. Here was a traditional company employing its existing product development metrics against an entirely new market. Our cheap and cheerful disruptive product Enterprise was deemed too early, slow, and insecure for the high performance, high-security needs of investment bank financial trading.

In fact, they were correct; it was too slow and too insecure at that time. However, it was clean, simple, contained the essential functionality, and was highly user-friendly, all the traits of a disruptive technology opportunity. Despite being too early, had we stayed on that path, performance would have improved logarithmically, and security was eventually sorted out. As a result, we might have had a very early entry and first-mover advantage in the internet financial trading arena, which ultimately became dominated by Bloomberg.

From this point forward, Reuters Financial Trading systems began their decline and ceded market dominance to Bloomberg. This was a significant lost opportunity for Reuters and was my greatest career mistake and regret, albeit providing a valuable but tough lesson. This reminds me of a valuable quote I once heard from Esther Dyson, the Swiss angel investor: "Always make new mistakes!"

TRIZ—Inventive Problem-Solving[29]

30

TRIZ, a Russian acronym for "A Theory of Inventive Problem-Solving," was invented by the Soviet engineer, inventor, and science fiction writer Genrich Altshuller. I was introduced to TRIZ by my innovation team technical architect, Andy, while setting up the TUI Innovation Labs. Genrich was a brilliant and colorful character who merits detailed study for those motivated and disciplined to use this complex but tried and proven methodology.

Genrich was an inveterate inventor, having built a rocket-powered boat in high school and developed an escape solution for submarines at age twenty. This earned him a post in the Russian Navy Innovation Center. At the time, Russian educators and scientists' overriding opinion was that creativity and innovation resulted from spontaneous flashes of insight and inspiration. However, Altshuller, an inventor himself, disagreed. Over the next few decades, he would analyze tens of thousands of patents to understand the patterns and criteria by which innovations were conceived and created.

At one point, he became so passionate about the deficient way innovation was being taught and sponsored in the Soviet Union that he wrote a letter to Stalin calling for a revision of the innovation procedures for the military. This landed him in the Siberian gulag (Soviet forced labor camp) for four years, where he encountered a host of other intellectuals of all academic disciplines. During his gulag detention, Genrich set up a knowledge exchange program among these intellectuals. This is another excellent example of the synergy of cross-domain "Medici Effect" style associations, despite far inferior conditions from that of the Medici's Florence patronage!

The time in prison in close interaction with many other incarcerated intellectuals solidified Genrich's theory that successful innovation could be systematically deconstructed and analyzed to identify repeatable patterns and distinguishing characteristics for problem-solving, including replicable methods for invention and innovation.

This body of work resulted in Altshuller developing the theory of TRIZ, which includes practical methodologies, tool kits, a knowledge base, and a specific algorithmic approach to solving problems and inventing new systems.[31]

His research on TRIZ produced three fundamental propositions:

1. Often, problems and solutions are not entirely unique, and similar classes of difficulties and failures are commonly repeated across different domains and industries.
2. Patterns of technical development and evolution are consistent and often repeatable across industries.
3. That learnings and innovations could apply and use previously proven scientific and technological solutions outside the industries or fields where they were initially invented.[32]

Over the following decades, he continued developing TRIZ through a growing community of TRIZ practitioners, analyzing and categorizing findings and solutions from thousands of inventions and patents. Altshuller and his TRIZ aficionados enhanced TRIZ to create the concept and tools referred to as "technical contradictions" and a matrix for constructing a system of forty fundamental principles for invention. Altshuller and his TRIZ associates distilled these forty principles from analyzing the solutions of tens of thousands of prior innovations and problem solutions. Then, they developed and documented these solutions that could be learned and reapplied to resolve new issues or problems.

The TRIZ methodology is initially somewhat complex and tedious to master and manage. Still, it has been proven extensively to be a valid and valuable approach and tool kit for problem-solving and innovation creation. If you have a serious and dedicated innovation initiative, I recommend exploring TRIZ. First, however, I'd suggest you seek out and employ a TRIZ coach to manage the process. It would be best to consider employing the TRIZ coach, much like using Scrum MasterScrum or Agile Coach to kick-start an Agile/Scrum initiative. This will help ensure the TRIZ initiative is set up professionally and sustained throughout the training and coaching. Implemented with commitment, rigor, and discipline, TRIZ can realize dramatic results in systematically identifying new solutions using previously successful methods from the forty principles tool kit.

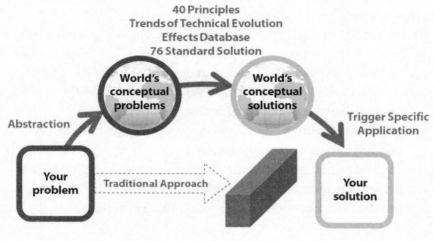

33

https://en.wikipedia.org/wiki/TRIZ

Ideation Strategy, Methods, and Technologies

We are all unique individuals with different knowledge, skills, talents, interests, and ways of expressing our distinct talents. While we all have the capability to be innovative, you'll need to embrace that diversity and approach innovation and change flexibly according to the diverse skills and talents of your team or workshop participants. Moreover, no one innovation style is best for everyone or every situation.

Recognizing the different ways we approach innovation is key to maximizing our contribution and working together successfully within an innovation team and the broader organization. You will find that those distinctive styles are often complementary to collaborate with others in meeting creative challenges through a combination of innovation approaches.

For example, one might be fortunate enough to have a creative genius somewhat akin to Steve Jobs with an exceptional natural instinct for products and design. Alternatively, there are other talents like Genrich Altshuller, with a highly scientific and analytical approach to innovation. Each has their unique talent, approach, and value.

Regardless of your particular style, you can draw on your past experience and then associate and combine insights and ideas from that experience with your current situation to discover hidden possibilities. This is simpler but not unlike the processes proposed by TRIZ. Then, further, extrapolate, extend, and evolve concepts and products from the present to envision and create future opportunities.

This is a technique and process we will discuss at length and which we used effectively in our innovation labs for envisioning future technologies and products. Finally, you must ensure you collaborate with your internal domain experts, line management stakeholders, and external specialist partners to build on your team and existing organization's strategy and capabilities.

In starting and stimulating an innovation initiative with your team, let's examine four typical macro-level innovation approaches you can use to create an innovation culture and methodology in your organization:

- **Visioning:** Envisioning a new state or ideal future
- **Modifying:** Refining and optimizing something that exists
- **Exploring:** Discovering new products or possibilities
- **Experimenting:** Combining and testing alternatives[34]

Each innovation style gives you a different method for meeting new creative challenges. By learning to use all four styles, including applying them in combination, you'll build an innovation framework providing focus to enhance and stimulate your innovation culture.

Two additional alternate dimensions can be applied to energize and empower each of these four innovation styles. Consider the following and ask yourself:

What can further stimulate and inspire this style's innovativeness?
Employing intuition, insights, and images (Steve Jobs)
or
Use of facts, details, and analysis (Genrich Altshuller)

How can you support the process approach of this innovation style?
Through broad, perceptive, and learning-oriented approaches (to build organizational capability)
or
By focused, well-planned, and outcome-oriented methods (to align with business objectives and realize quick wins)

Each innovation style can benefit from combining elements of these two dimensions. By developing your awareness, knowledge, and skillful practice of these various innovation styles within your team, you'll help guide your creative people to be more focused and productive in their innovation ideation activities.

As mentioned, each member of your team has a unique blend of innovation styles. Once you understand how these styles influence their innovativeness, you'll appreciate your teammates' styles better and how to leverage their collective skills to the best advantage. You'll also be more effective in getting them to buy into your vision and take part actively in generating innovative ideas and approaches instead of pursuing their own independent activities.

Further, for ideation purposes, depending on the type of challenge, you'll be able to select an appropriate mix of innovative people, realize higher participation, reduce relationship tension, and build greater synergy and motivation within your teams. You may also want to employ a

team-building methodology, such as Belbin, to enhance your team alignment and work as a precursor to your ideation and innovation work.

As you and your colleagues become more experienced and confident
in your creativity and innovation experience, you can cultivate innovative
solutions in virtually every aspect of your everyday work and challenges.
As you practice and stimulate a richer variety of ideas and approaches,
your innovation skills are reinforced and become habitual in your work,
which, as a result will become more motivating and productive. You can
apply these creative approaches and solutions successfully to challenges
in virtually any area of work, and in particular in areas of:

- Strategic planning
- Sales and marketing
- Organizational change
- New product/service development
- Quality or process improvement

These are some high-level innovation styles. However, having creative
ideas and building an innovative culture and team are only the starting points. Remember, innovation is the successful commercialization of
ideas. Thus, taking action and executing are the ultimate keys to making
a real, sustainable difference. So let's dig deeper and look at a number of
tried and proven innovation strategies and methodologies for innovation
implementation, execution, and delivery.

Innovation Strategies

One of the first and most important decisions and challenges in setting up an innovation program in your company will be creating the overall organizational design for the initiative. You may choose to do innovation in situ, in other words, within the context of the existing organization, or to set up a new separate organization as a "skunk works" to catalyze and lead innovation as an extension or adjunct to the current organization, or potentially even externalize your innovation activities to a third party.

Innovation Approaches

Considering the organizational design, there are many ways to set up and run an innovation initiative; however, the four most common and tried and proven approaches are:

- *Innovation Incubator*—creating a separate internal dedicated innovation team
- *Culture-Driven*—Innovation is embedded and immersed in, thus permeating the entire organization
- *Outsourcing*—Outsource or externalize innovation to a specialist third-party
- *Acquisition*—Identifying and acquiring an innovative external organization

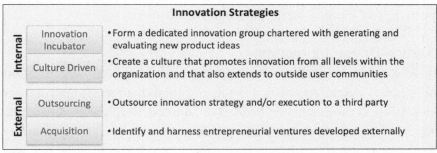

35

Each of these approaches has been implemented successfully by multiple different companies. The best choice for your company depends on your organization's culture, current innovation maturity, and level of leadership commitment. Drilling down into some of the details and nuances of each will help you understand which is best for your company and culture.

Innovation Lab Initiatives

A number of highly successful companies have recognized the value of creating dedicated "innovation labs." These comprise teams of people whose exclusive job is dedicated to stimulating and catalyzing innovation across the company.

A good example is Google, which ran a dedicated innovation lab, "Google X," for the first ten years of its operation from 2002 to 2011, with the mission to create a "moonshot factory" and recently announced it would restart its innovation labs in 2023. One notable example of Google's moonshot-level initiatives is Waymo, the self-driving cars that emerged from the labs to become the first robotaxi service certified to offer taxi service without support drivers in the vehicles. Further, Google DeepMind is a dedicated research and innovation lab that is a world leader in artificial intelligence.

Other notable companies that currently operate formal innovation labs are Unilever, Microsoft, IBM, LG, and Samsung. These organizations recognize they can realize breakthrough ideas from creative people in dedicated teams who are not directly immersed in, and therefore bogged down in, operational roles. This frees them up to adopt new perspectives and interject fresh ideas into the company.

Culture-Driven Innovation

There is also a compelling argument for "culture-driven" organizations like Apple, Google, Amazon, Toyota, and Intel that have innovation systemically and thoroughly embedded or "burned" into the organizational ethos and operations. In these organizations, innovation is genuinely "business as usual." This pervasive innovation-driven culture is a critical competitive differentiator for these modern digital technology and online media companies.

Apple, Google, and Amazon are outstanding current innovation examples, but let's look momentarily at Toyota, an exceptional case of a hundred-year-old, superbly innovative company. Within Toyota, innovation is built into and pervasive throughout the corporation's history, culture, ethos, and operations. Toyota follows the Japanese concept of *kaizen*, a process of continuous and constant improvement. Significantly, every employee of Toyota knows that an integral part of their job is to improve whatever they do. Whether it is the automotive designer, the finance manager, the machine assembly line worker, the administrative worker, or the cleaner. Innovation is an integral part of everything they do in this culture, and all employees are consciously aware of it. We will analyze some of Toyota's critical success factors shortly.

Ideation-Driven Innovation

The next model for innovation is where companies follow an "ideation-driven" approach to innovation. This model enhances the existing organization and organizational processes with formal Ideation methodologies comprising innovation initiatives, ideation campaigns, and portals. This methodology is an updated, modern approach to the old "suggestion box" campaigns of the past century. Companies successfully using this methodology are Sony and General Electric. This ideation approach may also be used as an innovation "campaign methodology" in conjunction with other organizational models.

Open Innovation and Outsourcing Innovation

The final high-level model comprises companies that recognize the value of partners and external specialist companies, such as IDEO and What*IF!*, who bring novel, fresh external ideas to the existing company. Companies that have used this model successfully are American Express, Bosch, and BYD Corporation. Again, these models are not necessarily mutually exclusive and can be used in conjunction with each other.

In some cases, innovation is "partially outsourced" using the "open innovation" concept to augment internal capabilities. The objective of open innovation is to leverage external knowledge and skills to stimulate and kick-start new ideas and products within your company. Open innovation can use existing partners, suppliers, customers, industry forums, research universities, consultancies, or contractors. By widening the net of external partners, you can dramatically increase the number and quality of ideas generated and available to survey and analyze. There are even open innovation intermediaries who specialize in scanning the marketplace for specialty innovation partners as a service to customers.

Open Innovation

Considering the compelling leverage that open innovation offers, it warrants a bit of further detail. The term "open innovation" was coined originally by Dr. Henry Chesbrough,[36] a professor and organizational theorist from the University of California, Berkeley. Dr. Chesbrough has researched, published, and consulted extensively, beginning with his groundbreaking book *Open Innovation: The New Imperative for Creating and Profiting from Technology.*[37]

The key concept is that in the complex information-based world of business today, no organization or person has a monopoly on knowledge. Therefore, no company needs to depend exclusively upon its own organization for research or ideas on innovation. Open innovation advances the idea that an organization should be more permeable and widen its innovation vision and approach to include other organizations, universities, research firms, suppliers, contractors, and even customers.

The graphics below vividly depicting open innovation are courtesy of Dr. Chesbrough:

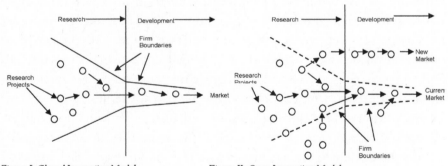

Figure I: Closed Innovation Model   Figure II: Open Innovation Model

Following is a further detailed open innovation model:

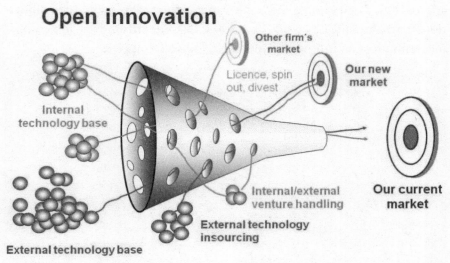

Open innovation

Other firm's
market

Licence, spin
out, divest

Our new
market

Internal
technology base

Internal/external
venture handling

Our current
market

External technology
insourcing

External technology base

39

Closed Innovation Principles	Open Innovation Principles
The smart people in our field work for us	Not all the smart people work for us, so we must tap into the knowledge \ expertise of bright individuals outside our company
To profit from R&D, we must discover, develop and ship it ourselves	External R&D can create significant value; internal R&D is needed to claim some portion but not all of that value
It we discover it ourselves, we will get it to market first	We don't have to originate the research in order to profit from it
If we are first to commercialize an innovation we will win	Building a better business model is better than being first
If we create the most and best ideas , we will win	If we make the best use of internal & external ideas we will win
We should control our intellectual property so that our competitors don't profit from our ideas	We should profit from others' use of our IP, we should buy others' IP whenever it advances our own business model

Combining Approaches

Naturally, some savvy companies hedge their bets and combine the above approaches. For example, here is an interesting adaptation and elaboration of an annual BCG study of 1,400 CEOs identifying the top companies using formal innovation methods and technologies:

	Which global companies do you consider the most innovative?	
Rank	Company	Headquarters
1	Apple	United States
2	Google	United States
3	Microsoft Corporation	United States
4	IBM Corporation	United States
5	Toyota Motor Corporation	Japan
6	Amazon.com	United States
7	LG Electronics	South Korea
8	BYD Company	China
9	General Electric Company	United States
10	Sony Corporation	Japan
11	Samsung Electronics	South Korea
12	Intel Corporation	United States

Culture Driven – Innovation is deeply embedded in the company ethos and ways of working

Innovation Lab – A dedicated Innovation Team is created to catalyse, create & concentrate innovation

Ideation Driven – An Innovation methodology to stimulate idea creation through campaigns or portals

Outsource – A method to tap external skills and resources to augment internal capabilities

Combination – Companies may start with Innovation Labs and progressively develop other methods

Source: BCG Consulting – Innovation a Return to Prominence – a survey of 1400 CEOs

40

As you can see, each innovation model has been and can be employed successfully; therefore, the challenge is to determine which approach is most appropriate to your particular culture and marketplace. If innovation is already systemic and pervasive in your culture, then perhaps building on and reinforcing the innovation culture is the most appropriate approach.

However, if your company is not fortunate to have a robust embedded innovation culture already, exploring one of the methodologies above or combining them can provide crucial catalysts for innovation in your organization. Further, your innovation culture and needs may evolve over time. We will explore a middle- and long-term innovation maturity road map in due course.

Centralized or Decentralized?

Along with assessing the organizational culture, you must look at your corporate leadership and governance model based on the degree of leadership commitment and involvement in product development. For example, is your organization a start-up, SME, large centralized multinational, or highly decentralized conglomerate? This will help you determine the best approach to organizational buy-in, support, and management for your innovation initiative.

Again, there is no one ideal model; what works best for your organization is a function of its culture, structure, and governance.

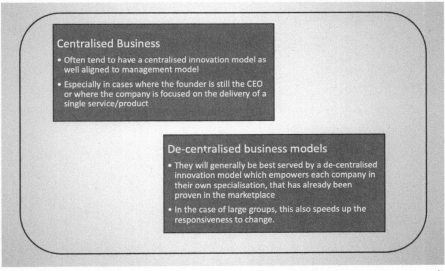

41

Centralized Innovation

If you have a centralized organizational business such as Facebook or Google were in their early days, you will likely need a centralized innovation initiative. If the visionary founders are still at the head of your company, you'll need their support and top management's involvement to lead and champion the innovation initiative.

- Organizations like this often tend to have a centralized innovation model aligned with their management model.
- Central initiatives apply in cases where a founder is still the CEO or when the company is focused predominantly on the delivery of a single product or service.

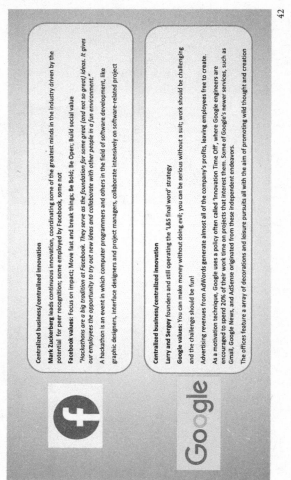

Centralized business/centralized innovation

Mark Zuckerberg leads continuous innovation, coordinating some of the greatest minds in the industry driven by the potential for peer recognition; some employed by Facebook, some not

Facebook values: Focus on impact; Move fast and break things; Be Bold; Be Open; Build social value

"Hackathons are a big tradition at Facebook. They serve as the foundation for some great (and not so great) ideas. It gives our employees the opportunity to try out new ideas and collaborate with other people in a fun environment."

A hackathon is an event in which computer programmers and others in the field of software development, like graphic designers, interface designers and project managers, collaborate intensively on software-related project

Centralized business/centralized innovation

Larry and Sergey founders and still operating the 'L&S final word' strategy

Google values: You can make money without doing evil; you can be serious without a suit; work should be challenging and the challenge should be fun!

Advertising revenues from AdWords generate almost all of the company's profits, leaving employees free to create.

As a motivation technique, Google uses a policy often called 'Innovation Time Off', where Google engineers are encouraged to spend 20% of their work time on projects that interest them. Some of Google's newer services, such as Gmail, Google News, and AdSense originated from these independent endeavors.

The offices feature an array of decorations and leisure pursuits all with the aim of promoting wild thought and creation

42

Decentralized Innovation

If you work in a large global decentralized business like Toyota or Philips, you will require a decentralized innovation approach. In this case, you will need functional or regional innovation steering boards for individual business lines or markets. In this case, each company or entity is empowered to operate within its own market and product specialization. This model works best in a mature company with a long history of a deeply embedded innovation culture.

- These organizations will generally be best served by a decentralized innovation model that empowers each company in its own specialization and geographic market.
- In the case of a large global multinational organization, innovation decentralization speeds up marketplace and product/service alignment and adaptability to change.

De-centralized business/de-centralized innovation

Toyota operates 11 region centers around the world (4 Japan, 2 Asia P, 2 US , 3 EU). Whilst models and strategies may vary, they use the same production lines across the world. All employees are encouraged to offer and share ideas in a global network to improve efficiency, according to company principles

Toyota leading principles: Jidoka (eliminate waste), Kaizen (continuous improvement), Just in time (reduce inventory and associated carrying costs, thereby exposure to risk of failure)

Toyota sees it as their duty to begin a design (or a redesign) by going out and seeing for themselves what customers want in a car or a truck and how any current versions come up short (genchi genbutsu). Each region has the power to interact with their consumers and address their needs

De-centralized business/de-centralized innovation

Each sector and specialization is responsible for driving progress from within. Motivation to excel technologically is engrained in the company culture

The Philips values: Delight Customers; Deliver great results; Develop people; Depend on each other

Innovation Leadership Gateway is a Philips-wide program designed to match young professionals' talent and ambitions with the company's desire to strengthen its innovation pipeline. They require 7-12 years of working experience, with 6-8 yrs in R&D/ innovation/ technology to drive innovation projects across the group

43

Toyota again is an outstanding example with its strong central direction and control. As discussed, their innovation strategy and culture recognize that innovation must occur everywhere in the company, both functionally and geographically.

In addition to Toyota's internal innovation culture, it works actively and systematically throughout its partner network. Toyota adopts a decentralized "open innovation" approach where suppliers and innovation partners are encouraged to innovate continuously, keeping them aware of their competition and close to their customers across the globe.

Further, with their innovation culture, they foster innovation across their entire automotive ecosystem, including:

- New car design comprising all-electric and autonomous vehicles
- Production systems innovation, including *kaizen* and robotics
- New approaches to lean manufacturing and kanban
- Organizational design innovation, including new ventures
- Safety and sustainability innovation
- Innovative approaches to leadership and management[44]

Toyota innovation is the topic of many books and dissertations. Yet, despite the rigor and complexity of fostering innovation across the world's largest automobile company, their overriding advantage is a pervasive and ubiquitous innovation culture throughout the company. This results in almost 400,000 employees and their vast network of suppliers who recognize that one of their key objectives is to make whatever they do, every day and in every way, just that little bit better. That alignment is a tremendous organizational advantage and provides an extraordinary opportunity for innovation and new product creation.

Takeaway: Based on your culture, determine the best innovation design for your company.

- Incubator, culture driven, outsourcing, or acquisition.
- Elect a centralized or decentralized innovation model.
- No company has a monopoly on ideas; employ open innovation with partners, suppliers, academia, and even customers.

Ideation Methodologies

Input Process
Innovation portal
Innovation team ideation
Business partner ideation

Ideation Processes
Visioning
Horizon scanning
Radar
Trend tracking and trendspotting
Exploring and insights
Association and extrapolation

Ideation Generation
Brainstorming
Experimenting
Idea management
Innovation platform
Campaign management
Scenario planning
Play

Analysis
Ethnography analysis—observation
Extrapolation from other domains by products or services
Market research
Opportunity identification
Identify opposites

Modification and adaption
The following is the most comprehensive list of innovation techniques and tools I have run across in my innovation research and work. This list is courtesy of David Straker[45] and http://creatingminds.org/[46] and was assembled by my colleague Neftis in my innovation team at TUI/Hotelbeds.

	TOOL	KIND OF ACTIVITY *Focus of the activity*	TIME FRAME *Estimated duration of the activity*	PARTICIPANTS *Recommended number of participants*	FORM *Link to the Activity Form*
					IDEATION TOOLKIT
Absence Thinking		Ideation	< 1 hour	Small Group (2-6 people)	Absence Thinking
A day in the life of...		Creative energizers	1-2 hours	Small Group (2-6 people)	A day in the life of...
Analogies		Ideation	< 1 hour	Medium Group (7-12 people)	Analogies
Assumption reversal		Creative energizers	< 1 hour	Medium Group (7-12 people)	Assumption Reversal
Assumption Smashing		Creative energizers	< 1 hour	Medium Group (7-12 people)	Assumption Busting
Attribute Listing		Problem analysis	1-2 hours	Medium Group (7-12 people)	Attributing List
Basadur Simplex process		Problem solving	1/2 day	Small Group (2-6 people)	Basadur
Brainstorming	Traditional	Ideation	1-2 hours	Medium Group (7-12 people)	Traditional Brainstorming
	Directed	Ideation	1-2 hours	Medium Group (7-12 people)	Directed Brainstorming
	Reversal	Ideation	1-2 hours	Medium Group (7-12 people)	Reversal Brainstorming
	Kaleidoscope	Ideation	1-2 hours	Small Group (2-6 people)	Kaleidoscope Brainstorming
	The Charette Procedure	Ideation	1-2 hours	Large Group (+12 people)	The Charette Procedure
	Phillips 66	Ideation	< 1 hour	Large Group (+12 people)	Phillips 66
	Electronic	Ideation	1-2 hours	Large Group (+12 people)	Electronic Brainstorming
Braindrawing		Ideation	1-2 hours	Small Group (2-6 people)	Braindrawing
Brainwriting		Ideation	1-2 hours	Medium Group (7-12 people)	Brainwriting
Brainwriting 6-3-5		Ideation	< 1 hour	Small Group (2-6 people)	Brainwriting 6-3-5
Camelot		Problem analysis	< 1 hour	Small Group (2-6 people)	Camelot
CATWOE		Problem analysis	1-2 hours	Small Group (2-6 people)	CATWOE
Circle of opportunity		Ideation	< 1 hour	Small Group (2-6 people)	Circle of Opportunity
Concept Screening		Decision making	1-2 hours	Medium Group (7-12 people)	Concept Screening
Context Map		Problem analysis	< 1 hour	Medium Group (7-12 people)	Context Map
Crawford Slip Method		Ideation	< 1 hour	Large Group (+12 people)	Crawford Slip Method
Cubing		Problem analysis	1-2 hours	Small Group (2-6 people)	Cubing
Delphi method		Decision making	1/2 day	Large Group (+12 people)	Delphi Method
DO IT		Problem solving	1/2 day	Small Group (2-6 people)	DO IT
Excursion Technique		Ideation	1-2 hours	Small Group (2-6 people)	Excursion Technique
Fishbone diagram		Problem analysis	1-2 hours	Medium Group (7-12 people)	Fishbone Diagram
Force-field Analysis		Decision making	< 1 hour	Small Group (2-6 people)	Force-Field
Force-Fit Game		Ideation	< 1 hour	Medium Group (7-12 people)	Force-Fit Game
Fresh eyes		Problem solving	1-2 hours	Medium Group (7-12 people)	Fresh eyes
Gordon/Little		Ideation	< 1 hour	Medium Group (7-12 people)	Gordon/Little
How-how diagram		Problem solving	1-2 hours	Medium Group (7-12 people)	How-How
Idea bits and racking		Ideation	1-2 hours	Small Group (2-6 people)	Idea Bits and Racking
Idea board		Ideation	1-2 hours	Large Group (+12 people)	Idea Board
Input-output		Problem analysis	1-2 hours	Small Group (2-6 people)	Input-Output
Kepner-Tregoe		Decision making	1-2 hours	Medium Group (7-12 people)	Kepner-Tregoe
King of the mountain		Problem analysis	< 1 hour	Medium Group (7-12 people)	King of the Mountain
LARC		Creative energizers	< 1 hour	Medium Group (7-12 people)	LARC
Lion's den		Ideation	1-2 hours	Medium Group (7-12 people)	Lion's Den
Lotus Blossom Technique		Problem solving	1-2 hours	Medium Group (7-12 people)	Lotus Blossom
Mind-Mapping		Ideation	1-2 hours	Small Group (2-6 people)	Mind-mapping
Morphological Analysis		Ideation	1-2 hours	Small Group (2-6 people)	Morphological Analysis
NHK method		Ideation	1/2 day	Large Group (+12 people)	NHK method
Nominal group technique (NGT)		Ideation	1/2 day	Medium Group (7-12 people)	NGT
NUF Test		Decision making	< 1 hour	Medium Group (7-12 people)	NUF Test
Pattern language		Ideation	< 1 hour	Small Group (2-6 people)	Pattern Language
Pin Cards		Ideation	1-2 hours	Medium Group (7-12 people)	Pin Cards
PINC Filter		Decision making	1-2 hours	Small Group (2-6 people)	PINC Filter
Post-Up		Ideation	1-2 hours	Small Group (2-6 people)	Post-Up
Problem reversal		Problem solving	< 1 hour	Small Group (2-6 people)	Problem Reversal
Question Summary		Ideation	< 1 hour	Medium Group (7-12 people)	Question Summary
Random input	Random word	Creative energizers	< 1 hour	Medium Group (7-12 people)	Random Word
	Random Picture	Creative energizers	< 1 hour	Medium Group (7-12 people)	Random Picture
	False Rule	Creative energizers	< 1 hour	Medium Group (7-12 people)	False Rule
Relational words		Creative energizers	1-2 hours	Medium Group (7-12 people)	Relational Words
Role-play		Creative energizers	1-2 hours	Medium Group (7-12 people)	Role-Play
SCAMPER		Creative energizers	1-2 hours	Medium Group (7-12 people)	SCAMPER
Serendipity		Creative energizers	< 1 hour	Medium Group (7-12 people)	Serendipity
SIL method		Ideation	1-2 hours	Medium Group (7-12 people)	SIL Method
Six Thinking Hats		Problem solving	1-2 hours	Small Group (2-6 people)	Six Thinking Hats
Sticking dots		Decision making	< 1 hour	Large Group (+12 people)	Sticking Dots
Squeeze and stretch		Problem analysis	< 1 hour	Large Group (+12 people)	Squeeze and Stretch
Storyboarding		Problem analysis	1-2 hours	Small Group (2-6 people)	Storyboarding
SuperHeroes		Problem solving	1-2 hours	Medium Group (7-12 people)	SuperHeroes
Swap-Sort		Decision making	< 1 hour	Small Group (2-6 people)	Swap-Sort
Synectics		Problem solving	1/2 day	Small Group (2-6 people)	Synectics
The Hundred Dollar Test		Decision making	< 1 hour	Medium Group (7-12 people)	The100$Test
The 7x7 technique		Decision making	1-2 hours	Small Group (2-6 people)	The 7x7 Technique
The two-words technique		Ideation	1-2 hours	Small Group (2-6 people)	The Two-words technique
TKJ Method (Rice Storm)		Problem solving	1-2 hours	Small Group (2-6 people)	TKJ Method
TRIZ	40 Innovation Principles	Problem solving	1/2 day	Small Group (2-6 people)	TRIZ - 40 Innovation Principles
TRIZ	76 Standard Solutions	Problem solving	1/2 day	Small Group (2-6 people)	TRIZ - 76 Standard Solutions
TRIZ	ARIZ	Problem solving	1/2 day	Small Group (2-6 people)	TRIZ - ARIZ
Unfolding		Ideation	< 1 hour	Medium Group (7-12 people)	Unfolding
Walt Disney Creativity Strategy		Ideation	1/2 day	Medium Group (7-12 people)	Walt Disney
Whising		Creative energizers	< 1 hour	Medium Group (7-12 people)	Wishing
Why-why diagram		Problem analysis	< 1 hour	Medium Group (7-12 people)	Why-Why diagram
Workouts and other group approaches		Problem solving	1 day	Large Group (+12 people)	Workouts

Managing the Innovation Process: Innovation Objectives

Your innovation initiative's strategy, objectives, and start-up activities are critical stages of the buy-in, mobilization, and lock-in of innovation into your organization. Here are some principles that will help you get on the right track.

- Leading innovators create systematic, reliable, and repeatable innovation.
- Reliance on a single "one-hit wonder" product or "hit-or-miss" innovation is not a sustainable business model.
- You will definitely need some quick wins and, ideally, some opportunities based on alleviating some key business points of pain or new incremental product opportunities in collaboration with the existing lines of business.
- Finally, your organization will benefit enormously if you can identify and deliver some major future "game changers" for your products and businesses.

The table below depicts these issues and demonstrates representative innovation objectives and a model for approaching innovation opportunities.

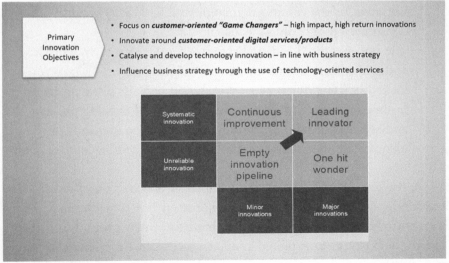

The x-axis represents a scale from minor to major innovations in the matrix. The y-axis is the scale from unreliable or ad hoc innovation to systematic innovation.

The matrix depicts various opportunity quadrants for ease of understanding; however, recognize this scale is, in reality, a continuum across the x and y axes. This matrix is a valuable tool to help focus your efforts on the optimal objectives.

- The lower-left "Empty Innovation Pipeline" quadrant of unreliable and minor innovations represents an ad hoc approach focused on minor innovations.
- The lower-right "One-Hit Wonder" quadrant of unreliable and major innovations is common in many companies without a formal innovation culture or initiative. This is a typical situation where a new product or business line was initially invented, only to fizzle out over time without significant follow-on innovation.
- The upper-left "Continuous Improvement" quadrant of systematic and minor innovations is a useful sustainability metric for evolving existing products or services. This is an invaluable objective for all products and services. However, it does not present a strong case for creating a dedicated innovation initiative, as the results are incremental and likely result in a continuation of business as usual.
- The upper-right "Leading Innovators" quadrant of systematic and major innovations focuses on "game changers." Once you've locked in some quick wins, this should be your ultimate target innovation objective. Here, you break free of existing product and service boundaries, employing innovation methods to identify significant and fundamentally new products or services.

As we consider game-changer innovations, it is worth mentioning Kim and Mauborgne's bestseller *Blue Ocean Strategy*.[49] A Blue Ocean Strategy is an entirely new product or service that breaks new ground in its field. These nonexisting, unexplored market spaces present tremendous new opportunities to create and own new market spaces. This book is an excellent follow-up to Christensen's *The Innovator's Dilemma*.

Again, I mention the Innovator's Dilemma as, when charting new market space territory, you may encounter the challenges Christensen discusses in forecasting and selling proposals to management without existing historical financials or marketplace track history.

I'll add a brief additional comment on marketing and product development. Even a generalist manager should be familiar with Geoffrey Moore's *Crossing the Chasm*. A quick review of the concept and book is vital to understanding the challenges inherent in bringing new high-tech products to market. It is a harsh reality that the vast majority of new ventures fail. Those who survive must hurdle the "chasm" between the more adventurous "early adopter" buyers to capture a sustainable beachhead within the larger mainstream marketplace.

A side note: distantly and orthogonally related to market growth is Moore's law, named after Gordon Moore, cofounder of Intel, not to be confused with Geoffrey Moore above. Moore's law accurately predicted over fifty years ago the exponential doubling of computer processing power every two years.

Peter Thiel's *Zero to One* is a must-read on creating and fostering genuine innovation versus me-too commoditized product or service imitation.

Innovation Portfolio Planning

Once you have some quick wins under your belt, have recognized some continuous improvement activities, and ideally identified some potential game changers, you can begin to mature your planning and execution by creating an innovation portfolio plan.

Through the use of "ideation portals, tools, and technologies," which we review shortly, you can systematically identify potential innovation prospects to evaluate for proof of concepts, prototypes, and, eventually, formal business cases.

Following the previous four-quadrant matrix, you can create a long list of innovation candidates to analyze with knowledgeable internal domain experts using an "efficient frontier" tool we discussed briefly in the creativity chapter. This powerful but easy-to-create tool can be developed further into a sophisticated analytic assessment using formal quantitative analysis metrics.

In the efficient frontier graph, adapted to the innovation portfolio context, you assess, measure, and plot the benefits/profits versus projected effort/cost of all proposed innovation projects and PoCs on a grid to identify potential tactical, strategic, and game-changing projects. This is an invaluable tool to help business and finance departments develop an innovation project portfolio and business cases.

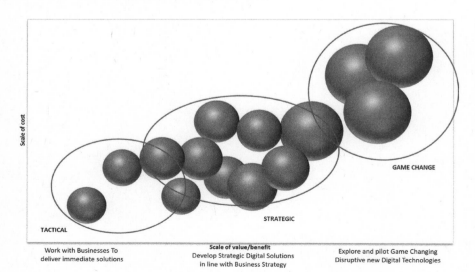

Scale of cost

GAME CHANGE

TACTICAL

STRATEGIC

Scale of value/benefit

Work with Businesses To
deliver immediate solutions

Develop Strategic Digital Solutions
in line with Business Strategy

Explore and pilot Game Changing
Disruptive new Digital Technologies

The "bubbles" depicted in this example were for an actual innovation portfolio efficient frontier exercise from one of my innovation labs. I've removed the project names for confidentiality purposes. However, this analysis and visualization aided the team considerably in crystallizing our innovation strategy and plans and developing our portfolio, budgets, and investment business cases. It was also a powerful visualization for presenting and selling various benefits cases to senior management.

The Innovation Journey

Now that you've identified your target innovation model and organizational design plans for creating an innovation program, recognize that initially catalyzing innovation is very different from creating a profitable innovation pipeline and long-term sustainable innovation culture.

In my experience launching my innovation labs, our immediate objective was to mobilize the innovation initiative rapidly to create awareness and receptivity to innovation as a critical business development metric. We then strove to innovate swiftly and assertively to achieve some quick wins to gain internal management buy-in and broader organizational support.

Once you have some initial quick wins and set up prototypes and proofs of concept, you must establish supportive champions and governance to ensure buy-in and traction across the organization. Then, to scale and accelerate further, you may want to explore the concept of "open innovation" across the partner and supplier network, as no one has a monopoly on innovation.

With successful quick wins, potential game changers, supportive champions, a solid business case for growth, and a network of innovation partners, you can start fostering innovation mentoring and training across the company. Innovation mentoring will aid in embedding a sustainable innovation culture across the organization. Realizing a permanent company-wide innovation culture and embedded innovation methodology is the innovation "Holy Grail" for any organization.

The following innovation journey is a high-level road map of innovation models and steps toward creating a permanent innovation culture within your organization.

Takeaway: Leading innovators create systematic, reliable, and repeatable innovation.

- Plan for quick wins to build internal support for innovation.
- Strive for some future "game changer" innovations.
- Use an efficient frontier graph to model your innovation initiatives.
- Consider an innovation portal to progress ideas with the business.
- Develop handoffs of mature innovation projects to the business.

In summary, innovation represents the future livelihood of any organization. But it must be carefully nurtured, managed, and championed, as long-range plans and investments are always vulnerable to the short-term vagaries of the current market conditions, the profit-and-loss statement, and the annual budget plan.

Additionally, innovation is as much of an art as a science. It will benefit from tapping a robust cross-section of the creative and analytical skills from across your team, organization, and partnership's diversity. Combining the innovation art and science creatively and systematically can foster and optimize innovation.

With strong leadership support, appropriate investment, and a talented and creative innovation team aligned to the business, an innovation initiative can be a vital asset to the improvement and evolution of your company's products and services and even for the future transformation of the organization itself.

For further detailed information regarding the setup, operations, and governance of an innovation initiative or lab, please see the appendix at the end.

To have a great idea, have a lot of them.

—*Thomas Edison*[52]

Key Takeaways—Leading Innovation

- Creativity and Innovation are inextricably connected. Creativity is the inventive process, and innovation is the implementation and commercialization of that invention.
- Innovation is not just a blinding flash of inspiration by a creative genius; innovation must be consciously catalyzed, and further, it must also be carefully cultivated, developed, and implemented.
- The Medici Effect comprises associative thinking and breaking down the barriers between domain boundaries, resulting in expansively creating new ideas and products at the intersection of the disciplines.
- Innovator's Dilemma—traditional companies perpetuate historically successful behaviors that may be inappropriate for new emerging and disruptive products in new markets, which may lead to their demise.
- Open Innovation—no one has a monopoly on knowledge and can depend solely upon their organization for innovation ideas. Therefore, they should widen their approach to include other organizations.

CHAPTER 2

Leading People and Teams— Do the Right Things Right

For those of you who started our journey with *Lead! Book 1—Finding Your Leadership Identity*, we now have a solid foundation and understanding of the theory, philosophy, strategy, and constructs of leadership.

Further, to become a successful leader and to develop your own unique leadership style, one must be experienced, skillful, and adept at leading people in teams and delivering organizational objectives. This chapter of concepts, case studies, tools, and tips is a compendium of leadership learned behavior and best practices from over four decades of frontline leadership experience.

I won't embark on an encyclopedic overview of these subjects; as for the topics selected, there are entire books, extensive articles, and courses available. Instead, I will elaborate on practical, actionable, real-life techniques, tips, hints, and case study experiences that provide value-added context, flavor, and expertise from an on-the-ground, line-management leader's perspective.

As a field guide providing immediate pragmatic value, concentrate on deep dives where relevant material will provide you essential guidance, and feel free to skim areas that may not apply to your highest priority requirements, e.g., some technical topics. However, don't forget the "Medici Effect" and remember that related and orthogonal material can augment and enhance your broader experience and give you valuable understanding and appreciation of your cross-functional peers.

Further, realize that today, all companies are, in one way or another, technology companies. Therefore, the high-level overviews of technical topics are relevant to virtually all leadership responsibilities regardless of industry.

Finally, as mentioned from my personal experience, related or tangential topics will contribute to your evolving expertise. One day, they may become the core critical path of your career.

LEADING THE ORGANIZATION

The launching platform for our discussion of leading people and teams starts at the macro-organizational level. Leaders need to understand and operate flexibly according to the needs of the organization and teams. Sometimes, a strategic leader is required to set direction and define objectives. Other times, tactical management skills will be necessary to guide people and deliver projects.

Leaders and managers of these teams must consider or create the overall organizational culture as well as respect functional tribes such as finance or development. This is where a leader must be experienced and adaptable to ensure they are effective in each diverse context.

Designing and building effective teams is fundamental to delivering projects and creating high-performing teams. However, crafting collaborative teams and ensuring optimal teamwork is both a complex and delicate task. We will explore a number of techniques and designs that will help you develop the right resources and structures for each unique requirement.

Once the objectives and structures are established, the glue and catalyst for effective operations will be open and fluid communications from leadership to the teams and people, as well as effective feedback loops from the teams back to management and within and across teams.

A vital enabler to the staff, teams, and overall organization will be the creation of a "learning organization" where formal and informal mechanisms of training and development ensure teams have the capabilities to deliver their objectives and that the organization develops the knowledge and skills it needs to grow and evolve in the future.

These topics and techniques covered in this section will be the organizational cornerstones upon which we will build the subsequent practical leadership skills necessary to lead people in teams.

When to Lead—When to Manage

There is often considerable confusion between the concepts and practices of leadership and management, as they are not mutually exclusive, with substantial overlap in certain areas. Clearly, there are many inspirational managers as well as efficient leaders, but the differences are subtle and important. Once you are clear on the primary principles and key differences, these distinctions are easy to identify. It's important to recognize that both are essential to any organization, but the requirements change depending on the state of the business, what activity is being performed, and by whom. They are the classic flip sides of the same coin, as both roles are needed, just at different times and places and for different people.

A leader is strategic, focused on the big picture, sets the vision, and leads people by inspiring, motivating, and influencing them. A manager is operational, tactical, and dedicated to running the business, coordinating, organizing, and controlling people and activities. However, as you can appreciate, the boundary between the disciplines is not solid and rigid; rather, it is blurred and must be flexible depending on the situation. Further, both can be exhibited and performed by the same person. Let's examine.

You can easily envisage how important it is for an executive to know when to function as a leader or manager. If you have a senior and capable team with the knowledge and skills to perform the job requirements, then you need a leader to set the vision, change course as necessary, and motivate and encourage the team. You can let the capable members attend to the details without micromanaging them.

On the other hand, if you have tactical, junior, or new people who need guidance, detailed information, continuous monitoring, or have a short-term crisis, everyone needs clear focus, concise direction, and ongoing supervision. In that case, they need you to be more directive as a hands-on manager.

The leadership versus management issue refers directly to previous discussions in Book 1 about identifying employee maturity and motivation through models of Situational Leadership, Blake & Mouton's Managerial Grid, and Broadwell's stages of competence.

The difficulty arises when the leader/manager doesn't understand or confuses these roles. Alternatively, perhaps the requirement changes momentarily because of altered circumstances, and the leader or manager does not adapt rapidly enough or appropriately to the new conditions.

The classic manager/leader problem often occurs, for example, when a manager who has not fully grown into a leadership position is promoted or reassigned to a role where there are highly experienced and capable staff who do not need tactical hands-on supervision. The result is likely to be frustration and irritation on the part of the seasoned team, who don't need and are not accustomed to micromanagement. Also, leaders can lose credibility if they don't recognize the problem or know how to lead through people instead of managing staff. Without conscious awareness of these issues, the leader can become threatened and be inappropriately strict with the team, which becomes increasingly resistant to the leader's inappropriate behavior.

The flip side of the leader/manager conundrum is if you have a visionary leader who finds themselves in a situation where the team is more junior, needs direct supervision, or when a crisis occurs. The leader might respond by trying to motivate and inspire them with new visions or grandiose ideas that are not pertinent to the problems and required tasks at hand. Again, the team will be frustrated, possibly dysfunctional, and more likely to flounder or even fail without the proper guidance and supervision they need to deliver. Again, the Situational Leadership model can help identify leader and team disconnects and how to manage the teams more effectively.

This is likely to be a situation where there is a misalignment between the leader and the organization. In this case, the leader may not have sufficient knowledge about the organization's operations and thus can't give the contextual guidance the team needs. In that case, you can change the leader if necessary or identify a capable team member to take on a support or supervisory role. This experienced team member can assist the leader and provide the functional guidance needed for the team.

The mature leader/manager will recognize when to set a vision, motivate and work through people, and the other times when more direct guidance and supervision are required. This decision or action becomes a function of the requirement needed at the time, the team's knowledge, and capabilities considering the immediate tasks pending. The experienced leader/manager will shift naturally and fluidly between modes as the team or task requirements change. Additionally, with time, trust, and knowledge of the group, a leader will often need to employ diverse styles with new or distinct staff types.

Another critical situation is when there is a leadership or management change if their styles are very different. For example, replacing a "control freak" tactical manager with a servant leader committed to training and empowering staff could be a true "godsend" to the staff. Unfortunately, the reverse situation will have a dramatic opposite effect as well. You and the organization must recognize that a change in leadership or management will probably have some disruptive impact on the staff, which you should anticipate, carefully communicate, and tactfully manage.

Therefore, an adaptable, mature, and successful leader/manager must operate highly effectively in both modes and even concurrently. However, it's crucial and in everyone's best interest that the leader/manager is placed in a role closely aligned to their primary leadership style, preference, experience, and skill set.

Corporate Culture vs. Tribes

We touched on corporate culture briefly in Book 1, in our review of Charles Handy's *The Gods of Management*[1] and subsequent works, where he describes the 4 Classes of Corporate Culture: Power, Role, Task, and Person. His key insights on corporate culture nuances are:

1. A Power Culture is a highly centralized organization dominated by an influential, charismatic leader(s), frequently the founder and CEO. The power remains predominantly in their hands, and they make most of the critical decisions. He terms this a *Zeus* Culture after the omnipotent king of the gods in Greek mythology.

2. A Task Culture is a project-oriented or task-based organization. It is based on teamwork, where teams of people with specific skills are structured into specialist groups formed around organizational goals with common objectives. The Task Culture is an *Athena* culture, named after the goddess of wisdom.

3. Person Culture is an informal culture dominated by employees and individuals acting primarily out of self-focused interest. This culture represents flexibly structured organizations like start-ups, artist studios, and consultants where creative types work in small groups. This is a *Dionysian* culture based on the god of wine.

4. Role culture is a highly structured organization based on functional and specialized roles. Employees are assigned roles and responsibilities according to their skills and experience. The *Apollo* organization represents solid structures, governance, and processes. Apollo was the most complex and important god.

Beyond these classic definitions, every reader, from their own experience, undoubtedly, consciously or subconsciously, profoundly understands and appreciates the concept of corporate culture. Whether you have thrived and flourished or suffered and been stifled by one, undeniably, each company has an over-arching corporate culture that can invariably be identified and described. Moreover, interestingly, most companies also have ecosystems of departmental or functional subcultures or "tribes" that, while heavily influenced by the corporate culture, are not entirely superseded or supplanted by them. An example might be a technical team in a retail company.

There are also frequent variations and nuances to a multinational's corporate culture based on nationalistic, geographic, and functional structures. For example, a strong national cultural influence might be an American subsidiary of a Japanese multinational or vice versa. Important geographic nuances are also relevant, for example, a French subsidiary of a German company. Further, functional organizational tribes, even in the same company, can have radically different cultures, for example, marketing versus technology or sales versus finance.

Accepting the geographic and cultural differences and then overlaying the functional tribe element to the organizational culture, you comprise a fascinating corporate and subcultural diversity in many companies. For example, you might have 1) a company's national corporate culture (e.g., General Electric—US corporate culture), 2) the geographic and country cultural nuances (e.g., a GE subsidiary in China), 3) the departmental functional (e.g., a GE software development unit in China).

This wide variety and diversity can often provide a bubbling ecosystem of creative innovation. Yet, despite that, these contrasting dimensions can sometimes be conflictive, creating dysfunctionality and causing culture clashes. Occasionally, this can result in miscommunication, misunderstanding, and disruptive behaviors that can derail or compromise the best strategies and intentions.

There are countless examples of both positive and negative cultures. Whether it is the mind-boggling creativity of Google or Apple or the toxic, soul-destroying cultures that will remain nameless, no one can deny corporate cultures can bring out the best or the worst in us. Undoubtedly, some organizations have negative, destructive, or toxic environments that cry out for change in the unfortunate employees' best interest.

Therefore, organizational culture is a critical dimension to consider when surveying companies for a new job. One good resource is the annual Harris Poll[2] for America's best and worst corporate cultures. Regardless, in our role as leaders, it is critical to be constructive agents of change within our teams, departments, and companies.

Through the upcoming Reuters usability and design team case study, I discuss several corporate culture challenges, particularly in the interplay between an innovation initiative and the business and technology organizations in the context of a major transformation.

However, beyond the major Reuters transformation, I do not undertake exhaustive coverage of the challenges of wholesale corporate culture change transformation programs in this book. Those are major, complex, lengthy, and risky undertakings that are the subject of many reputable books dedicated exclusively to that topic and are also a focus of professional service firms.

The critical first step is to recognize any dysfunctionality, muster the courage to call it out, and then embark on an effort to address the fundamental issues. If you have a culture transformational change challenge, you will find excellent resources in Book 1 in the Leadership Gurus chapter, including John Kotter and Rosabeth Moss Kanter.

My focus and work here for leaders are targeted primarily at the departmental, team, or tribe level, where the rubber meets the road. Here, there are unlimited opportunities to create high-performing, highly cohesive environs where people in teams can thrive, perform, and self-actualize in conjunction with or even despite the overall enterprise culture.

There is a type and level of professional knowledge and expertise that differentiates those in business into tech experts, finance professionals, marketing specialists, and product designers. For example, I've run marketing, sales, and operational teams in America, training and development teams across Asia, and technical development, consulting, and innovation teams in the UK and Europe. However, despite these layers of knowledge and experience, human nature remains essentially the same. Human nature lies deeper within the psyche and behavior constructs than the specific functional domain knowledge and practices. Thus, constructive and effective leadership and management experience are highly transferrable across industries, cultures, and functional domains.

The fundamental issue is whether the corporate culture, values, tribal customs, domain ethos, departmental practices, and management style reinforce and motivate your people and teams. Or do they rub people the wrong way, chafe on people's psyche and values, or grate on their nerves? Is the team, department, or company a place where people thrive and flourish, or is it caustic and toxic, resulting in either a virtuous or vicious cycle, creating positive or negative feedback loops that become self-reinforcing and self-perpetuating?

Regardless of the company culture, country nuances, and functional disciplines, a strong leader can create successful and pleasurable high-performing teams at the departmental level anywhere. Whether your company is enlightened, progressive, forward-thinking, or antiquated and less advanced, you can still create a safe and secure enclave where you can create a constructive and collaborative ecosystem, regardless of whether the larger organization actively reinforces, benignly neglects, or fights it. However, the extent to which your constructive team and departmental cultures align with the overall company culture will determine the effort required to maintain this positive climate in your area vis-à-vis the broader organization.

As a leader, you create the vision, determine the direction, set the tone and chemistry, and are the secret sauce that establishes the work climate and, therefore, your departmental culture. It all starts with your attitude and the atmosphere you create, perhaps as a servant leader, but certainly with heightened emotional intelligence. Then, your vision, purpose, and ethos of encouragement, empathy, trust, and respect will foster an environment where people thrive and perform.

In today's work world, especially because of the COVID pandemic, many new organizational structures exist, including new virtual and remote models and emerging types of workers, from employees and contractors to external consultants. These diverse structures and workers require careful attention to ensure these new hybrid organizations are efficiently and constructively incorporated into your team, department, or tribe's culture. Managed carefully, collaboratively, and effectively, your high-performing team culture can be a valuable asset to any organization, as well as a creative, empowering, and engaging place to work for all.

Team Building and Teamwork

As a former training director, I strongly advocate formal training and development, motivating off-site workshops, and team-building efforts. However, as a long-term line manager, I'm conscious that training, mentoring, and team building should be full-time day jobs for leaders and managers, not just a once-a-year, fix-it-all panacea for everything.

Nevertheless, these occasional events can be highly beneficial for a change of ambiance, pace, and location to interact with and bond with team members in a neutral environment and to "reset" and refocus individuals and teams. Further, you will find that groups can be refreshed and realigned and realize renewed behaviors through a well-facilitated team-building activity. However, again, this cannot be a substitute for continuous business-as-usual inspiring leadership and empathetic management.

Relative to formal team building, I have experienced and effectively used two of the most successful models in the market. First is the excellent Belbin Team Roles Model, which we discussed extensively in Book 1 within the Leadership Tips and Assessment Tools chapter. The Belbin assessment instrument does an exceptional job specifying the requisite roles in an effective team and identifying the capabilities and gaps in any particular group. The critical issue in the team-building exercise and in constructing an effective team is ensuring that all required roles are filled, there is not too much duplication and competition in similar positions, and no critical functions are missing. Referring to the Belbin Instrument, the essential capabilities are three action-oriented roles—Shaper, Implementer, and Completer-Finisher; three people-oriented roles—Co-ordinator, Team-worker, and Resource-Investigator, and three cerebral roles—Plant, Monitor-Evaluator, and Specialist.[3]

Another highly complementary model is the Tuckman Stages of Group Development methodology. I don't view this specifically as a "team-building" model, although many people do. Instead, I consider the Tuckman stages of group development as a group process model; however, it is directly related and highly relevant to team building, particularly for new teams and projects. Tuckman postulates, and I fully concur, that groups in their formation go through the predictable stages of

Forming, Storming, Norming, Performing, and, a more recent addition, Adjourning. See the review of Tuckman's Stages of Group Development in Book 1 for more detail.

I've used both models extensively and attest to their value and usefulness. I like to use both simultaneously and complementarily. First, I use Belbin to identify and establish the required roles for any significant project or team. Second, I use the Tuckman model to mobilize, develop, and mature the team.

Once you have set up or realigned a team, you must recognize that you need to monitor and nurture continuous teamwork within your organization and teams beyond formal interventions, such as team building. This becomes more of a continuous process of establishing a team-based culture that aligns with and reinforces the vision, purpose, and mission you have laid out. Part of that culture involves establishing a pervasive atmosphere of trust, honesty, open communications, and a climate of psychological safety. Next, communicate and ensure clear expectations, the modus operandi and outcomes, and individual and team-wide clarity of roles and responsibilities. Finally, you'll need to monitor the teams regularly to ensure individuals continue to collaborate cooperatively and stay aligned with the group and project mission.

Perhaps the two most important things to monitor are continuing team trust and continuous communications. Both should be a natural function of the collaborative trust culture you've established in your organization. However, as projects and challenges ebb and flow, you may need to gently tweak the relationships, roles, and tasks to ensure everyone is aligned and contributing and that everything is running smoothly. Again, Belbin is also an excellent tool and system for the occasional ongoing alignment of a mature team, as team members often come and go over the course of months and years in an established group or long-term project.

If you run into any serious team-based hurdles, a brief review of Book 1, chapter 2, "Leadership Concepts and Culture," and Chapter 5's Assessment Tools can help identify the issues and chart a course of corrective action.

Let me provide two relevant examples: the first is a case of a successful team-building exercise, and the other is where team building and teamwork happen continuously. Both are valid and effective approaches to building effective, high-performing teams.

The first example occurred when I was Asian training director for Reuters during an off-site team-building event for my Singapore training team on Batam Island. Batam is a large island off Sumatra, Indonesia, an hour's ferry ride from Singapore. We arrived late afternoon, and about a dozen of us decided to have a casual pre-course "bonding dinner," which I share as an amusing aside.

We requested a local Sumatran restaurant, not an "expat tourist" place, from the concierge. A fifteen-minute cab ride brought us to the perfect small, quaint, and local restaurant. As there was no English menu, we managed to order house specialties and pitchers of beer for the tables. It was a lively evening, and my colleague Mike and I dug into what we agreed was the best barbequed chicken ever. After demolishing the large oval plates of food, we drank more beer and discussed the barbequed chicken again.

Again, agreeing that it was the best we had ever had, we decided to order two more. I called the waiter and asked, with the help of a dictionary, for two more barbequed chickens, and to his and our surprise, he responded they did not have barbequed chicken. I insisted, saying we had just had some, and they were excellent. He looked and, with a laugh, said through the dictionary, "No, we have no chicken; those were fruit bats!" We were temporarily stunned and initially quite taken aback. Then I reconsidered and said, "Mike, we just agreed these were the best chickens we'd ever had and loved them. Since we wanted more, why were we turned off upon discovering they were bats?" We debated, steeled ourselves, and ordered two more. They were delicious! It was going to be an interesting two days.

For the team building, I had decided not to facilitate it myself since, as the leader, I was a part of the team and wanted to take part as a team member. Hence, I contracted a well-known "outward bound style" adventure team-building consultant to run a series of outdoor bonding exercises for the team.

The first day was a big success with the typical outdoor exercises. Everyone was deeply involved and agreed it was good fun and created a sense of "esprit de corps."

The second day started much the same with building a tower, and we began constructing a raft. Suddenly, the coach called me out and said: "Greg, come over and help me out." I complied and joined him at the side. He said, "Let's watch together for a while." The team seemed a bit confused, but they proceeded with the task with our encouragement. Unfortunately, the raft was not viable, and the exercise was scrapped. A further two activities proceeded, with each as faltering as the former.

The teams couldn't get organized and asked me lots of questions, which the coach rebuffed. Ultimately, the coach called a coffee break and took me aside. "Greg, what do you think is going on?" I responded that they perhaps needed some guidance and thought I should dive back in to give them direction. He countered, "Greg, that is the problem. They are floundering without your leadership, but you will not always be there, and they need to develop their own decision-making and leadership skills." I protested that, as a training director, I had spent a good deal of time training them. However, he did not give up and stated emphatically: "Greg, with your strong hands-on leadership style, you have engendered a leadership dependency on yourself! Without you, they are leaderless, lack direction, and have not sufficiently developed their self-confidence, creativity, and decision-making skills. If you don't delegate and give them more responsibility, you won't achieve as much for the organization, but worse, you will stunt their professional and personal development."

This message was striking and slightly unnerving, but a vital insight and learning for me about being too dominant in top-down communications and decision-making. Further, I needed to actively encourage and ensure my team's involvement, empowerment, and development. Despite my deep caring for the team, I immediately saw that I needed to hold back, take some risks, maybe even stumble, and allow others to take responsibility in order to learn. Otherwise, I would have a group of loyal team members with a heavy but unhealthy dependency on me for leadership and decision-making. As I wouldn't retire there, it was my responsibility to help them develop and grow for the future.

When I returned to the office, I took this learning on board and promoted and empowered a new layer of supervisors, one for each major work stream. As a consequence, several team members flourished, were recognized, and advanced even further, and the whole team subsequently benefited. This was initially slightly unsettling but turned out to be an excellent learning point for me as a lesson in egoless servant leadership. Moreover, it reinforced for me how critical it is to encourage team participation and empower staff in supervision, decision-making, and communications.

For the second situation, I'm reminded of when I was running the Reuters Usability Team in London and also the TUI Destination IT Teams. We had highly motivated, collaborative, and exceptionally high-performing teams in each case. I recall reflecting at the time and, on several occasions, commenting, "We don't need an off-site team-building event! We do team-building every day!" In this scenario, for which I provide a virtual team case study in the penultimate chapter, we established and nurtured a highly developed culture of teamwork and "esprit de corps."

In both circumstances, we were charging full steam ahead with highly motivated and high-performing teams. In these cases, we had created and articulated a clear vision and challenging mission and had been explicit with the objectives and expectations. Fortunately, we had hired and inspired outstanding teams of individuals and had zero turnover in both groups. In addition, the jobs and roles were attractive and empowering for all the team members. Finally, the leadership was directly engaged with the teams and had solid, supportive communications with all staff members.

In the case of Reuters, we guided, encouraged, and mentored the teams daily. I believe we wouldn't have benefited further from an external team-building activity. Teamwork, trust, and team cohesion were critical factors in those high-performing teams, which resulted in strong affinity, morale, and team spirit.

A caution on external team-building, which I hope would not occur today, is that you must ensure the facilitator and management are aligned with the team-building's expectations and objectives. For example, in one company where I worked, people were reluctant to attend external team-building courses. This was due to two prior occasions when the team-building assessment found that the team interworking was dysfunctional due to some problematic personalities. Those individuals were then terminated at the end of the team-building exercises! This may have been warranted in those specific cases, but it meant the team-building activities were now invalidated, as the team composition had changed, albeit for the better.

One of the recent intriguing but challenging developments in this regard is the complexity and differences in teamwork and team building in a hybrid or remote work-from-home context. As discussed in the communications section, managing a mixture of team working scenarios, including on-site, hybrid, and remote workers, requires extra care, creativity, the intensive use of new technologies, and heightened people skills.

The devil is always in the details. The challenges are amplifying communications and collaborative work using new conferencing and whiteboarding technologies and balancing the various support and emotional needs of the diverse staff working contexts.

I've been doing intensive collaborative working using high-bandwidth videoconferencing since the mid-nineties at the Reuters usability labs. Therefore, I can assure you that despite the promises of high-quality telepresence videoconference and virtual reality conferencing, they are not the same as an in-person meeting, and each needs to be managed accordingly. Having said that, these new VC technologies like Zoom more than proved their worth during the COVID-19 pandemic lockdowns. It is difficult to imagine how most businesses would have coped without them.

However, along with the creative use of conferencing technologies, leaders must be at the top of their game, communicating, managing, and building mixed teams of hybrid workers. The critical difference between teamwork and team building is that we are not just discussing a leader's effective communication with staff. Instead, the challenge is how a leader can encourage and help the team collaborate. The keys to team building and teamwork in the remote context are setting the right expectations, providing the right tools, and training to ensure everyone is comfortable with the technologies and the new working context. Often, this requires appointing someone (not necessarily a supervisor) in the team to train, monitor, and support staff to use the tools competently. Finally, blogs, e-learning, and VC recording tools will assist in bringing everyone up to speed asynchronously due to challenges in remote working availability.

Again, I refer you to the penultimate chapter on remote working to understand the diverse challenges of team building for leaders, colleagues, staff, partners, and suppliers in the remote work context.

In summary, among your most important leadership and management responsibilities are leading and managing your teams in real time, 250 workdays a year, rather than just waiting for an incremental ad hoc off-site with a facilitator to resolve your interworking problems. Therefore, a teamwork and team-building culture should not be just a token, annual, knee-jerk, or one-off artificial event designed to gloss over more fundamental team issues or personality problems.

With those provisos, as stated, I firmly believe that these occasional off-site team-building activities can be beneficial to inspire, motivate, and reward the teams. Moreover, continuous on-the-job team building in the office, plus team development, are a constant day-in and day-out process and leadership responsibility.

Effective Communications

Decades ago, my good friend Ernie Lopez sent me a fascinating conference handout on the etymology (origins of a word) of the word
"Dialogue" by David Bohm. "*Dialogos*" comes from Greek, where "*Dia*"
means "through" and "*Logos*" means "the word." Dr. Bohm explains that
true dialogue is to think together, nonjudgmentally, to come to a collective understanding through a shared "stream of meaning" within a
group.[4] This collective shared meaning is an essential and vital basis for
effective communications.

Communications are especially critical in business as they encompass
virtually everything we say and write and touch virtually every aspect of
your leadership role. For that reason, it was one of our core leadership
characteristics in Book 1. So here, let's explore some additional practical
tips on effective communication. It can be a great advantage and enabler
if done effectively or a stumbling block and genuine risk if not managed
carefully.

> **Honesty is always the best policy.** First, as much as possible, given
> your leadership situation, company, culture, and ever-present politi-
> cal climate, always endeavor to be honest. Anything else is a "fools'
> game" that, whether or not you believe in karma, will almost always
> eventually circle back to bite you. Modifying or altering the truth
> will often land you in hot water, complicate issues, or certainly
> undermine your word and credibility. Trust, as elaborated in Book 1,
> is one of the critical tenets of effective and excellent leadership. Thus,
> honesty in communications is fundamental.
>
> Coupled with the virtue of honesty is the efficient and effective
> practice of **being immediate and in the moment.** As the content
> and context of any issue are continually changing, the honest and
> prompt response to most situations will often ultimately be the eas-
> iest, simplest, and most appropriate for everyone. Further, any delay
> in response always runs the risk of the issue changing over time and
> evolving contextually away from the initial situation, even to the
> extent that a delayed response may no longer be appropriate to the
> new conditions.

Be decisive, don't beat around the bush, and attempt to make decisions efficiently and constructively to the greatest extent possible. We will discuss decision-making in detail shortly, but recognize that effective and timely decision-making is critical to good communication. Further, decisiveness implies an element of self-confidence, and sound, honest messages delivered decisively and with conviction inspire staff and instill confidence in your listeners.

Be direct, as people will always see through diversions or smoke-screens and perhaps mistrust your mincing of words, or worse, potentially even doubt your integrity. **So, know when to use your head and when to speak from the heart.**

Use **allegory, metaphor, analogy, and executive storytelling** to help people associate the communication's context and situation with familiar personal experiences to understand better and relate it to their everyday lives.

Know when to be serious and when to use humor. Ensure you are always respectful, but where appropriate, be adaptable, assertive, and adventurous with humor. The places and reasons where humor can lift staff spirits and cut tension will surprise you, as they are often counterintuitive. Enthusiastic humor is an excellent way to de-stress, encourage, and motivate staff, especially in challenging circumstances.

Be brave and bold and have a high tolerance for risk. The greatest risk you will often take is not taking enough risk, even in your communications. Dull, boring, monotonous, and predictable verbal and written communications can subliminally label you as much the same. On the other hand, powerful, adventurous, atypical, humorous, and individualistic communications can set you apart as a unique, intelligent, thoughtful, and even congenial leader or colleague with whom to work.

An effective leader should foster fluid and effective communications across the organization. Communication should not be just one-way, top-to-bottom. To motivate and empower people, remove all formal and informal barriers to communications and decision-making. Encourage the free flow of ideas and feedback up and down and across the organization, allowing communications to cascade efficiently and seamlessly. This will stimulate autonomy, catalyze creativity, streamline decision-making, and accelerate action. Furthermore, this helps to realize genuine *dialogue* in its original context, coming to a common understanding through shared meaning within a group.

Finally, the post-pandemic world we now work in has dramatically altered the context, form, and timing of verbal and written communications in the workplace. Besides powerful new digital communications technologies, the way we communicate has transformed as well.

The leader managing teams remotely must be sensitive to new constraints and challenges employees and teams have working from home. This requires significant additional care and attention on the part of the leader to connect with and empower staff by increasing virtual versus physical engagement. This will often be through an array of new communication channels. These include email, text, chat, phone, videoconference, and whiteboarding using enhanced communication tools like Zoom, Slack, WhatsApp, WeChat, Google Meet, Skype, and Teams. Furthermore, recognize that along with increased communications through multiple new channels, the leader must also enhance and adapt the quality and quantity of their leadership people skills to compensate for the lack of face time and personal attention that hybrid or remote working imposes.

Refer also to Chapter 3 on Remote Working and Work from Home for a detailed discussion of the communications opportunities and challenges this new style and form of working presents for us now and in the future.

A footnote on the pandemic imposed virtual communications. Some legacy strictures and structures will remain, even with returning to some semblance of normality in the post–COVID-19 future. Clearly, remote and hybrid working will be a lasting fixture in the employee work landscape, and the aggressive use of remote conferencing technologies will persist well beyond the pandemic. Therefore, learned behaviors of employing remote leadership soft skills and robust digital communications will remain and become increasingly crucial for on-site, hybrid, and remote workers.

Training and Development

In the mid-1980s, I jumped ship from American Express to join a technology start-up a half-mile from Apple in Cupertino, California, which would eventually become the heart of Silicon Valley. Eighteen months later, on one fateful Friday afternoon, when the start-up was in what looked like a death spiral, my old boss, Tim Cashman from American Express in San Francisco, called me up. He implored: "Greg, I know you left for a start-up, but we've decided to create a training department on the West Coast, and you've done just about every job for me in the past. Is there any way that I could convince you to come back?" I'm not sure I ever told him, but I was likely about to be out of a job with a wife who was six months pregnant! So, instead, I told him I'd always enjoyed working for him (which was true), and yes, I would be delighted to return as the new training manager for American Express Travel Services. Whew!

This kicked off a new training and development career at American Express and Reuters Group for the next ten years. Now, not only is training and development in my corporate DNA, but it is something that I fervently believe in for my staff and myself. As a personal testimonial, through continuing education, my education finished not in college almost forty-five years ago but with my professional reading last night. Whether it is on-the-job training, online learning, corporate training events, executive education, or business books, I'm a continuing education and lifelong learning devotee and champion. Consequently, I'm a huge advocate for maximizing the personal and professional commitment to conscientious formal training and continual informal education for staff, teams, friends, and family.

The investment made to train and develop your staff will almost always have a significant payback in the quality and effectiveness of your team's performance. At the same time, it will also increase the motivation and loyalty of your staff and teams. Your love of learning and development will be contagious and inspire your staff to seek out and make the most of any training opportunities. Hopefully, they will apply themselves to the available on-the-job learning, related professional courses, and reading to augment their knowledge and skills and further their career.

In Book 1, we discussed Peter Senge and the concept of the Learning Organization in his book *The 5th Discipline: The Art and Practice of the Learning Organization.*[5] This comprises an organization where learning is pervasive and continuous within the company's culture and processes. This goes beyond traditional on-the-job training (OJT). It means that every product, service, and process is consciously designed to encourage and facilitate learning and training.

In addition to embedding self-learning and training into the products and processes, enlightened modern companies offer ongoing online learning, product training, on-the-job operational training, and formal skill and career development training.

To support and develop staff, line management, and training departments in conjunction with human resources, talent management, or people operations, ensure you conduct knowledge and skills capability assessments to evaluate competence gaps within the team and with the employees relative to their operational responsibilities. This is also important to determine if staff have the training and expertise needed to perform their jobs and what training is required. It is also invaluable for recruitment assessment and identifying future staffing skill requirements. This is particularly pertinent for identifying reskilling requirements for adopting new technologies and enabling transformational changes.

Once the skill assessment is complete and the staff recruitment plan is outlined, training and development can determine the best approach to closing any knowledge and skill gap. This could be on-the-job training, management mentoring, corporate training programs, external training coursework, or, failing that, new recruitment or outsourcing of the necessary skill sets.

Regardless of the technique or tool, the organization and leader should consciously consider embedding learning and training into every aspect of their business. In this way, knowledge acquisition and an organizational learning culture become pervasive across the company, much as we discussed imbuing the organization with a quality culture or, as in Toyota's case, a pervasive, continuous improvement innovation culture.

Another recent hugely popular and beneficial educational phenomenon are the "massive open online courses" (MOOCs) at top-rated universities, available directly from the colleges themselves or, for example, at Coursera.org. Further, many of these programs are for free or virtually free! These courses provide professional skill development programs, personal knowledge, abilities, avocational training, and development coursework. This provides an intriguing and compelling, orthogonally related learning and education opportunity closely associated with the previous discussion of the *Medici Effect*. This is where additional learning and education provide further knowledge and aptitudes to enhance job and career-related growth. These continuing education opportunities ensure you and your teams continue to develop valuable new experience and talents instead of languishing with the same old, increasingly stale expertise!

Developing a love of learning, you may find that these job-related, as well as avocational and recreational courses, can dramatically enrich your work and even personal life. For example, over the past ten years, I have substituted fascinating and personally enriching courses and studies for mindless television and have taken perhaps twenty-five to thirty world-class university courses. Moreover, instead of this being a tedious self-development obligation, it has become our enjoyable evening's entertainment. Experiment with a wide range of potential interests, such as travel, history, psychology, languages, food, music, art, or anything that interests or intrigues you.

All of this avoids the previously discussed situation as to whether one has twenty-five years of experience or one year of experience twenty-five times! Be ambitious and adventurous!

Takeaways:
- A leader is strategic, sets the vision, and leads people by inspiring, motivating, and influencing.
- A manager is operational, tactical, and dedicated to controlling people and running the business.
- Corporate culture has industry, social, and geographic elements with functional tribes.
- Be conscious of when to lead strategically or manage operationally.
- Team building is a daily role, not just an annual off-site activity.
- Teams go through stages of forming, storming, norming, performing, and adjourning.
- Communications are critical, encompassing virtually everything we say, write, and touch.
- Effective communication is more important with remote staff.
- Learn and teach something daily. The world is moving too fast to stagnate and become marginalized.
- New, different, and orthogonal learnings may become the critical path to your future career.

MANAGING TEAMS

The following managing the team section delves into the critical nitty-gritty details of how to lead and manage people. There is hardly a skill and activity more important yet trickier than hiring an effective, well-balanced team. We will examine designing the team, spec'ing the role and required capabilities, and conducting the interview.

Once you've designed the team, then comes the essential but complex task of setting "stretch" but appropriate goals and objectives. With a good team in place with clear and concise objectives established, depending on the seniority and experience of the team, you will need to monitor performance and conduct timely and honest work assignment discussions to ensure team members are on track.

Finally, we review the all-important performance discussion topic. Along with hiring, setting goals, and work assignment discussions, the performance appraisal discussion is equally or more delicate and complex. Setting the right context, climate, and communications for these four activities is delicate and daunting. Still, it is perhaps the one area where developing exemplary leadership skills is both vital and valuable. This is also one of the most significant areas where leaders and managers fall down in their emphasis and efforts, and thus, is an area where aspiring leaders should concentrate their development efforts.

Hiring the Team—The Job Interview

Hiring and building a great team are crucial organizational requirements and, thus, an essential leadership skill set. However, like all
management disciplines involving people, recruiting the right people
and conducting job interviews is both a science and an art. Abraham
Lincoln reportedly once said that if you gave him six hours to chop a
load of logs, he'd spend five hours sharpening the ax. This is a fitting
analogy to reinforce the effort you expend in carefully ascertaining the
skills and capabilities required, defining the type of individuals you
need, and writing the job descriptions. All this advance work will help
ensure you identify and recruit the right team. In addition, this role
specification will be an invaluable guide for recruiters to select and vet
suitable interview candidates. This investment in detailed preparation
prevents a common recruitment pitfall of overreliance on interview
chemistry only to discover missing competencies, skill gaps, or a poor
candidate/role fit later.

When planning a new team and identifying the requisite role skills,
you should first consider the availability and quality of internal and
external skills and competencies.

Robert Townsend, the visionary ex-CEO of Avis, makes the pertinent point that *"The key to great corporate performance is not employing
great people, but letting existing people flower."*[6]

Look to Hire Internals: For any effective team, you will likely need
in-depth knowledge of the existing company, its culture, and essential
expertise in what works in that particular company. People already within
the organization know the company, the market, products, processes, and
systems underpinning and operating the company. Moreover, they have
extensive existing relationships and the know-how to get things done in
that company. This is a convincing argument for identifying and recruiting mission-critical internal staff to form the cornerstones of any new
team. Beyond the value of the existing competencies, tapping current
employees for staff and leadership roles is also tremendously motivating
for all employees across the organization. Several studies, including those
by LinkedIn and *Harvard Business Review*, contend that up to 50 percent
of new external hires fail within the first eighteen months! This raises

considerable concern about hiring externals and is a strong argument for internal hires![7]

Interestingly, I have frequently found "hidden gems" who were vital "number two" employees to management or were working underneath a high-profile department or functional heads. These hidden treasure resources are often the actual experts in their teams and the workers responsible for performing the essential specialist work. These staff have often been overlooked in the past; nevertheless, their colleagues already know they are the essential coworkers who can consistently be depended upon for requisite information and delivery.

An excellent example of this approach to recruitment was when I was running the European three-company carve-out from TUI Group and Hotelbeds, which I've mentioned previously. As a part of this process, we had to create an entirely new company, TUI Destinations, and, correspondingly, a completely new IT team. For the above reasons, I intentionally identified only internal staff for the key roles. Due to respect for Hotelbeds, our parent, we chose and agreed not to cripple them by poaching any top functional heads and therefore tapped the current number two in each functional domain. The incumbent leaders in each function at Hotelbeds were first-rate; however, so were the hidden gems beneath them. We ended up with an excellent team of highly motivated internal transfers who could hit the ground running at full speed on day one!

Some of the "number twos" who had been plateaued previously because of their supervisors' presence were able to break through the glass ceiling to become managers and supervisors in their own right. They were all eminently ready for advancement and just needed the chance to break into the open and soar. Further, it was highly motivating for everyone to see these well-deserved promotions and how well they had stepped into the new roles. As a result, the new IT team was highly motivated and competent and a high-performing team from the outset.

Recruiting an entirely new team would have been nearly impossible, caused significant delays, and presented a major potential risk to launching and running the new company.

How to Hire Externals: Once you've created a competent core team of internal managers, supervisors, and staff and rewarded the existing staff for their hard work and commitment, you will have established a loyal and qualified internal team. Next, you may need to enhance that team with fresh blood, particularly for specialist or emerging roles. Despite management's best intentions, any organization can become stale, complacent, and outdated over time, especially in disruptive new industries. Thus, it's vital to interject new life and energy into the company. After rewarding internals first to create a new team, you may need to reinvent, modernize, and reengineer how you work, the technologies you employ, and the products you deliver.

This is a rare opportunity to transform rather than replicate the old entrenched ways of doing things. Therefore, beyond the existing core competencies, make sure that you identify any unique new skills and knowledge that will enhance your organization with the latest state-of-the-art business models, processes, and technologies. Hiring recent graduates or people with specialty skills will help augment the existing organization with fresh ideas and modern technologies.

Along with selecting "perfect fit" candidates for new roles, be adaptable and bold, selecting some "wild cards" who might not be initially perceived as ideal but bring exceptional new skills or insights that might be game changers for the new organization. Be open to cultural and ethnic diversity to recognize unique skills from different backgrounds, genders, and ages. Besides this diversity, I have benefited from both young hires with cutting-edge new skills, as well as retirees who frankly were overqualified but thrilled to have a job when others might have seen them as "over the hill"!

I have also benefited enormously from exceptionally talented individuals who, perhaps in the "old days," might have been passed over due to biases that would not be accepted today. Some examples of incredible staff I've had who at the time were creative hires; I hope this does not offend anyone, as my intention is to demonstrate the value of embracing diversity:

- I hired a brilliant mathematical quant, data visualization expert, and tribal chief from Zimbabwe in the early 1990s to design financial futures and options trading systems.

- I've also found brilliant technologists who might be classified as individuals with autism spectrum disorder (ASD), a common condition, especially in very senior technology leadership roles.
- An interim technical head for one of our businesses was a retired IT director who had seen and done it all before. So it was a relief to have an interim who didn't have to be trained or mentored.
- We had a highly respected senior developer who had not previously been viewed as a manager. I promoted her to manager, and she became one of our best team leaders.
- We hired an amazingly talented but novice graphic designer directly out of college. Subsequently, I took him with me to three different companies, and eventually, he became the head of design for one of the world's largest computer software companies.
- Without going into the details, I also hired two disabled technologists who, through overcompensation for their disabilities, excelled dramatically in their own domains.

This is evidence from my experience that looking for the best talent always pays off, regardless of other extraneous and, therefore, irrelevant personal criteria.

With this background to frame your candidate interviews, your interview plan will comprise conversations, role-plays, demonstrations, or tests of the knowledge, skills, and behaviors required for the job. Regardless, I also believe in giving the interviewee every opportunity to show their best hand. Interviews are stressful enough as they are without applying undue pressure. Therefore, I always try to create a friendly and positive atmosphere to allow them to perform at their best. Also, recognize that the candidate is evaluating you as well, as a potential leader they may or may not want to work for. Therefore, don't be too relaxed, flippant, or too informal. They are assessing you not only as a good manager or leader but also as someone they can respect and look up to for help and guidance. Thus, a constructive and professional rather than a high-pressure or overly casual interview is critical to successful recruiting.

A quick caveat is that in those positions where a high tolerance for stress is vital, as with air traffic controllers, the medical field, or police enforcement, appropriate additional situational role-plays will be required to evaluate a candidate's resilience to stress and pressure.

Further, recognize that an individual identified as a potential candidate and asked to attend an interview has likely spent days, nights, and weekends preparing for the interview. They typically will have made a considerable effort and undoubtedly have high emotional aspirations in anticipating this meeting. Therefore, even if you recognize they are inappropriate early in the interview, give them the expected scheduled time, make an effort to probe, and discuss naturally.

Finally, if you are definitely sure that they will not be selected to proceed, compliment their assets, thank them for their efforts, and honestly explain why you will not proceed with their application. It is far better to gently and graciously let them down with an honest conversation, along with praise for their assets and abilities, rather than give them false expectations and prolong their anxiety. Your feedback can be very helpful to them for any future interview and role.

I recall once interviewing a candidate for an IT security officer role who was, in my assessment, undoubtedly better suited to an IT manager role, which I didn't have available. I explained at the end that I liked him and valued his capabilities but did not see him as good a fit as some other specialist security candidates. As it turned out, we got to know each other afterward through various industry gatherings. Eventually, he became the CIO for another company and, years later, one of my consultancy clients. My sincere and constructive letdown on the security role at the time was accepted and appreciated, and thus, we later became close industry partners.

When hiring new staff, you must be careful to respect the current employees and ensure you have not overlooked any qualified, loyal, long-term internal candidates. At the least, interview and give internals a fair chance even if you select an external candidate. If you first recognize and reward internal staff and position new joiners as people bringing essential new specialty skills, your existing team will often embrace them constructively and even enthusiastically. This is essential for ensuring their successful integration into the team.

Interview Examples

As learning points of perhaps what not to do in an interview, I will share a couple of vivid interview experiences that, to this day, still leave an unpleasant taste in my mouth. Both, I would contend, are perhaps the worst and among the shortest interviews in the history of interviews, and both happened to me!

The first was when I was training manager for American Express in San Francisco. I received a recruitment call and an invitation to interview for the global training director position at the world's largest soft drink company, Coca-Cola. Living in San Francisco at the time, I was a health food aficionado, but it was a terrific job, so I agreed to an interview. So, I bought a pack of Coke and went home and drank a whole one!

The following week, at 9 a.m., I arrived at the exclusive Huntington Hotel on Nob Hill with a new tie and shirt and was guided to the Presidential Suite. The Coca-Cola SVP of HR ushered me into the presidential suite and put me at one end of the twelve-foot walnut boardroom/dining room table. He then opened the fridge at the other end, took out a six-pack of Coke, and slid it rapidly, scraping the entire length of the lovely polished table, exclaiming, "Would you like a Coke?" Despite it being 9 a.m., I kept from laughing. Still, I cleverly responded: "Ah sure, orange juice isn't just for breakfast anymore!" (Coke had just bought Minute Maid Orange Juice and was running a prominent ad campaign: "Orange juice isn't just for breakfast anymore!") Which I thought was a rapid uptake and creative response! (In other words, if you can drink orange juice all day, you can also drink Coke for breakfast!) But he turned beet red, walked briskly to the door, and said: "Thank you for coming!" I responded, "Yes, very happy to come along." He opened the door as wide as possible, gestured to the exit, and repeated slowly and menacingly, "Thank . . . you . . . for . . . Coming!" I was dismissed. I thought my response was brilliant, but evidently, I had just insulted the world's most popular brand! Obviously, I was the wrong cultural fit! I couldn't have been in the room for more than ninety seconds.

The second interview was in 1994, in the early days of the internet. I was headhunted to interview for the CTO role for the top web search engine at the time, and flew to Los Angeles to meet with the CEO. Well prepared, suited, and booted, I arrived to be ushered into the CEO's office overlooking LAX airport. As I walked over to the table, he shouted with, I think, a Texan accent, "Sit down!" And without a break, continued. "We're growing 140 percent monthly; technology can't keep pace with the explosive growth, we're melting down, and the system is crashing continuously! What would you do?" I swiftly responded, "The first thing I'd do is a quick analysis of the situation and do a traffic capacity forecast to look at the growth projection—" He cut me off, screaming, "WRONG! F**KING, WRONG!!! You'd buy 20,000 servers and then come to me and tell me it's all sorted. You're the wrong F**KING guy; get the hell out of here!" I did better than the first example; I think I lasted almost two minutes with this guy! I can only imagine the pressure he must have been under to lose it like that.

Years later, now that my ego has fully recovered, I can reflect back and say that I think my responses were appropriate and correct in both cases. Regardless, I still take umbrage at the rudeness and callousness of the treatment. In both instances, I was there at their invitation, had prepared extensively, and was friendly, enthusiastic, and earnest. While the times have changed, they still stand as good examples of what I said earlier: to respect your interviewee, at least give the politeness and respect they deserve for the time allocated.

I will add a humorous interview story, not as an interviewer story, but as an interviewee story. I was at the Gore Hotel in London circa 2014 with Andy, my enterprise architect, interviewing candidates for the innovation strategy director position in our new TUI Group Innovation Labs. We had some highly qualified candidates, including Bill. Bill was an exceptional individual with a global New Media strategy pedigree. He arrived and sat down and, with no further introduction, promptly announced that he wanted the innovation job and was the best-qualified candidate we would find because he was a genius! I kept my cool, didn't laugh, and stated, "Well, yes, we're all smart people here, and that's why we're looking for another smart person to join the team. Tell us about your strategy experience." Bill said, "I'm an exceptional strategy guy and particularly follow military strategy, having read *The Five Rings*" (a popular strategy book at the time). This was his second mistake and just the opening Andy wanted. Andy immediately responded, "Yes, nice little book by Miyamoto Musashi; if you follow military strategy, then you must have read *On War*, von Clausewitz's classic Prussian military treatise dissecting the Thirty Years' War?" Unfortunately for Bill, he had just met more than his match in Andy. He turned white and stammered, "No, not yet, but I'd like to." Ultimately, despite two glaring faux pas, we decided Bill was a capable and talented guy, and we liked him. However, it didn't work out from a compensation perspective. The morals of the story are 1) For the interviewee—be humble even if you are a genius 2) For the interviewer—give creative types a break; they're human too.

Setting Goals, Objectives, and Tasks

Setting goals and objectives is a notoriously delicate issue, as it's not simply a function of deciding how to divide up the overall strategy into chunks that you divvy out to staff. As Newton astutely stated: "For every action, there is an equal and opposite reaction." Bending this to my purpose, in other words, you've got to consider your staff's objectives, capabilities, and desires in the equation or transaction. What are the tasks, and who has the capability, time, and motivation to carry them out? Further, how to apportion the tasks equitably across the team. What are the current workload levels in the group? Should the task go to the most capable person, or is it a better stretch goal to provide growth for another? There are a multitude of questions of this nature, but suffice to say, consider the task and carefully assess the individuals and the team collectively to ensure you "select the right tool (staff member) for the task." Let's analyze this further.

There are several key issues to consider when setting staff goals and objectives. There are the annual formal written objectives, plus ongoing necessarily adaptable project-based goals, objectives, and tasks. A leader needs to coordinate team, project, and individual objectives that require collaboration and delivery by multiple people and then adapt individual objectives to accommodate the collective goals. Then, you can assess the individual employee's maturity, experience, and capabilities relative to these objectives through the aforementioned models of Situational Leadership and Competency Maturity Models covered in Book 1.

You need to be more prescriptive and granular for junior, inexperienced, or less mature staff performing low-level and repetitive tasks. You must define the specific activities, anticipated tasks, required outcomes, and the overall KPIs and metrics they are expected to achieve. Conversely, for mature, experienced staff, you can specify higher-level objectives to provide latitude for capable individuals to contribute their ideas and abilities to successfully deliver or exceed with the more complex and challenging objectives.

Your company's HR organization will provide specific formal methodologies and extensive guidance for preparing your annual staff objectives. These processes are highly mature and precisely defined in most companies. However, it is helpful to reiterate a standard accepted approach for setting goals, harkening back to Peter Drucker in his book *The Practice of Management* and further refined in Hersey and Blanchard's *SMART* objectives.

Sometimes, *SMART* objectives initially seem a bit tiresome to align precisely with many managers. Nevertheless, you should make a reasonable effort as it is a beneficial qualitative and quantitative model for writing demonstrable and trackable staff objectives. The *SMART* model represents the following attributes: *Specific, Measurable, Attainable, Relevant, and Time-Based.* There are dozens of viable variations on writing *SMART* objectives, but in simple terms, here are the essentials:

S—*Specific goals and objectives* that are clear, simple, and well-defined, providing specific activities, tasks, and outcomes or deliverables that need to be accomplished.

M—*Measurable goals or outcomes* that can be quantified to help determine and evaluate successful progress, achievement, and completion.

A—*Attainable*, the objective must be realistic and achievable given the employee's available resources, time, and ability.

R—*Relevant*, employees' objectives must relate to and be aligned to the overall department and organization objectives to ensure relevance to broader team objectives.

T—*Time-Based* objectives set specific time frames and deadlines to ensure activities and outcomes are quantifiable and measurable.[8]

As mentioned, given other pressing issues, this may feel like a tedious, low-priority task for a senior leader. However, a large team can achieve great things when directed clearly and efficiently. Recalling Abe Lincoln's ax analogy, your effort to create clear, specific, and measurable objectives will yield tremendous results and benefits over the next assessment period.

Having discussed specific objectives for new or junior staff, let's move on to more experienced and senior staff. For middle-management and senior staff, you need to find an effective balance for annual objectives that gives general guidelines for objectives and precise specifics if required. You must also provide ample scope for the capable individual's initiative, creativity, and adaptability to the ebb and flow of business activities throughout the year.

For a senior person, if you write too specific and rigid objectives at the start of the appraisal year, ultimately, you might find yourself disappointed in their achievements. Moreover, you won't want senior staffers to focus on a laundry list of finite objectives at the expense of taking the initiative, coming up with innovative new ideas and solutions, and helping manage the changing business needs in real time. Therefore, it is preferable to identify general areas of responsibility and high-level objectives with expected outcomes and empower them with a measure of independent decision-making to deliver results.

When considering senior management, greater freedom and flexibility may be required to deal with situations comprising ambiguous challenges or emerging markets/products. Therefore, empowering managers to think and act adaptively and expansively is vital to inspiring and encouraging them to undertake unpredictable tasks or achieve new objectives.

One crucial nuance to objective setting is the frequent requirement for multiple people to deliver a task. This implies an element of personal motivation as well as teamwork. If both or all resources are on your team, it will be easily manageable, but occasionally projects require cross-functional effort. This can be more complicated. One mechanism I've implemented successfully within my organizations was a shared objective and bonus system, which I named "bonus buddies." This is where specific individuals and teams had targets and were evaluated based on their collective contribution and success. Of course, this is more difficult across functional and organizational teams, but you can still manage recognition across boundaries through shared objectives if not material rewards. This approach proved an excellent way to get different, even competing functions, to work together collaboratively.

A further word of warning is to set defined areas of responsibility to ensure clear boundaries between departments, functions, and projects to avoid conflict with other senior managers on the team or within the organization.

In my career, I've directly and indirectly experienced some senior management who have the misguided impression that there might be some benefit in setting senior managers in competition or giving over-lapping responsibilities. Evidently, they believe this conflict might have a challenging motivational use in stimulating new projects or "separating the wheat from the chaff" to see who might best deliver a critical new initiative. Unfortunately, those of us who have been thrown into this sit-uation found this approach disrespectful, inefficient, disruptive, conflic-tive, and hugely demotivating. It can also result in losing respect for the initiating leader/manager or even a valuable employee's sudden departure.

To complete this section about setting objectives and how to manage different types of staff based on competence and motivation, I'll provide two real-to-life, personal examples.

My first example is a detailed case study, which I will elaborate on later. In the late 1980s / early 1990s, when I was training manager for Reuters Asia, I was grappling with the flood of new derivative financial service products. While struggling with the products' poor usability, I began urgently building computer-based training and e-learning to scale to the challenge of training thousands of customers across half the globe. Finally, I proposed to the group board that we build "performance sup-port systems" into the core systems during development. The proposal was approved, and I was relocated to London to kick off the initiative.

I reported for duty on January 3, 1993, and went to see Peter Job, the Reuters chief executive. I walked into his office, and he sat me down and said: "Greg, your assignment is simple. Fix our product line." That was the mission and sole instruction. However, that was precisely the right direction. Had I had more prescriptive objectives, I might have only built the e-learning performance systems. I wouldn't have conceived of or set up the help desk incident tracking system, the global network of usability labs, or the usable design labs. The ultimate result dramatically exceeded the original task requirements.

The following example was when I was at TUI leading a large trans-formational project when it came time to set the annual objectives for the new year. Despite my awareness of the importance of the activity, I recall a fair amount of frustration with the "administrative work" while being in the heat of battle with multiple transformational challenges. After managing all the other staff objectives, I only had Andy, the enterprise architect, remaining. Andy was intelligent, motivated, and fully engaged with me in the transformation. We sat down for the mutual objectives setting, and despite my scribbled notes for the discussion, I recalled the previous situation with my boss at Reuters. Finally, I just blurted out: "Andy, you know what's happening; you know what we are trying to accomplish. Over the next six months, your objectives are: To Do What Needs to be Done!"

I'd realized that he was so capable and engaged that any prescriptive list of objectives or tasks would be obsolete within the month. He and I would be managing the transformation in real time, and the best thing to do would be to motivate and empower him to "Do what needed to be done!" We laughed about this many times over the next year. When it came to his appraisal the following year, his list of accomplishments far exceeded whatever objectives and tasks I might have set for him in that objective setting the previous year. This is an interesting example of managing, motivating, and empowering a consciously competent, willing, and able employee.

Let's fast-forward for a moment in that the flip side of setting objectives is ultimately the associated performance appraisal against those objectives. In cases like Andy's above, where you have a "willing and able" employee, both Peter Drucker and W. Edwards Deming would agree with a "light touch" on performance objectives and appraisals. Drucker felt the job appraisal erodes the senior employee's self-confidence and the manager/staff relationship by focusing on the staff's failures rather than reinforcing and building on their positive behaviors and achievements. Deming felt the appraisal process was akin to management by fear, which again focused on the negative aspects of the behavior instead of building on the positive. Both suggest that better hiring, robust training, good communications, encouragement, and support of valuable employees were far better ways to achieve top performance in capable staff than the tactical appraisal mechanisms.

These caveats regarding senior staff objectives should not be an excuse for "bucking the system" within your organization by neglecting the responsibility for doing proper *SMART* objectives when required by the company. However, also recognize the enormous benefits of assertive empowerment, good judgment, responsible flexibility, and adaptability when managing capable senior staff.

Work Assignment Discussions

Setting work and task assignments are largely similar to SMART objectives, as the principles are broadly the same, although the scale is different. There is, however, a nuance that is worth a few words. Not every task assignment will excite and motivate the staff and may seem beneath them or be perceived as a reprimand. Regardless, as a leader, you still need to get the whole job done across the board.

It is vital to exercise your best judgment to balance the workload of difficult or unattractive assignments throughout the team to give the feeling of equanimity and equality. The same holds true for the assignment of plum projects or attractive assignments. Likewise, ensure the appealing ones are allocated to the team as equitably as the unattractive ones. This way, you will establish a reputation and recognized track record for fairness. This balanced impartiality will help avoid objections or conflicts about playing favorites or fairness.

The best way to handle unattractive or unpleasant task assignments will be an open and honest discussion of the overall team's objectives and how these tasks, however mundane or disagreeable, are an essential part of the team's responsibility to deliver a complete solution. You can even have a forthright discussion about an unattractive assignment with a top performer if they have high emotional intelligence without them feeling the work is beneath them or denigrating them. Of course, this may be a challenging discussion in some cultures. However, if you position it as a leadership learning point, they will probably understand and appreciate the leader's role in delivering the results while managing the team equitably.

Tracking and Incident File

Ages ago, I took a time management course from Alan Lakein, who wrote the book *How to Get Control of Your Time and Your Life.*[9] During the course, Mr. Lakein gave me a terrific piece of advice. He said you'll never remember everything beneficial (or not) for each of your employees at appraisal time at the end of the year. This is especially true if you, unfortunately, and inadvisably, as often happens, have too many direct reports.

Therefore, he recommended creating an "incident file" for each employee in the form of a simple folder in your drawer. Whenever anything significant happens, quickly scribble it on a scrap of paper or Post-it Note with the date and drop it in the file. This invaluable and simple system has helped me throughout my career to capture and retrieve valuable information on employees over the year to use at appraisal time. During the appraisals, managers and staff were occasionally amazed at my apparent near-photographic memory of what they'd achieved during the year. I'd then share my simple tip about the incident file to provide clear, valuable, time-based incident evidence about performance (positive and negative).

This was also indispensable documentation for staff mentoring, performance counseling, and especially employee salary reviews to defend proposed salary increase recommendations to management.

It's perhaps a sad comment on overall management effectiveness, but the reality is that in most cases, promotions, salary increases, and bonuses are a zero-sum game. In other words, there are only so many perks and money to go around. While I don't mean to be Machiavellian, you have your department to run and your teams and people to manage. Therefore, to the extent that you are proactive and disciplined and have the information and data, including that of the incident file, you will be more effective and successful than most in advancing your requests and proposals to leadership. That means that your budgets, proposed promotions, and salary increases will have superior justification and, thus, better chances of success.

Moreover, I am conscious that my staff were acutely aware of my ability to secure promotions effectively and achieve aggressive salary increases. These successes were, in part, a direct result of the background performance data evidence I had and the disciplined documentation efforts I made on their behalf. Undoubtedly, this positively impacted staff motivation and, ultimately, their performance.

Performance Discussions

Performance discussions and performance appraisals are always tricky situations. Still, you can learn to make them valuable and as natural as any other management or leadership skill with honesty, appropriate techniques, practice, experience, and a bit of courage.

Your corporate HR or people operations will have extensive documentation on performance discussions and likely have videos or training programs that will model and train management in their accepted corporate and legal requirements. My comments provide some leadership procedural best practices and contextual overlay rather than a substitute for any officially required company processes.

The challenge with performance appraisals is that people and even leaders are often naturally uncomfortable with awkward situations and would just as happily avoid them if at all possible. Except, this is shirking your responsibility as a manager and a leader. Ignoring or glossing over missed targets or performance problems is failing your obligation to your company and likely letting down the wider team. Not dealing with these issues may also undermine your credibility with your high performers as a manager. Moreover, in the long run, it does not help the employee, who ultimately needs honest feedback, to understand where they are excelling or failing and how to correct their performance.

If you've set up a solid team-based trusting and collaborative culture, a positive "can-do" attitude, and a constructive "tolerance for error," performance discussions are much more manageable. At the very least, the culture and the team will be appropriately aligned. Furthermore, any letdowns or personal failures cannot be blamed on managerial or organizational dysfunctionality. Therefore, your appraisal challenge can focus on the individual and the suboptimal performance.

First of all, ensure you get your facts right and confirm the details on any issues wherever possible. Importantly, assess if any other internal or external extenuating circumstances affected the situation and, thus, employee performance. Make sure you root out any impinging events you may not have been aware of relative to the issue or problem through continuous and immediate communications. You don't want to focus on a comparatively minor performance issue to be told that the employee or spouse has a serious illness, a parent has passed away, or a child is sick!

During the appraisal discussion, occasionally, the employee will deny, divert, or denounce the performance gap by claiming it is incorrect or never happened, was someone else's fault, or not entirely their responsibility. Accordingly, you need accurate information or evidence that they own the issue and the outcome. There is nothing worse than "accusing someone" (don't!) of or reviewing something when the situation you are describing is, in fact, false! Don't get bogged down here or get defensive; just gently set the record straight and get back on track; remember, they are the ones receiving the behavior modification or corrective action, not you.

Next, ask the employee to review the situation, the circumstances, and the outcomes and ask for their assessment of what happened and what they might have done differently. Then, most importantly, provide an honest and fair evaluation of what happened in your estimation. What was the objective, what happened, what was the impact, and what, in your view, should have happened? Use relevant metrics, quantitative evidence, or qualitative feedback to support the discussion.

In delivering the appraisal feedback, you've got to be honest, fair, and nonjudgmental. They will not respect you if you waffle about, beat around the bush, and don't speak straight and to the point. Further, if you don't take reasonable but firm control of the discussion, you could have continued performance issues with this employee, as they will feel you are weak and that they can get away with anything. So, just honestly, "call it like it is" without being punitive or inappropriately judgmental. Point out what happened and, in particular, what impact it may have had on other people, overall projects, or the departmental outcomes. Then, ask the employee what they suggest they can do to improve the situation and their subsequent performance.

Ensure you get an agreement between the two of you to confirm it conforms to your requirements in the future. You then need to ask for regular updates about the situation and monitor their performance until you are comfortable it is sustainably headed in the right direction.

You will undoubtedly recall instances in your career where someone or something began to "go off the rails," and corrective actions were lacking or delayed. This can result in the situation getting out of control, missed goals, or compromised results due to deferred corrective measures. Further, this can eventually result in employee failure or even dismissal. In short, direct, honest, and immediate communication is always the best policy.

You need to use this honesty and immediacy to overcome your fear or reticence of confronting the situation or feeling uncomfortable or awkward with these discussions with employees. This is a routine, natural, and essential part of your job. If you conduct performance appraisal discussions as an "adult" conversation, with straight talk, your effectiveness and credibility as a leader, along with your department's objectives and operations, will improve dramatically.

Critically, ensure you conduct yourself as a servant leader, mentoring and guiding the staff, rather than acting as an authoritarian despot more interested in asserting control than helping the employee improve.

If you have established a climate of authenticity and trust within your organization, your performance appraisal discussions will be immensely easier and more productive. With honesty, mentoring, and feedback, there need to be few "secrets" or "agendas" between the leader and the staff, to the extent that the relationship is open, forthright, trusting, and supportive.

I have on numerous occasions told a staff member: "If you don't know there is a problem, then there is not a problem!" In other words, I try to deal with objectives and performance moment-by-moment (see Ken Blanchard—*One Minute Manager*)[10], which means that you "nip things in the bud" and deal with minor issues before they grow or escalate. The staff member will appreciate this, especially if they recognize this is a standard modus operandi to ensure objectives are clearly understood, tasks are headed in the right direction, performance is correct, there is a tolerance for error, and guidance is benevolent and prompt.

Takeaways:
- Explore hiring internal staff first.
- Current staff have proven knowledge, skills, and relationships.
- Internal hiring is motivating across the organization.
- Hire externally for new and esoteric skills that do not exist internally.
- Virtual hiring requires careful role specification and candidate scrutiny.
- Use specific, measurable, attainable, relevant, and time-based objectives for new and junior employees.
- For senior staff, ensure objectives provide latitude and flexibility.
- An incident file requires only seconds to maintain incrementally over the course of the year but saves hours and delivers enormous benefits at staff appraisal or promotion time.
- Establish a climate of authenticity and trust within your organization, and your performance appraisal discussions will be immensely easier and more productive.

MANAGING PEOPLE

Leading and managing people involves a delicate balancing act of exercising your corporate responsibilities and managing people effectively yet empathetically. Among the most complicated and emotive issues you will deal with as a leader are salaries and promotions on one hand and redundancies and terminations on the other. This is where you need to employ your disciplined management skills as well as your leadership soft skills to motivate and mentor staff.

It is a harsh reality of management that there is never enough time or money to satisfy both the needs of the organization and the desires of the staff. Further, occasionally, given the dynamics of market conditions and the diversity of human nature, difficulties arise that destabilize people and disrupt plans. These situations where there are conflicting needs and demands require astute, delicate, and diplomatic strategies and tactics to achieve acceptable solutions or compromises to seemingly intractable conundrums.

This section on managing people will provide insights and techniques to manage these complex situations to an acceptable result for both the organization and staff.

Salary Discussions

According to Herzberg and other psychologists, salary is primarily a hygiene factor, not technically a motivator. That may very well be true when you argue semantics; however, one thing I know for sure is that if the salary is not a motivator, then as Herzberg explains, a lack of it, or disputes with it, can certainly be a demotivator!

Regarding resourcing, staff skill needs will differ depending on the task requirement. Especially if, for example, you need four hands instead of two to perform a task. However, as a personal principle for knowledge workers, I'd rather have one supersmart person than two average people. Even the higher salary for one exceptional person will probably be lower than two average people's wages. Let's scrutinize this position and potential investment carefully.

I've always tried to hire excellent or exceptional people and endeavor to motivate good people to perform excellently. We discuss motivation in depth elsewhere, but let's look at it from the perspective of the related issue of compensation.

Through many salary negotiations over the years, I've developed my own philosophy and approach to compensation, which I've repeatedly validated in my tenure. First of all, there is often a local market industry standard salary for most specific roles. Specifically, many companies such as Hayes, Glassdoor, Salary.com, and the Bureau of Labor Statistics produce reliable salary information. There are even new laws regarding transparency for employees and their salary ranges. In addition, recruitment agencies, sites, and companies like LinkedIn are excellent references for comparative salaries.

For simplicity's sake, let's use an example of 100,000 for whatever currency you like to make the calculations easy and the example clear. As said, I will search for the best person I can for any particular role, and in this case, for an industry benchmarked 100,000-dollar or -Euro role. My view, and undoubtedly, the high-caliber prospective candidate's opinion, might be that they are worth a bit more than the "industry standard." There are then a few scenarios for handling their recruitment salary negotiation.

First, there is the outdated corporate approach for a new candidate, where the hiring manager repeats the standard political line: "We like you and want to hire you, but you are new and unproven. Therefore, we'll need to offer you 90,000 dollars/euros, and if you work out and perform exceptionally well in the future, we'll accelerate you rapidly, and you will be rewarded commensurately." What happens here? The manager and prospective candidate both know that the job level and industry standard for the role is circa 100,000 dollars/euros. However, if it's a good role and company, the candidate may reluctantly accept the lower starting salary to get a foot in the door.

Unfortunately, in a best-case scenario, it will take the employee some years to recoup this loss of initial wages. Further, this approach leaves a slightly bitter taste in the candidate's mouth, resulting in a disappointed or somewhat negative attitude toward you, the role, and the company.

As I've explained to many high-caliber candidates in the past, if the role is a 100K role, and I give you 90K, then you may subconsciously resent it, feeling that I've stiffed you 10K, which you might claw back in reduced motivation, effort, or performance. The result of your reduced performance, by the 10K you lost, initially results in you delivering perhaps an 80K performance.

Second, if I pay you the 100K the job is worth and you deserve, accordingly, you perform appropriately and deliver an appropriate 100K performance.

Lastly, suppose I want exceptional performance and am attempting to hire an outstanding person. In that case, I expect that person to make a big difference in the future and be a critical key success factor for the team. Therefore, my approach is this: I will source the best person possible and argue the following in advance with HR and my management, who are accustomed to me hiring great people and delivering reliably well.

I will explain this in advance to the prospective candidate during the salary negotiation: "Listen, this is the way I work, and I review the scenarios above." I go on to explain: "You and I both know that this job is a 100K role by industry standards. However, I don't want an industry-standard performance or outcome. Therefore, I will believe in and invest in you from the outset, and I'm going to offer you 110K. I presume you will recognize our investment in you, and you will perform accordingly. Therefore, I assume that if I pay you 110K, I'm likely to receive 120K worth of exceptional performance!"

The three scenarios above show that the difference between saving 10K or investing 10K in a high-caliber person is not 20K. It is the difference between an 80K and 120K performance, a 40K uplift in the final result in delivery achievement terms! Clearly, this is a very "blunt" tool, and one can debate the numbers and the resulting performance impact, but the principle holds true. This is a simple approach and an easy metric. Still, it has served me exceptionally well over the decades with star staff and never failed to produce tangible results in negotiations, employee motivation, and exceptional delivery.

Let's look at another scenario: Negotiating to hire a superstar performer who knows their worth. However, perchance the company salary band and requirements are unfortunately less than the superstar's expectations. Again, I've had this situation on numerous occasions. The best approach, as above, is full disclosure and an honest conversation. This will also start the relationship off on the right foot.

In this case, I'll sit down with the person and say: "I want to hire you, and we both know that my situation is not unique to my or any other company. We have organizational financial constraints, not the least of which is keeping equality with the other high-quality internal staff. Let's have an open conversation to do our best to try to get you on board. We both have two metrics. You have your bottom-line minimum acceptable salary and your desired expectations. Conversely, I have my absolute top wage that I can afford and sell to management, and then I have the company's desired compensation level. Based on the principles I explain in the scenarios above, I appreciate it is in my best interest to try to motivate you or at least not to demotivate you, or there is no sense in either of us proceeding. Therefore, let's see if, at a bare minimum, my top line meets your bottom line."

Hopefully, we can identify an overlap between my top and the candidate's bottom lines through this open and honest discussion. If there is, then I offer my top line rather than their bottom line, thus achieving the return-on-investment principles discussed in the scenarios above. The candidate will recognize my good intentions to treat them fairly by investing in them rather than being a heavy-handed negotiator manipulating or pressuring them to come on board.

If there is a significant disconnect between my top-line possible salary and their bottom line, then at least we have everything out in the open and have established a climate of honesty and trust. Further, I will do my best to communicate an exciting vision of their future role and the team and demonstrate my integrity as a manager, which the candidate can factor into the career decision. At that point, I offer my top line and leave it to the candidate to decide whether to accept the role at that salary.

Based on the honest and open salary principles and discussions above, I can only think of one case in decades where a candidate and I failed to find a common ground salary position acceptable to both parties. That was with "Bill the Genius," we discussed earlier, but unfortunately, we had a gap of 75K, so regrettably, despite our desires to proceed, we could not bridge so large a chasm.

Additionally, a leader/manager must remember that staff behavior can change over time based on accumulated knowledge and skill development or obsolescence. Thus, you'll need to adapt and evolve your approach with this employee over time to accommodate this change in capabilities. If not, you risk constraining staff members' development, stifling their motivation, or potentially losing them. Also, be aware of alterations in staff motivation and attitudes that can relate directly or indirectly to the management style you need to employ.

For example, even if you are an employee advocate for all the best intentions, your ability to provide financial compensation will always be constrained by your organization's health and the state of the economy. Then, given individual circumstances (e.g., an employee's growing family), these limitations can affect an individual's behaviors if not carefully managed.

One example of salary-related motivational issues was early in my career when I managed my first office at American Express. I'd conceived, started, and received recognition for having built the first AMEX office to make money in its first full year. Shortly after that, Amex recruited some high-flying Harvard MBA trainees, one of whom was assigned to me. After bringing on my new trainee (who I did like), I discovered that my new trainee was making significantly more than me. This was a serious demotivator to me, which resulted in me calling my boss in Chicago and announcing I would be quitting. When he asked me whatever for, I announced I was resigning to reapply for my current role at an improved salary. He laughed at my boldness and immediately gave me a 15 percent increase. This was not at the level the new trainee was making, but it did placate me.

The lesson here was that despite having a Harvard MBA, the trainee was being trained by me to take on a role similar to mine and with a considerable disparity in salary. This was a clear demotivator for me, one of the current top performers. Therefore, be aware of maintaining some level of equivalence, even in unique situations such as graduate programs where new high-fliers will work alongside your current high performers or "solid citizens." Even if, on the rare occasion, nothing can be done about the discrepancy, open and honest communications go a long way toward maintaining trust, motivation, and loyalty.

Promoting Staff

I made the case earlier for hiring internal staff when we discussed interviews. In a related context, I'll expand on those thoughts with additional compelling reasons for promoting internal staff versus hiring externally. First, the internal team is proven; they have already acclimated to the company and fit into the culture. Further, internal staff have the established organizational relationships necessary to get things done that an external candidate would need to build from scratch over an extended period. Third, critically, existing staff have a wealth of knowledge and capabilities vital to performing the job. An expensive new external may fail to fit in or bond with relevant stakeholders, perhaps taking years to absorb what the internal has already assimilated.

Further, as mentioned, there is a high risk of external candidate failure. Finally, tapping current employees for new roles is enormously motivating for employees across the organization. This cumulative organizational impact should not be underestimated.

As mentioned, I have often found "hidden gems" internally, who were key employees working beneath current managers or supervisors and who thus were "glass-ceilinged" because of the incumbents in the role. These high performers may also be viewed as essential staff in their current position and often perceived as indispensable and too critical in their role to move. They may be the resident experts or have crucial capabilities. As such, they can languish in mission-critical functions for years, being passed over by highfliers who may not have an equivalent depth of experience or expertise as loyal, long-term corporate citizens. Further, don't forget this indispensable employee has all the knowledge, skills, and even motivation to train their replacement to backfill them to take the new role.

A case in point was Carmen, a senior development employee who once worked for me. Carmen was one of the crucial top technical development staff and, for years, had already been informally training and mentoring staff. However, with the most extensive experience with the legacy core system, she was so mission-critical no one dared move her on and lose seemingly irreplaceable departmental knowledge. Further, Carmen was well-liked, excellent with people, highly respected, hugely capable, and disciplined. She had all the management capabilities needed, except that she had never been given the opportunity or leadership visibility to break through the organizational management glass ceiling.

The merger carve-out of a new business required establishing two parallel development teams in separate organizations. This provided precisely the right opportunity for Carmen to advance. Her current boss remained in the parent company, and I tapped Carmen to be the IT manager of the core systems department in the new company. Everyone who knew Carmen was delighted, and she flourished overnight. Her team comprised former colleagues who had known her for years and, in most cases, had worked closely with her and had been trained and mentored by her. Her colleagues, now her staff, were excited for her and to be working for her. There was no internal jealousy or competition, and everyone immediately fell in line with Carmen's natural leadership capabilities. Carmen blossomed rapidly as a leader for her team and as a valued contributor across the organization.

Carmen's example is a clear and vivid example of tapping one of the hidden internal gems I've referred to. In setting up the new organization, she was not the only one, as there were three other similar senior promotions. I recruited and promoted the entire top tier of my IT directorship team internally. Promoting and placing internal staff in these leadership roles was the right thing to do for everyone due to the exceptional capabilities of these long-term capable and qualified staff. Additionally, it had a significant positive motivational impact across the organization. Everybody was pleased with the newly appointed managers and encouraged that management recognized the existing talent and promoted the entire directorship team internally.

Further, a considerable additional benefit was an extremely high-performing leadership team that hit the ground running immediately. The quick mobilization and rapid acceleration of the new team occurred literally in days instead of potentially many months or even a year or two (or never) had we needed to source new externals to fill the same roles. Finally, the entire team knew each other, and there were no issues like having to incorporate a new member into an existing team.

The tremendous benefits of this new team were felt well beyond the IT team and throughout the whole company, which profited immediately from a highly experienced and mature IT organization. The newly

formed organization began to operate seamlessly, technically, operationally, procedurally, and organizationally. Any alternative strategy comprised a multitude of potential points of failure.

While I received significant accolades for this terrific team, I'd have
to say the immense success of this team came down to their years of
preparatory labor in the trenches before their promotions. All I had to do
was recognize their talent, negotiate their release, and assemble and motivate the teams. Selecting a great internal team for a new task is likely the
easiest and most effective way to achieve your immediate objectives. I was
successful; they got promotions, and the company realized the benefits!

Employee Redundancies and Layoffs

In the course of business, structural and organizational changes occur now and then. Whether it is a market transformation or contraction, a restructuring, or a skill's obsolescence over time that requires downsizing or, as is said now, rightsizing. When this occurs, human resources is an essential business partner to help you through the procedural mechanisms and legal maze to effect this change correctly and legally. However, your role as the leader is even more critical to cushion the blow for the redundant staff and the remaining team, who may have lost collegial friends and will have to pick up the slack.

Often, to affect the organizational change, again, you will have to conduct a skills assessment to determine what skills and competencies will be required in the future and which employees have the requisite skills to support the business going forward. This is not a popularity contest but rather often a survival exercise, which must leave the remaining team and organization fully equipped to operate the business with reduced or altered resources. In light of this, the objective is to retain critical essential skills. However, you will also need to consider the potential effectiveness of the remaining team to ensure that they can work together satisfactorily.

Once you have identified who will remain and who will regrettably depart, you must create a plan to manage and mentor both parties. For the redundant employees, with HR, you will need a communication plan, an implementation plan, and, as much as possible, an outplacement program. This process will be formal through HR and informal through your leadership initiatives to guide and support the redundant staff to land on their feet as rapidly and effectively as possible. Remember, these were your loyal team and colleagues, and you have likely hired, trained, and mentored them. Therefore, you must execute the redundancies or terminations as responsibly, supportively, and benevolently as possible. Ideally, through formal outplacement and informal networking, you, the leader, the management, and the retained staff can assist the redundant employees in securing alternative employment. Finishing something well, especially like the layoffs, is just as important as starting things out well!

Some communications and team-building interventions will probably be necessary to realign the new team. Further, you will need to reallocate responsibilities, acknowledge the separation anxiety of lost colleagues, and attempt to facilitate the new team's bonding to ensure and maintain effective continuing collaboration.

The following example is a good case study, with various nuances, on managing large layoffs effectively.

Large Redundancies and Layoffs

In January 2000, I was headhunted for a role as CIO/CTO for Worldsport Networks. In hindsight, I should have taken the safe route and stayed with AOL, which had just merged with Time Warner. However, despite this merger, cited as one of the worst mergers of all time, my job as director of mobile and broadband for AOL Europe in 2000 was a terrific role in a nascent emerging market.

When contacted for the Worldsport role, I went along to the interview primarily out of curiosity because of the attractiveness of the CIO/CTO role and the dramatically increased compensation and options. Moreover, the chief executive and managing director were great salespeople who sold me on the vision of promoting and advancing sports for youth globally. We were not solving world hunger, but we were promoting sports to help improve the health of youth, which appealed to my sense of purpose and altruism.

I joined Worldsport Networks in mid-February 2000 as CIO/CTO, only to have Boo.com fail two weeks later in late February 2000. This incident catalyzed the catastrophic global dot-com collapse, causing severe erosion of confidence in internet businesses right at the time Worldsport needed a new round of funding. According to CEO Alan Callan, Sky Sports had offered him 2 billion pounds the previous year for Worldsport Networks, with their monopoly of webcasting rights for the GAISF sports federations, including all major global sports federations, with the exception of the Olympics.

Unfortunately, a perfect storm of the dot-com collapse compromising the next round of investment funding, along with the simultaneous discovery of Alan Callan's bone cancer caused a series of successive implosions of Worldsport Networks. We struggled desperately for funding for weeks, with a final offer of $40 million from Hicks Muse Tate and Furst from Dallas, for controlling interest. Alan was furious; he wanted a minimum of £100 million, and from his sickbed at the Mayo Clinic in Rochester, Minnesota, he snapped, "Over my dead body," which we feared would be the case. As the situation deteriorated after the collapse of Boo.com and the dot-com bubble burst, rolling layoffs were necessary to maintain the company's survival through successive contractions.[11]

What happened next is a poignant example of how to execute a dramatic and painful but necessary staff downsizing in an ethical, caring, and effective manner for the team and the company.

Starting with 256 IT staff, when I joined in February, by a fateful week in mid-June, I was told on a Tuesday that I needed to reduce my staff by 50 percent by Friday of that week to cut costs. For the next three days, my directors and I analyzed the situation. What were the critical skills we needed to survive, who were the key essential technical staff required to save the company, and were there any extraordinary circumstances of individual staff we needed to consider when identifying the redundancies? The team knew we were in trouble, as the rumor mill from sales and marketing told them redundancies were imminent. First, we compared the identified skills we needed with the staff who had the requisite skills. Next, we discussed their circumstances and potential options with all the staff. The process was complicated, but I decided to have discussions as open as possible to ensure we had all the information on the table.

I announced a whole team "town hall" on Friday at high noon. At the appointed time, I called all 256 staff together in the open-plan office and asked them to gather around.

I began, "Team, unfortunately, sometimes things happen that are beyond our control, that have dramatic and unavoidable consequences for us, through no fault of our own. You all know that Worldsport Networks is in severe financial trouble. The board and I have done everything we could to rectify the situation to avoid a catastrophic collapse of the organization. Unfortunately, the efforts have been unsuccessful, and to survive and try to save the company, we must cut the costs by a full 50 percent immediately. I sincerely hoped and prayed that we could avoid this, but unfortunately, the situation is desperate, and we must reduce the staff and cut the costs to survive. Therefore, at the end of my speech, we will have to lay off half of the team in the room. I sincerely apologize, but this is unavoidable. We all joined with the hopes and aspirations of success of this grand venture that Alan and the Board painted. However, we are now in survival mode and must make some difficult and tough decisions. We have carefully determined what skills we need and which staff were qualified and best placed to provide those skills. In many cases, it is the most qualified resource we need, but in other cases, the decisions were made based on some unique skills required for survival."

I closed my speech with tears in my eyes and a catch in my throat: "It is easy to start out well, rush ahead with enthusiasm and excitement, and gear up and mobilize rapidly. Finishing well is more challenging. However, we should consider the company's and employees' needs in both situations. Therefore, when we make this staff cut, we will not cease until each redundant employee finds a new situation. We are a team, and we remain a team that will support each other through this difficult challenge. Now let's do it, and do it right; let's care for each other and take care of our own!"

I sat back on the back of my chair with an unashamed mist in my eyes. Then, to my complete shock, all 256 staff leaped to their feet and gave me a standing ovation! The most moving and significant moment of my leadership career was being given a standing ovation by the staff I was about to terminate. In retrospect, this taught me that you can even do difficult things well if they are done with honesty and sincerity. Further, you can do it in a heartfelt manner to respect, honor, and support your teams who believed in your vision, followed your mission, and have been dedicated to your program.

We executed the redundancies with honesty, respect, and compassion and with the full cooperation of all the staff. We then set up counseling sessions with each of the redundant staff to determine how to help them find a new situation. Within two weeks, we found new jobs for all but one employee, who eventually found a role after about six weeks. This experience gave me a firm belief and faith in "leading with the heart" through servant leadership and in the spirit, courage, loyalty, and integrity of the staff you lead.

Employee Terminations

Inevitably, in business, as occasionally in life, things don't always work out. At these times, good leadership is tested and proven by effectively overcoming challenges. A particularly thorny issue for leaders and organizations is employee terminations. Further, this is not a "zero-sum" game where one party automatically wins and the other loses. Instead, I believe effective employee terminations or layoffs can be concluded professionally and humanely, with a reasonably successful result for both the employee and the company.

There are many reasons for employee terminations. It can be for unacceptable performance, a change of functional departmental circumstances, the evolution of the industry or technology, or the result of an organizational contraction and redundancy. The termination procedures and approach will differ depending on whether it is a termination for cause, an employee inadequacy, or a redundancy necessitated by market conditions. Regardless, when terminating a subordinate, be sure to have every meeting and conversation with that employee fully documented, with a cc to HR. This includes a brief notation for an informal discussion or other related employee comments. This should follow the same principle as the incident file we discussed for employee achievements. Just remember that a disciplined quick note to file can prevent a thorny future issue if the termination regrettably ends up in a dispute.

In terminations due to performance problems or "by cause," this matter must be handled in close consultation with human resources. They will have specific formal procedures and governance complying with company policy and local country laws. I'll address some of the direct leadership and management steps and behaviors to be completed in conjunction with HR to ensure as good and positive an outcome as possible for both parties. Remember that corrective guidance is the preferred solution for the manager, as turnover is costly, disruptive, and painful and should be the last course of action. But if it is necessary, it should be done courageously and decisively.

As mentioned in the performance discussions section, I have often reassured staff members by stating: "If you don't know there is a problem, then there is not a problem"! Conversely, when there is a problem, the employee should be acutely aware of the issue and what should be done to correct and improve the behavior and performance. As stated multiple times, early and honest feedback is essential to "nip problems in the bud" before they mushroom out of control and become real performance issues. There should never be any surprises relative to performance-related deficiencies or failures. This is an essential part of management monitoring that should be done immediately and consistently. Avoidance of the issue or delay in feedback will always exacerbate the problem.

Initially, corrective performance discussions should be informal and cordial mentoring feedback sessions, ideally with brief informal notes dated and archived in the staff incident file. Should the problem persist, then you need to get to the bottom of the issue. Is the problem related to any externalities on the part of the staff member? Is it a knowledge, skill, or training issue? Are there any internal conflicts or impediments you may not be aware of? What does the employee attribute the issue, deficiency, or problem to? Does anyone else need to be consulted or involved? What can be done to correct the situation?

If, after several informal mentoring and monitoring managerial efforts, the problem persists, then you should formally document the issue and have a review meeting with HR to discuss how to proceed. This will likely be the time for a friendly, firm, unambiguous discussion, including HR, with the staff member to advise them that the situation will need to be addressed, what specifically needs to be done, and how it should be rectified within an agreed time frame. Depending on the urgency or issue, it typically takes a month or six weeks. As this conversation will probably be threatening and anxiety-producing for the employee, make an extra effort to communicate your belief in them and your sincere desire for their success. Ensure you or a supervisor stay in contact and monitor the staffer to get regular progress feedback.

After the designated period, schedule a formal assessment review, then agree and document the result. If the issue continues, gently but unambiguously advise the staffer that you will now enter a formal HR-led corrective performance process. Again, HR will guide you, but this will be for setting "SMART" objectives within defined short-term time frames and with regular reviews.

Eventually, if there has been no improvement, you will arrive at the stage where you will need to terminate. This should not come as any surprise or shock to the employee or colleagues. Often, the employee will have already sourced another job, as they will have recognized that the "handwriting is already on the wall." You will need to be serious, firm, and decisive at this stage; in other words, "know when to hold them and when to fold them" to use a card-playing analogy. If you have done your best to guide and help the employee to no avail, then make a firm decision to deal with the issue rather than prolong the agony for everyone. I'm reminded of another saying: "If you find yourself in a deep hole . . . stop digging!"

When termination is required, ensure you work through the processes carefully in advance with HR. Try to facilitate and execute the termination as humanely, constructively, and professionally as possible. Plan the meeting with the employee and HR present in a quiet, out-of-the-way place, and have an honest and open conversation with the employee. Explain your sincere, ongoing efforts to help them succeed, but this has not been successful despite the substantial effort. Listen to what they say, but do not lose control of the conversation, and do not lose resolve or capitulate. Then again, with the HR staff in attendance, firmly and carefully communicate the termination and terms for separation. Next, try to encourage them considerately and benevolently. Explain what has gone wrong and give them guidance about what they might do next, given their positive attributes and considering their shortcomings. Try to leave them with a sense of self-respect and a feeling of hope for the future. Close the meeting promptly with a final word of encouragement.

Next, communicate clearly and honestly to the former colleagues' coworkers what has occurred, including your considerable efforts to help and guide the former employee to rectify the situation. The chances are the other employees will be acutely aware of the terminated employee's performance issues, which may have adversely impacted them by this employee not pulling their weight or even being disruptive. Colleagues may be sad, but relieved and grateful that management has taken the appropriate action. Next, explain the termination result, respecting the terminated employee's legal rights, privacy, and honor. Finally, brief the team on what will be done to fill the responsibility gap left by the employee and any plans for realignment, replacement, or recruitment.

Finally, officially document the issue with HR and prepare any necessary communications to leadership and the wider organization relative to what actions are being taken to resolve the outstanding problems and reassign responsibilities.

Dealing with Difficult People or Situations

One of the areas that differentiates a top leader from a novice or ineffective leader is their ability to deal with difficult people or problematic situations. An effective leader will have a firm foundation of principles and a substantial measure of self-confidence and courage as a starting point. From that personal foundation of strength, as discussed, immediate, honest, straight talk is generally the right policy and the best approach.

In some troublesome cases, the first thing you may have to do is defuse a situation. If the problematic situation entails a previously trusted and loyal staff member, you can rely on your existing relationship to help calm and reassure the employee. With a good prior relationship, you can sit them down, calm them, and reassure them that you are concerned, you will listen, and you will provide them with as fair a resolution as possible within the constraints of your role and company requirements.

Ensure you stay composed and don't enter into the heat or heart of the debate; try to rise above it and maintain some emotional distance while verbally de-escalating the situation. Once you've cooled things down, ask them to explain the situation carefully. Listening intently will somewhat defuse the situation and help you understand more precisely their concerns. Don't jump to conclusions or assume you know the issues; wait and listen.

Don't prejudge the situation and show respect for them as individuals beyond the issue at hand. Attempt to see and acknowledge their point of view. If they have a valid point and you agree with it, acknowledge it and collectively look for a joint solution to the problem. If you are not in accord with their view, if appropriate, you can empathize with the situation from their perspective, but be careful not to agree or commiserate with it, which might put you in a compromising position regarding your company responsibilities. Acknowledge and address the situation directly; then, you can give your perspective, offer help/guidance, and encourage them wherever possible.

Attempt to reach a mutual understanding and common ground and endeavor to get their agreement to an appropriate course of action or compromise if required. Try to be positive and put things into perspective. Strive to paint the bigger picture, reminding them of what their colleagues, the team, and the organization are attempting to achieve. Reiterate and emphasize your vision and its purpose, lift their attention out of the passion and minutiae of the specific problem, and try to get them back on track with the big picture, the mission, and how their role and responsibilities contribute to it.

Occasionally, the problematic situation may have to do with something outside of the work responsibilities that is affecting them and their performance. If this is the case, and they are coming to you for advice, follow the general pattern above. Being friendly but not necessarily familiar, attempt to understand the situation, empathize with it, and look for suggestions and a potential solution without you owning it. Then, mentor them as their leader to attempt to help them resolve or cope with the situation as well as possible.

Dealing with Cultural Nuance

At Reuters in the early 1990s, we migrated our Reuters operations from Hong Kong to Singapore because of the unrest and protests in Hong Kong after the Tiananmen Square incident in Beijing. Consequently, I consolidated most of our Asian training and development operations to our new headquarters in Singapore Science Park.

However, as we had a critical mass of competent technical trainers in Hong Kong, I left the East Asia technical training operations there under Thomas, my Hong Kong Chinese technical training manager. Thomas was technically excellent, and I identified and mentored him for a middle-management role. However, with his team of six technical trainers in HKG, two in Japan, one in Australia, four more in Singapore, and two in Bahrain, the learning curve was steep with the monthly flood of new product launches.

I organized several extensive London-based product technical "train the trainer" sessions for Thomas, who was subsequently to conduct comprehensive training sessions for the Asian technical teams. Unfortunately, the complaints began to trickle in from various regional offices, indicating that the technical teams were floundering and not performing as well as expected. To ensure his in-depth knowledge acquisition, I then sent Thomas over to the development labs in New York and scheduled more Asian training sessions. When things did not improve, I talked to several regional trainers who reported not receiving adequate information and sufficient training to install and support the new systems.

I called Thomas from Hong Kong to Singapore to understand what was happening and explain the situation. I inquired, "Thomas, the technical trainers report they have not been properly trained. You went to the "train the trainer" sessions and the development labs and then conducted local "train the trainer sessions." Are you sure you covered everything about the products, services, and technologies to ensure they are fully trained?" Astonishingly, he responded candidly and directly, "Mr. Garrison (formalities in Asia were common at that time), I did cover many things, but not everything." To which I responded, "But why not?" Thomas responded incredulously: "Mr. Garrison, if I told them everything, they would know everything I know!" Instantly, to my surprise and dismay, I saw the heart of the matter and recognized that full disclosure of all training information would reduce his advantage and potentially threaten his "rice bowl," meaning his seniority, employment security, and career advancement.

There was no recourse; I needed to be straight and directly challenge his rice bowl. I continued calmly but firmly and with no ambiguity, "Thomas, as the technical training manager for Asia, I have invested months and thousands in your training to ensure that you, in turn, fully train and develop your staff. If you are not motivated and committed to fully training your staff to complete competency, I will need to terminate or demote you, reduce your salary, and appoint Daniel to take over your responsibilities." Thomas got the point. Despite my suspicions that he would never fully disclose all his training knowledge, the quality of his training improved to the extent that the complaints ceased and the services improved satisfactorily.

In summary, ensure you understand the problem, its origins, and any mitigating factors, including any actions deriving from cultural biases outside your normal operational context and behavioral experience. Encourage the employee to share their perspectives and any potential influencing considerations they may be aware of before assessing the situation and devising any appropriate actions or solutions.

In summary, when dealing with difficult people, adhere assiduously to the following techniques. Communicate with the individual, carefully assess the situation, ensure there are no extenuating circumstances, solicit their feedback and recommendations, propose a solution, take and communicate a firm decision, and get the employee's agreement and compliance with the approach.

If they still do not agree but are required to comply, secure and document their acknowledgment of your decision, their understanding, and expected compliance. Then, set a time frame for a follow-up checkpoint for a review and confirmation of competition or progress. If they object or do not comply, you may have to formalize the counseling/compliance, which we will address within the upcoming notification and termination procedures.

Politics—Good News/Bad News

When we think of politics in business, it often evokes negative connotations of a shifty, deceptive, underhanded, or untrustworthy person. However, politics in and of themselves are not inherently malevolent; it is the intent or actions that drive either the negative or positive behavior. For example, if we consider being political in the context of Bashar al-Assad, president of Syria, some might consider him dishonest, self-serving, and manipulative. Conversely, António Guterres, the UN's Secretary-General, is an astute, powerful, and highly ethical politician. As both are politicians, let's think of politics and being a politician as someone who is highly influential, has strength or power, and perhaps has highly developed networking and social skills, regardless of whether they are good or bad, ethical or unethical politicians.

In the case of bad, dishonest, or disreputable politicians in business, we need to beware and be cautious to defend ourselves and protect our team and organization. A word to the wise is to be careful what we say and do and, if possible, avoid or minimize contact with unethical individuals. Further, align yourselves with ethical and honest work colleagues to create a wholesome network of individuals with whom you can collaborate honestly, effectively, and with integrity. Finally, if the overall company culture is toxic and dysfunctional, unless you are in charge, in which case you need to do something to rectify it, otherwise isolate yourself, or if that's not possible, it is probably best to move on.

Having said all that, let us focus on good politics. In any large organization, there are inevitably politics. Therefore, it is necessary to become adept at communicating, collaborating, and navigating the organizational politics for your initiatives, team, and career. While many individuals are naturally social and gregarious, many are not, but that should not impede them from becoming successful politically. I'll refresh your memory from Book 1 regarding Joseph Badaracco's research into *Leading Quietly*.[12] Perhaps the best advice, as we have said, is to be true to yourself, honest, and sincere. That will help you build a vital internal organizational reputation of credibility and reliability. This internal favorable standing will take you a long way toward building the networks, support, and resources you need to be politically influential and effective.

If a leader does not have the requisite influence and a supportive network, it will be challenging to sell their ideas to leadership, secure approval for initiatives, and attract and retain high-caliber staff. Whether astuteness in politics is already a natural strength you can build upon or need to work on, developing effective communications, influencing management, and networking skills are essential for the team's activities and your career success.

These skills are often formed over time and through experience. Therefore, be sure to bolster yourself with the courage and confidence to persevere, even if sometimes that growth, particularly with politics, comes through awkward or painful experiences. Ultimately, your sincerity, integrity, and honesty will be recognized and rewarded. See the Leadership Characteristics topics in Book 1 on diplomacy, courage, and confidence for further guidance and support.

Takeaways:
- Believe in and motivate your staff and new hires with aggressive salaries. Investing in staff will deliver much more significant benefits than penny-pinching savings can ever yield.
- Tapping current employees for new roles is enormously motivating for employees across the organization.
  This cumulative organizational impact should not be underestimated.
- Redundancies—these were your loyal team and colleagues you hired, trained, and mentored. Therefore, execute redundancies responsibly, supportively, and benevolently.
- Terminations are challenging and costly in the best of circumstances. Avoid them if at all possible. If you've exhausted all alternatives, be empathetic but disciplined and take decisive action.
- Deal with objectives and ongoing performance moment-by-moment as a "one-minute manager."
- Deal with minor issues immediately before they grow or escalate and exacerbate.

OPTIMIZING OPERATIONS

In addition to the management techniques and soft skills we have been discussing in the previous sections, there are also a number of methodologies and tools in our leadership repertoire that are indispensable to effective operational and fiscal management.

In this section, we will elaborate on critical skills, proven techniques, and robust tools for:

- Efficient time management
- Effective project management
- Achieving quality
- Sound decision-making
- Wise fiscal budgeting

TIME MANAGEMENT AND SETTING PRIORITIES

I mentioned the time management course by Alan Lakein, which I took earlier in my career; I recall another great piece of advice from that course and his book *How to Get Control of Your Time and Your Life* that stuck with me. The instructor said: "All day long, every day, ask yourself frequently: What is the best use of my time RIGHT NOW?"[13] By challenging yourself continuously, he said you could keep focused on the essential things and keep from frittering time away minute by minute, which eventually adds up to hours or days.

He was exactly right, and once, when my father gave me a small silver John Audubon commemorative ingot, I scratched this saying on it and stuck it in my pocket before work every day for decades. This slight weight in my pocket reminded me continuously to reflect and act on the question: What is the best use of my time right now? Over the years, the impact of this simple but effective reminder undoubtedly helped my focus and efficiency measurably. Similarly, while the CEO of Avis, Robert Townsend, kept a poster on his office wall that read, "Is what I'm doing or about to do getting us closer to our objective?"[14]

Over the years, to maximize time and capture valuable moments, I've always tried to remember to keep a book in hand while waiting for appointments, on transport, and during flights. As a result, I've found that the number of books one can fly through is astounding.

When I read Stephen Covey's *7 Habits of Highly Effective People*,[15] I found the following model extremely effective when prioritizing and managing tasks, incidents, or projects. Delving deeper into this model reveals that this model evidently originated with US President Dwight Eisenhower, a supremely productive, efficient, and effective president, military commander, and university president. Thus, the Eisenhower Matrix, later popularized by Stephen Covey, has become my "gold standard" model and approach for time and priority management. I've modified it over the years according to my needs.

This classic four-box model uses time urgency and issue importance as the axes. We end up with the following categories:

A—Important and Urgent
B—Important and Not Urgent
C—Not Important and Urgent
D—Not Important and Not Urgent

Activity Prioritization

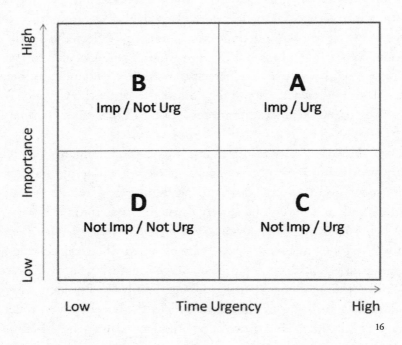

16

Let's work through each quadrant to challenge and optimize how we apply our time and priorities in each context.

First, everyone would agree that your top priority and target would be the As—the important and urgent tasks.

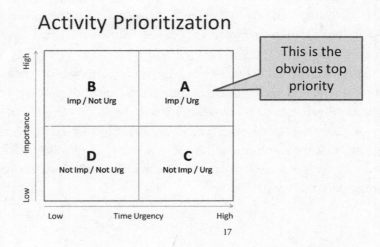

Secondarily, following a similar logic, we would all likely agree with the following scenario where we eliminate tasks within category D—not important and not urgent.

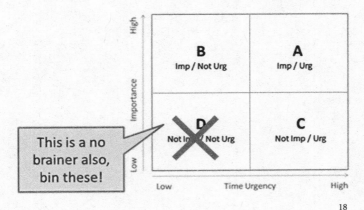

However, in the course of our daily work and the heat of battle, we often become focused on being action-oriented. We all like to feel productive, so instead of reverting automatically in our work to the important As or Bs, we often become reactive and respond to the urgent, but perhaps simpler and easier, but less critical tasks represented by the Cs.

This focus on Cs is one of the biggest mistakes we can make in time management and task prioritization. If a C is unimportant, then it is just a time-waster and of no greater value than a D. Therefore, we must continuously challenge ourselves to consciously stop ourselves when we begin to tick off small but unimportant tasks. They might make us feel good and appear productive, but in reality, these time wasters should be disregarded along with the Ds.

Another critical time management and prioritization issue is that if we focus on the Cs due to their urgency, we rarely get around to the important but not urgent Bs.

Activity Prioritization

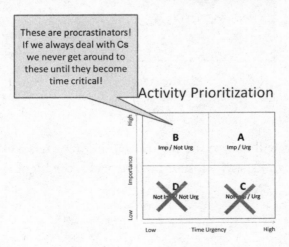

This is the biggest mistake people make! We like to feel productive and like to knock off lots of urgent tasks from our to do list. However if they are no more important than Ds, kill them too!

19

By wasting valuable time on unimportant tasks, in other words, the Cs, we procrastinate by not focusing on the Bs, which are important but not urgent, until time slips away and the Bs become time urgent and become As.

The problem here is that despite the Bs not being time urgent, the time and effort spent on the unimportant Cs are wasted when they could have been spent productively on the critical As and to progress the important Bs. Despite the lack of time urgency for the Bs, undoubtedly prioritizing them and completing them in a timely manner is bound to be value-creating. If something is important, it must be important enough to do swiftly.

These are procrastinators! If we always deal with Cs we never get around to these until they become time critical!

Activity Prioritization

20

Therefore, our one and only path of time and project prioritization for work allocation should be to dedicate our time and effort only to the essential tasks and ignore the unimportant work entirely, regardless of whether it is urgent or not.

Work first on the As, and when they are completed, or you have spare time, revert to the Bs. This is the only truly productive and efficient workflow rule.

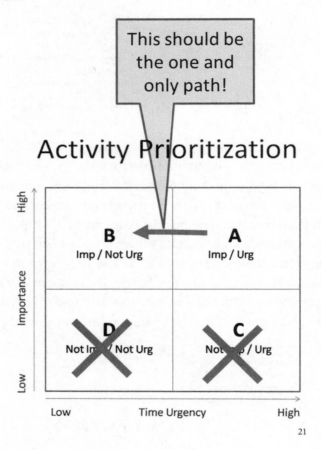

21

By now, you will appreciate, for time allocation, that concentrating solely on critical tasks, incidents, or projects yields the highest results.

This follows the 80/20 Pareto Principle of delivering much greater value for the time allocation.

Further, besides focusing on the important and urgent issues, keep in mind the big, hairy, and scary tasks as well. You will do well to attack the big, daunting, and complex tasks first, or at least early on.

Often, there will be unforeseen complications you'll be well served to identify and deal with early on. Further, supplies or approvals can take much longer than provisioned or anticipated. Not attacking large and long tasks can potentially put them at risk when difficulties occur, compromising the critical path time. Additionally, deal with these significant troublesome issues first, if for no other reason than to reduce your anxiety.

Activity Prioritization

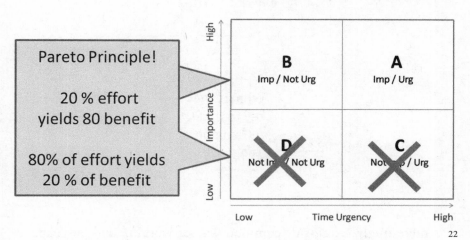

22

The final recommendation is for the benefit of socializing this methodology across your teams. You can create a common methodology and a communal language, modus operandi. This way, you have an immediate and rapid collaborative way of setting priorities and communicating actions between team members.

Activity Prioritization

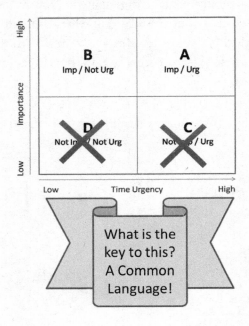

23

Interestingly, using this common way of working and language as a team leader, I have often gone to a team member and asked them to do something for me quickly. Occasionally, which I strongly reinforce, I would get a response somewhat like this. "Greg, can you tell me the priority on that? I'm working on an A; if your task is more important, I'll drop what I'm doing. But if your task is an urgent C, then do you really want me to shift over from what I'm working on?" The answer will invariably be no; stay on your A task, and I'll either find someone else who has spare time, do it myself, or decide it is unimportant. [24, 25]

The Pareto Principle—80/20 Rule

Most of you will have heard of the 80/20 rule. While this rule-of-thumb metric has suffered somewhat from a highly liberal application, with a thoughtful application, it can be very effective as a high-level tool.

It's useful and interesting to know some background on the 80/20 rule. Its formal name is "The Pareto Principle," from the eponymous founder of the concept, Vilfredo Pareto (1848–1923). Pareto was an Italian economist, engineer, and sociologist who initially observed that 80 percent of the land and wealth in Italy belonged to 20 percent of the population. He subsequently conducted the same analysis in other countries and discovered a similar trend.[26]

In addition to Pareto's groundbreaking work in economics and sociology, the "Pareto Distribution Efficiency Principle" has been successfully applied in science, mathematics, and, more recently, in business. The 80/20 rule has been observed in multiple business contexts, including sales, products, customers, staff, etc. Examples are: 80 percent of sales come from 20 percent of customers, 80 percent of revenue from 20 percent of products, and 80 percent of sales from 20 percent of staff.[27]

There are many other business examples and contexts. While the 80/20 principle is not a hard and fast "law or rule," it is nevertheless a valuable management tool to help rapidly identify efficiency and productivity. Interestingly, I remember my father telling me when I was appointed to my first management job many years ago: "If you have an urgent task, give it to your busiest person!" At the time, this made little sense to me, but it clearly does in the context of the Pareto Principle.

Mobilizing Projects

A well-known quote circulating in management circles states that it's not so crucial how you start something; rather, the critical thing is how you finish it. As discussed in the large-scale redundancies commentary, I agree with the importance of finishing things well. However, I would also stress the importance of starting things well, efficiently, and effectively.

In business, habitually, by the time you are ready to mobilize a project, you can generally assume that you are already later than you would like to be and that time is marching on urgently. This relates to the typical time lag and long delay from an idea conception through the business case development, funding approvals, team selection or supplier proposal, and procurement processes. Therefore, starting well helps avoid incorrect targets, disastrous missteps, and redundant restarts.

I'll remind you of prior discussions of Tuckman's Stages of Group Development relative to the initial stages of project mobilization: forming, storming, and norming. There are several essential elements that must be carefully structured and nurtured to ensure you start on the right foot.

Critically, you must select the right program or project leader to set the appropriate culture and climate for the activity. Often, a good team leader who leads by example, motivating and nurturing the new team, will be a more effective and sustainable choice for a major long-term project than an aggressive, hard-driving command-and-control manager. A hard-driver autocrat risks alienating people or partners, burning people out, or losing vital resources at critical junctures in the program. After all, large projects are not delivered by a single person but rather by a sizeable cohesive team working together.

With the right leader setting a suitable culture, that person will also select the correct composition of team members who can be mentored, nurtured, and empowered to create a high-performing team.

Once you've established a constructive, can-do culture and selected the best team and the right external partner, you must align everyone, particularly the external partner team, to your agenda and ways of working.

I've discussed previously and will elaborate on the critical concept of "One Team" in mobilizing and managing programs and projects in the external supplier section. As I've stated, it is only a historical accident of fate that planted the team members into different companies and organizations. However, with careful and respectful team mobilization, each team member can be inspired and motivated to align with the project vision, purpose, and the "One Team" operating principles. The upcoming Project Drive Case Study we will discuss is an excellent example of careful and successful attention to Project Mobilization.

Another interesting case occurred during my stint at AOL, which led to an important learning for me. My boss at AOL, the director of business development for Europe, was Chris Hill, who taught me a powerful lesson. Never sell just to the person in front of you. Instead, put yourself in their shoes and imagine to whom they must sell the proposition internally! In other words, understand what the win is for your prospect's stakeholders and refocus your pitch on what your prospect's pitch needs to present to their boss, leadership, and stakeholders. Then, ideally, craft your pitch and presentation so they can easily extract relevant details from your presentation to pass on to their management.

Chris was the consummate pro at initiating projects and working with partners. His unwritten motto was initially to forget the lawyers, management, contracts, and prices. When you want to get something started, just start.

I recall a major proposed mobile initiative with BT in London. We had the initial meeting with the top brass for BT Mobile. About 20 minutes into the session, Chris intervened and suggested: "We all know this is important and that it is going to be big. Also, we are both likely to need each other in the future. So why don't we just get together and try to kick-start the initiative to see where it goes and if there is enough value in it before we get bogged down and waste time and energy in legal red tape and politics?" "How about we both select a crack team of mobile engineers from both companies, throw them into a room together for a week, and see if they come up with anything useful? I can give you half a dozen engineers to come to you, or you can do the same and come to us?" BT cautiously opted for "you send your engineers to us first."

Chris immediately accepted and suggested meeting again in two weeks to see if it had been valuable, and we all agreed on the BT and AOL team exchanges. A month later, after respective visits, the teams were working together, prototyping and developing core technologies for mobile internet services in early 1999. His enthusiastic and casual "just do it" manner kick-started the projects well before the lawyers and finance managers could stifle the nascent relationships. We got the joint projects up and running with enough critical mass and product traction to demonstrate the proposition's viability before intellectual property impediments and business case complexities could kill the projects still-born. This was the consummate example of "Just Do It!"

Project Management versus Agile/Scrum

In this leadership discussion, it is not our task to elaborate extensively on technical or operational issues such as project management, agile development, DevOps, etc. However, as these issues influence and impact all companies, especially technology-dependent companies (which frankly make up all companies today), I will digress briefly into these areas to share relevant nuances from personal experience.

With an extensive project management background, including being a certified Kepner Tregoe Project Management Instructor, I am biased toward detailed and disciplined project management. However, as a CIO/CTO, I subscribe to the hyperefficient Agile/Scrum philosophy and methodologies. In today's Agile/Scrum world, there is often no requirement to chart the critical path through a Gantt Chart, let alone a Pert Chart. But that does not mean that occasionally robust project planning is unimportant or superfluous.

Take the case of the TUI Merger Case Study we've discussed. With 150+ people working simultaneously to synchronize multiple business, process, financial, application, and infrastructure work streams with an 11-month drop-dead deadline because of critical work stream dependencies, just "iterating" our way forward to delivery milestones was not practical or even possible. We delivered software code development sprints through agile scrum methodologies within the application development work streams. However, those sprints needed to fit into multiple interrelated business work streams such as new business entity creation, back-office finance, new company set-ups, and restructuring of products.

Therefore, in multinationals versus dot-coms, agile/scrum and project management are not "mutually exclusive" and often must effectively coexist within other macro-level organizational activities. Digital Natives are often passionate about agile/scrum. As a CTO, I am fully aligned with Agile benefits, and I grew up in the industry with SDLC and RAD in the early 1990s, developing into extreme and lean programming, then Agile and Scrum. Therefore, I fully support these methodologies for software development activities. But there is a caution to quote the old saying, "If you only have a hammer, everything looks like a nail!" [28]

Having seen and proven the benefits of formal project management, even "waterfall" activities have their place, as do agile/scrum development sprints and activities. The key is that different requirements and tasks require different tools. Therefore, using the right tool for the right task, a leader can successfully deliver major cross-organizational, cross-functional programs through robust project management methodologies while managing hyperefficient, agile scrum developments within the work streams. The challenge for a leader is to work with and align these potentially diverse delivery communities, including people with different work philosophies, disciplines, approaches, and tools, into an effective team.

As a leadership, not a technical discussion, I'll offer a couple of critical learnings from my various Agile/Scrum implementations. I've run traditional technology operations and transitioned traditional technology to agile/scrum and several dot-coms. While all new media and dot-com technology companies natively use Agile/Scrum, most traditional companies have also embarked on complex digital transformation programs over the past decade.

The challenge is managing this transition. To be fair, I've struggled to move traditional IT wholesale to Agile/Scrum despite extensive training programs and expensive Agile/Scrum coaches. In any conventional IT organization, there are always some early adopters who will be fully on board and excited to embrace new technologies and approaches. Like any change program, there will also be some qualified people who will initially be skeptical, but once they understand the benefits, they will eventually hop on board and make the transition. As always, there will be a few people who will remain skeptical and resist the change through rigidity or inability to learn or adapt. Regrettably, the reality is that the latter group will often ultimately need to move on or retire.

While you can successfully manage this transition and transformation, I've found that the best approach for me was to create a new digital team seeded with some native agile/scrum technologists. With a new team having a critical mass of native agile/scrum staff, you can add the enthusiastic traditional early adopters to the new team to be coached and mentored by the native agile technologists. It's often best to retain the skeptics in the original organization to manage the legacy systems and, hopefully, to retire at some point in the future; ideally, at the same time, the legacy systems will also be obsoleted and retired. This was always more successful than attempting to fully transition the entire old team to the new technologies by themselves.

It is not my intention to create an extended discussion on Agile or Project Management; however, there were several relevant project management lessons to be learned within the merger program at TUI. Multiple types and levels of project managers are required for major programs and their associated projects. First, for a major program, you need a senior program leader/project manager who sits on the steering committees and faces off to other internal work streams to keep the program and all the projects linked up and aligned. This person must be an inspiring, disciplined, courageous, and politically adept leader.

However, you will also need a highly focused, detail person to manage the complexity of an exhaustive project plan. In the case of "Project Drive," I was the program lead. Fortunately, we also had an extremely thorough operational project manager in Joaquin Piera from Accenture, who rigorously and continuously managed the constantly changing four thousand-plus tasks within the ever-evolving project management system.

Critically, working across major program work streams internally within your own company is complicated enough. However, invariably, with transformations and large programs, you will often need specialist external resources and sometimes just additional hands beyond business-as-usual activities. In these cases, you'll need to employ external contractors and often external consultants and suppliers to help carry the extra burden of an extensive program. This supply complexity demands a robust project management discipline to keep alignment across project work streams and a heterogeneous supplier network.

The final chapter will detail these opportunities, challenges, and the complexities of working with contractors, consultants, and external suppliers.

Quality Initiatives

Building on the philosophical underpinnings of quality we discussed with Robert Pirsig and the quality processes of W. Edwards Deming, Joseph Juran, and Philip Crosby in Book 1, let's explore some powerful technical and procedural quality concepts, many of which emanate from Japan. Crosby's Do It Right the First Time and Zero-Defect concepts provide numerous insights into product design, testing, and development.

Systems thinking, do it right the first time, *kaizen*—continuous improvement, kanban—just in time, and zero defects are the subject of many books in their own right, so I'll touch on each just briefly to whet your appetite for more in-depth study if they are appropriate for your interest and work. In addition, many of today's advancements, such as Agile/Scrum, just-in-time supply chain, and lean manufacturing, to name a few, have their origins and foundations in these disciplines.

Do It Right the First Time (technical topic)[29]

"Do it right the first time" is a powerful management practice in the context of quality, excellence, product development, processes, and time and motion. It provides the principle and modus operandi for almost everything you do, from handling a piece of paper or email once, dealing with a staff issue without endless procrastination, and developing technical systems properly without quick fixes that require future rework or replacement. While this mantra seems self-evident or obvious, it is a necessary discipline to remember and practice as time pressures often cause us to compromise standards and quality to meet deadlines.

Kaizen—Continuous Improvement (technical topic)[30]

Kaizen is a Japanese word for "improvement" referring in a business context to the Japanese concept of "continuous improvement" or "change for better" popularized by Toyota.

In the "Toyota Way" corporate vision, every employee of Toyota knows a part of their job is helping to improve whatever they do. Everyone is aligned with this vision, whether they are the marketing director, automotive designer, administrative, assembly line, or cleaner. In this culture, innovation is an integral part of everything they do. Instead of being single monotonous, anonymous cogs in a tedious production wheel, individuals and teams share multiple tasks, taking responsibility for the quality of products and productivity through *kaizen*'s continuous improvement processes. It emphasizes removing waste, eliminating rework, and improving processes like operations, logistics, or lean manufacturing.[31]

The following diagram depicts how *kaizen* achieves an optimal development trajectory through positive improvement initiatives and rapid cycle times (e.g., agile development) aligned with continuous improvement.

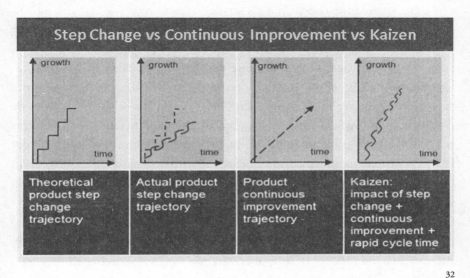

[32]

Kanban (technical topic)[33]

Kanban is another efficiency methodology that also originated in postwar industrial Japan as a "signposting system" supply chain process for lean manufacturing at Toyota. This concept has developed as a "just in time" system for hyperefficient supply chains to minimize costly excess inventory and systematize and optimize assembly line operations.

This process was fundamental to the process innovation of such suppliers as Dell Computers and Amazon and has been institutionalized across most global manufacturing and supply chain companies.

Zero Defect (technical topic)

My final takeaway from quality as a critical concept and methodology for leadership is the concept of zero defect. Zero defect represents more of an aspirational goal than a practical objective. It means setting an objective within your team to "do things right the first time," develop for quality and continuous improvement and implement test-driven development to eliminate defects at the point of its creation. This avoids overreliance on functional, performance, or user testing to identify errors for refactoring or rectification at a later point.

I try to inspire the teams to strive for zero defects but not obsessively insist on its achievement, as evidence has shown that achieving the last 2–3 percent of perfection can consume 80 percent of a project's cost. These statistics are not absolute numbers, as each industry and system is unique. However, it drives home the point that perfection comes at a price and that an absolute zero-defect cost is not justifiable in the dynamic digital world we live in today. Many Agile/Scrum developments strive for rapid "good enough" delivery and a minimum viable product (MVP) instead of perfection. Regardless, nurturing a culture of high quality and excellence and inspiring teams to strive for zero defect at pace is a valuable slogan rather than a formal, rigid objective

A related process improvement topic is Six Sigma (6σ), a measure of quality that strives for near perfection. It is a disciplined methodology for eliminating defects in any process, from manufacturing to products or services.[34] In my context and industries, Six Sigma is not a necessary or practical objective; however, many swear by it. Thus, it is helpful to be aware of the process should you be in a mission-critical industry such as nuclear power that warrants an extreme level of quality.

Decision-Making

As mentioned, I was fortunate to be a training manager for American Express in the States early in my career. Learning the training curriculum in order to deliver it was a great opportunity and a sharp learning curve. Henceforth, presenting these courses multiple times allowed me to achieve mastery over many of these subjects.

At one point, AMEX decided to train all senior management in Kepner Tregoe Problem Solving and Decision Making and KT Project Management. As a result, we were given extensive train-the-trainer sessions to be certified to deliver these programs. Subsequently, I've found both methodologies beneficial throughout my career.

Given the importance of disciplined and successful decision-making for leaders, let's look at multiple decision-making processes and methodologies.

Kepner Tregoe Problem Solving and Decision Making

Kepner Tregoe Problem Solving and Decision Making (KT PS&DM) is a very effective methodology for analyzing and assessing problems and conducting structured decision-making.

In fact, during the Apollo 13 crisis, while returning from the moon mission, NASA engineers used this KT PS&DM methodology to help discover the critical air leakage problem and identify a viable solution. See An Abbreviated Use of Problem Analysis in Charles Kepner and Benjamin Tregoe's book *The New Rational Manager*. Summary at: www .kepner-tregoe.fr/linkservid/1BA87498-AD75–4EA4-A7403BAFE5182 96C/showMeta/0/ .[35]

Having seen and used the KT methodologies extensively, these methods and disciplines stuck with me and assisted on numerous occasions to crystallize issues and resolve problems. Following are some of the key principles:

Kepner Tregoe Problem Solving and Decision Making[36] is a structured methodology for systematically analyzing problems, identifying potential risks, solving problems, and making decisions.

Here is a brief overview of the methodology; also, review the diagram and link below for further information.

Situation Appraisal—Analyzing complex problems.

The situation appraisal is the initial starting place where you step back, get the overview, and form a brief and concise, *objective definition and description* of the problem or issue. Next, you *document the situation*, *problem*, and *objective*, list *risks* and *opportunities*, *set priorities*, and *create your analysis action plan*. This approach ensures you are clear on the challenge and have an objective perspective.

Problem Analysis—A systematic approach to deconstructing the problem.

The problem analysis activity is where you organize and analyze the situation thoroughly. Start by describing the problem in detail and identifying and confirming probable causes. Several powerful questioning methods are employed here, which I use regularly. For example, define carefully the following: 1) Identify the "distinctions and changes" from before and then after the incident or issue occurred. 2) Next, define—what it is: who, what, when, where, and extent? Then, in simple terms, just ask 3) What has changed, and further, *what is different*?

Decision Analysis—A formal approach to clarifying decisions.

In the decision analysis, you *describe, classify, quantify, and weigh your objectives*. Next, *generate and evaluate a range of alternatives*. Following this, *assess the associated risks and benefits*. Then, *make a preliminary informed decision, test it, and confirm your decision*.

Potential Problem Analysis—Clear thinking for managing risks.

During the potential problem analysis, you *anticipate threats* to the success of planned actions. *Identify the skills required for effective preventive and contingent measures to pinpoint and prevent potential problems*. Potential problem analysis helps prepare in advance and avoid unplanned and unprepared reactive actions as much as possible.

Potential Opportunity Analysis—Clear thinking for leveraging opportunities.

During the opportunity analysis, *identify potential risks and problems and associated causes*. Then, you formally *plan contingencies and develop preventative plans*. Finally, set trigger alerts to detect risks and implement contingency mitigation plans.[37]

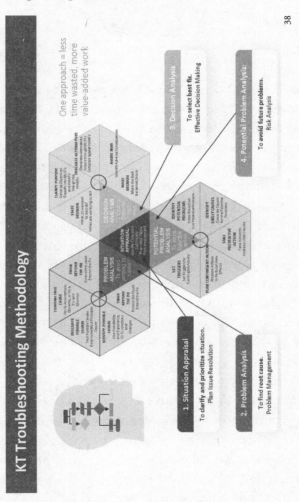

A valuable decision-making tip comes from Peter Drucker in *The Practice of Management*. Instead of jumping to conclusions, the critical, overlooked issue in decision-making is to identify the right question! Finding the right solution to the wrong question is a recipe for failure![39]

Daniel Kahneman—Thinking, Fast and Slow

40

A recent and fascinating study on decision-making comes from Nobel Prize–winning psychologist and economist Daniel Kahneman, which we discussed briefly in Book 1. His book *Thinking, Fast and Slow*[41] brilliantly covers the issue of knowing when and why one should and can make rapid, sound decisions based on extensive prior knowledge and experience. Furthermore, one should hold back in unfamiliar or complex situations where careful analysis and thoughtful, reasoned judgment and decisions are required. This might initially appear self-evident and straightforward. Nonetheless, in corporate politics and decision-making, there is great complexity and multiple actors who layer issues with complexity, risk, and, conversely, opportunity. Further, the element of time pressure for a decision often conflicts with a carefully reasoned solution to a problem.

The key to this decision conundrum is the conscious awareness and discipline of decision-making using these "two systems" as Kahneman refers to them. During our early development as leaders, we hear, are told, and are trained to be decisive in our actions, particularly in decision-making. Further, our growing confidence and the intense pressure to deliver create a propensity for managers and leaders to make rapid high-level decisions, which may or may not be the most appropriate course of action for any particular issue.

In business contexts and situations where you have extensive knowledge and experience and where you've seen it all before, all your knowledge, skill, and experience have prepared you to make rapid, robust, and correct decisions with a high degree of success. However, in new, unfamiliar, or complex situations where your previous knowledge and experience are inapplicable and inappropriate, you must recognize it, ensure you do your research, consult with domain experts, and employ slow and deliberate analysis, consideration, and informed decision-making.

You will likely have heard of the "10,000 Hour Rule" Malcolm Gladwell popularized in his book *Outliers*,[42] which originated from Dr. Anders Ericsson's work at Florida State University. This research regarding the study and practice required to achieve complete mastery of any skill or discipline equates to approximately five years of full-time work.

Reflecting on my years of decision-making experience, I can now clearly see examples of both situations and systems. For instance, in my early career, when I leaped or was thrown into the deep end with radical career shifts, I found it could take up to six months to grapple with the new context and assimilate the knowledge and skills to bed down fully in a new role. Therefore, having made a number of these significant job changes to new domains, I've discovered that these six months or approximately one thousand hours are sufficient to become highly competent and fully functional (although perhaps not mastered or to become a world-class expert) in most new disciplines and business domains. This is the time necessary to learn, absorb, and apply the newly acquired skills and knowledge to master the new position sufficiently and assimilate the knowledge and experience needed to deal with rapid and accurate decision-making in that context.

One harrowing but now amusing example of jumping into the deep end with a dearth of knowledge and experience was when I was head-hunted from American Express in San Francisco to become training director for Reuters Group in Asia. At American Express, I was responsible for developing and training travel and financial services, credit cards, and traveler's cheques. Reuters was also a financial services information company; however, it was the market leader in providing data, analysis, and technology solutions for investment bank trading systems. They had some minor similarities at a high level; however, they were entirely different at the operational level.

I flew to Hong Kong, interviewed, and was offered the job. Six weeks later, I reported to work with all my worldly possessions on a ship and my family in the Hilton. Moving from a stable role, where I essentially had the equivalent of "tenure," was an exciting but somewhat risky prospect.

Nevertheless, I was confident and enthusiastic about the new opportunity, at least until the first ten minutes.

I reported to the Reuters office receptionist in the Landmark building in Hong Kong, who then took me to meet with Jeremy, my new boss. To his apparent surprise, I walked into his office and said hello. He responded, "Ah, you're starting today? Excellent, that's great; good timing. We've just received our new Yen Bond Futures service and need to prepare for the customer launch. Would you develop the training courses for the Southeast Asia Sales teams and run the new product training in Singapore for the sales teams next week?" That hit me like a thunderbolt; this was not week one or day one, but the first sentence.

I was totally out of my previous sphere of financial service experience with credit cards, money orders, and traveler's cheques! However, my home was in the middle of the Pacific, and my young family was in the hotel. Moreover, I was committed with no way back. So, I said, "Sure! Just one question?" "Is that Yen Bond-Futures or Yen-Bond Futures"? After a week of eighteen-hour days, I flew down to Singapore, met the sales team, and successfully delivered the Yen Bond Futures training. But in retrospect, as you can appreciate, there was no way to "wing it" or "bluff" my way through this task. This exercise required "thinking slow," a heck of a lot of research and study to plan carefully and deliver the complex financial instrument trading system training.

When you find yourself in a new situation, attempt to identify and recognize similar patterns or conditions in your prior experience and understand what approaches, strategies, and behaviors are or are not appropriate in the new domain. Then, you can focus on what requirements, knowledge, and skills are necessary to perform effectively in the new context. With that as "background" to your decision-making, add a bit of lateral thinking and creativity, and you will be prepared to apply your past experience effectively and flexibly to similar situations.

As you assimilate the new skills and knowledge, you will be able to make rapid but well-reasoned judgments using appropriate, judicious, and quick-thinking decision-making on most management-related issues. Of course, as a leader, you are ultimately responsible for decisions across your organization. But that doesn't mean that you need to be the expert on everything or have to make every decision. Transferrable management-level expertise is distinct from the product or process-specific operational or executable knowledge and skills.

Critically, you must recognize when to draw upon other knowledgeable resources for support or even delegate to experts as required. You can rely on existing staff and functional experts to augment your current capabilities with domain knowledge and domain-specific skills and processes.

Depending on your work colleague's maturity, knowledge, experience, and self-confidence, you should learn when to manage and when to mentor. You'll need to adapt your communication and management styles along a spectrum of management and mentoring skills based on the application of "situational leadership," task or relationship practice. This will help guide you on when to lead, make a decision, or delegate and leave the decision to a capable colleague or knowledgeable subordinate.

According to Kahneman, unless you are a seasoned expert in the field represented by the challenge in front of you, it is always best to employ an objective methodology and consult other experts. This is preferable in those situations to relying on less analytical and reduced reliability gut instincts.

Understanding both of these "decision systems," knowing your own skills and expertise, appreciating your decision-making challenges, and consciously practicing them appropriately will go a long way in recognizing when to make fast or slow decisions. Then, using the suitable approach, fast when you are eminently qualified and slow when required, you can improve the quality of your decision-making and reduce errors to virtually zero.

There are many different approaches to problem analysis and decision-making. However, as in the case of Kepner Tregoe and the following one, Delphi, the critical thing is having objectivity coupled with creativity.

Delphi Decision-Making[43]

Another formal and valuable but somewhat complex methodology is the Delphi Method developed by Rand Corporation. I used this methodology at PwC in a UK consulting project for the UK Royal Mail. It was an interesting and effective process but required extensive hands-on facilitation. The Delphi method is a decision process framework of multiple rounds of anonymous questionnaires sent to a panel of stakeholders, with subsequent expert summary feedback and review sessions in between. We employed an online digital Delphi application tool that streamlined and sped up reviews, feedback, and decision-making. The iterative process continues with progressively reduced answers and solutions converging toward the correct or recommended decision.

A final word on decision-making, coupling robust discipline and practice with the previously mentioned "be brave and bold" will result in sufficient knowledge and experience to make a reasonably sound judgment. It is always better to make decisions promptly rather than procrastinating and postponing them. Any delay in making a decision will, at best, complicate the situation and, at worst, mean you may miss the opportunity to deal with it effectively, if at all.

Patrick Lencioni in *The Five Dysfunctions of a Team* reminds us of an "old military axiom that a decision is better than no decision. Militarily, they recognize it is better to decide decisively and be wrong—and then change direction with equal boldness—than to waffle, waste precious time, and let external events overtake you."[44]

Financial Budgeting

In this leadership discussion, since every company has its own methodology and tools, I won't go into excessive tactical details about budgeting, financial fundamentals, or company-specific issues. However, as all leaders and managers are required to manage operational costs and departmental budgets prudently, I'll share a number of valuable tips and learnings that have been advantageous to my fiscal management along the way.

As mentioned, I started my career as a management trainee with American Express Company in the United States. This was fortuitous, as it was and still is an extremely well-run organization. My first task as a trainee was to help with the annual budget, balancing the reams of financial printouts. So naturally, as a trainee, the excruciating detail of checking the history and projecting the future for hundreds of items, from resource requirements to sales projections, fell to me. As a result, I'm still a stickler for details.

Even if you are more of a creative type, giving appropriate attention to the budgets, P&L statements, and forecasts is an essential discipline for managing the business and establishing and keeping credibility with your leadership, who are often former finance executives. Nevertheless, some stumbling blocks relate to the annual budget process, the three-to-five-year forecast, and how to plan and get budget agreements for major systems' replacement.

Despite the difference in budget tools and processes, most companies begin the annual budget planning process with a high-level projection of the long-term plan. This would often be a three-year plan (depending on the company) about a month in advance of the following year's annual budget planning exercise. However, in most companies where I've worked, the long-term planning exercise announcement is not generally met with enthusiasm. It was viewed as non-mission-critical and, therefore, somewhat of a waste of time. Further, as the initial three-year plan was only a snapshot top-down review process, most of my colleagues would give it a very high-level cursory effort.

However, this meant a highly detailed and accurate bottom-up plan for me. It never made sense to me to make a broad, sweeping, long-term projection without as accurate as possible fundamentals underpinning it. Therefore, my exercise was essentially to create a three-year budget. Further, the effort I would put into the plan would make the subsequent mission-critical annual plan a relatively simple extraction from my detailed three-year forecast.

The critical thing I learned years ago is that once the cursory high-level plans went to headquarters, after the appropriate debates, they would "burn the numbers" into the overall projection for the board. Then, subsequently, any significant variation or modification, come annual budget time, would be nigh on impossible. So, with considerable effort and exceptional detail, I'd prepare a three-year plan with every conceivable requirement built in. Further, the fully loaded figures sailed through the cursory long-term review process since it was not the final annual plan. Then, come annual budget planning a few weeks later, I would simply update and extract year 1 of the three-year plan and my five-year forecast!

The annual plan I submitted would automatically align and comply with the high-level projections already posted for the three-year plan. Thus, my annual budget often passed review and approval with only minor challenges. All the while, my colleagues who had done only very superficial three-year plans would then begin a tedious trench warfare negotiation exercise with finance to build up a robust annual plan out of the wafer-thin skeleton forecast provided by their three-year plan.

The key learning here is that despite the perceived tedious nature of financial and budgetary planning, attacking the task with enthusiasm, vigor, and exceptional detail is essential. This will yield huge payback for your efforts throughout the year. Remember, adequate funding for your plans, projects, and staff is a leader's responsibility and one of the principal enablers of your entire operation.

The other substantial benefit of building a robust three-year plan and five-year forecast relates to the long-term planning for major capital investments, such as replacing large core IT systems. The issue here is that without significant forethought and advance planning, when you need a major IT systems replacement or transformation, finding tens of millions of dollars will be virtually impossible. Therefore, you must plan and act well in advance of when the requirement is needed to ensure funds are available when required.

With advanced foresight and strategic planning, I would typically build my three-to-five-year plan with careful forecasting of any new major systems replacement (e.g., a new CRM, ERP, or core operating system). So, for example, for the 30M needed, I might put 10M in the long-term forecast for each year from year 4 to year 6.

Generally, my direct management would quickly recognize the system's replacement requirement and, therefore, would not seriously challenge the issue that far in advance. No one would really be bothered yet, as it was not on the radar for the mission-critical three-year plan, and thus, my new system provision would sail through the five-year forecast submission.

The following year, I still had a legitimate systems replacement requirement, and now I had a forecast track history for the replacement with historical documentation and tacit agreement. Then, the requirement will flow automatically year over year from year 5 to year 4 and eventually into year 3 of the all-important three-year plan. Again, this is not a critical showstopper issue, as this is not the annual plan, and they don't have to take the pain yet. But now, the budget track history and requirements are well established.

For the subsequent two years, the major system replacement is already on the books, and the Board and the investors have previously burned these monies into the overall long-term forecast. Eventually voilà! The new system lands on the following year's annual budget plan. Now, the money is there, fully provisioned and planned for. My management, who understands and recognizes the importance of the replacement, is now pleased (or at least accepting) since the funds are available and their management has had long-term visibility of the requirement. Then, I could proceed with replacement and transformation. At that point, declining a long-term, well-planned, and provisioned budget allocation for a mission-critical system would need formal justification not to proceed.

What is the learning in both cases? First, get well in front of the process via advance planning and using the long-term forecast. Second, put in the effort to fully mature the long-term strategy, the associated plan, and the budget. Third, do a detailed bottom-up three-to-five-year plan with the same rigor as you would for the annual plan. Management will allocate funds for the three-year plan into the board-level forecast, and if your requirement is not in the three-year plan, you won't be able to make any material changes to the annual plan later. The considerable time and effort you have expended on the three-year plan will be recouped when it comes to the annual plan.

In summary, plan ahead for significant capital investments, such as major IT systems replacement. No system lasts forever, and typically, this is a painful process that eventually sneaks up to bite you. However, if you build it fully transparently into your long-range plan, the project and the funds will generate a line-item history year over year until the replacement is required. You will then have the funds documented, factored in, and fully aligned with management!

A significant additional benefit is that when everyone else is in a panic about the annual budget, you will already be prepared and much more relaxed, having done the detailed financial groundwork weeks earlier. It also gives you some strategic thinking time to do the management stakeholder alignment for the budget and prepare for the annual budget presentation and justification. As a result, you end up looking like a far-sighted hero instead of a shortsighted rookie.

Takeaways:

Time is a critical resource; develop robust time management disciplines.

- Focus tenaciously on important issues; start with urgent ones first.
- Ignore unimportant issues regardless if they are urgent or not.
- Urgent, unimportant tasks are the most significant time wasters.

Attention to Quality is an overriding tenet of any leader.

- Do it right the first time is a powerful organizational philosophy.
- Kaizen or continuous improvement is an operational imperative.
- Zero defect is a laudable attitude and objective, but is not always practical.

Remember Kahneman's *Thinking, Fast and Slow* decision-making.
- If you're confident and have the knowledge and experience, make a quick and decisive decision.
- If the situation is new or complex, research and consult with others to make a careful, measured decision.

Financial planning and budgeting are vital to everything you do in your organization. Be proactive and disciplined, get into the details, and plan well in advance for any major project funding.

Key Takeaways—Leadership and Management Tips

- A leader is strategic and focused on the big picture, and a manager is operational and tactical; however, an experienced leader / manager must shift naturally and fluidly between modes as required.
- Tuckman's Stages of Group Development—Be consciously aware of the nuances and management of teams based on their development through the stages of forming, storming, norming, and performing.
- Hiring the Team—After a careful recruitment capability assessment, look for "hidden treasures" within your organization first. Then, to re-invent, source new blood for specialist or emerging roles.
- Setting Objectives—For new or inexperienced staff, prepare S.M.A.R.T. objectives. For more experienced and senior staff, create objectives that provide latitude for staff empowerment and individual initiative.
- Decision-Making—Know when and why to make rapid, sound decisions based on prior knowledge and experience. And when to use careful analysis and reasoned judgment in unfamiliar or complex situations.

CHAPTER 3

Remote Living and Working— Leading from Anywhere

Lessons from Afar and from the Trenches

As an expat who has lived overseas for 35 years in Asia, the UK, and Europe, I am no stranger to the opportunities and challenges of extended remote working. Eventually, remote working evolves over time to become a broader type of remote lifestyle.

While I am based primarily in Mallorca along with San Francisco, I'll share remote working experiences and associated learnings from the decades as an international expat, as well as the recent remote working as a digital nomad.

We all endured a sudden, dramatic, and radical sea change with the onslaught of the COVID-19 pandemic. The impact of the pandemic and other personal circumstances precipitated my transition from expat life to that of a digital nomad for the past four years.

I mention this as a remote working case study, as I have continued to write this book and consult to clients in the UK, Spain, the Middle East, and India during 3.5+ years of extensive road trips, numerous ferries, and countless different accommodations in the UK, France, Spain, and four months on a world cruise.

The learning from this remote working, work from home (with our new definition of home—a place where we are for more than a week!) is that with Wi-Fi or often only mobile-enabled internet hotspot, and even with the painfully slow maritime internet on a ferry or cruise line, I can work virtually anywhere. This means a hotel, Airbnb, café or restaurant, a park bench, motorway rest stop, parking lot, or ship.

One interesting note is that for conference scheduling, the people I worked with were frequently confused where I was, thinking I was in Spain when in the UK and the UK when in Spain or on the high seas. But, other than the time differences, my volatile and diverse remote working had virtually no other impact on my work.

This has been my protracted and varied but fascinating remote working experience over these 3.5 years. However, I am only one of the millions of workers and families who have been accidentally or intentionally misplaced since 2019 and the onslaught of the COVID-19 pandemic.

However, extending beyond our personal experiences, these disruptive and displacement ramifications have touched all parts of our personal and professional lives and virtually every business and company on the planet. Therefore, let's explore the challenges, opportunities, and liabilities of the remote working phenomenon from a personal and corporate perspective. Further, how we have adapted, the impact and repercussions for companies, and finally, what changes are transitory, and which ones are likely to have altered forever the way companies and we work in the future.

It has been an existential shock for companies that cannot transform or adapt rapidly enough. We've seen cataclysmic impacts in retail, food and beverage, hospitality, hotels, aviation, and untold others. We are seeing that many of the changes to businesses that the pandemic has brought about are bringing permanent changes to how companies operate. One fundamental corporate issue is the critical health and safety requirement for most companies to move to "remote working" and "work from home" and, finally, a return to various flavors of "hybrid working."

In fact, remote working is not an entirely new phenomenon, as it has a long history associated with globalization and the proliferation of multinational corporations. It has also been fueled by the coinciding development of successive generations of communications technologies combined with the rapid expansion of international aviation in recent decades. Globalization, multinationals, family, and "social diaspora" have all been advanced and supported by the rapid evolution of international telecommunications with internet telephony, mobile phones, email, messaging, videoconference, and whiteboard technologies. Further, the dramatic international migration of remote expatriate knowledge workers in recent years would not have occurred without both robust communications and world-shrinking international aviation.

Despite our adoption and gradual acclimation over the past two decades to robust international collaborative working, there are some fundamental differences between traditional expatriates, international communications, and the nuances of effective remote working. What is dramatically different is the scope and scale of the urgent requirement for work from home (WFH) that has exploded because of the pandemic social distancing requirements, office closures, and lockdowns.

The pandemic imposed international border closures and associated travel constraints, resulting in a virtual collapse of the aviation, transportation, and hospitality industries. Consequently, the COVID-19 health risks, plus the associated traveler anxiety, international travel restrictions, and the resulting company business travel bans, further contributed to the demand and exponential growth of remote working. Fortunately, during the COVID-19 crisis, new digital tools such as Zoom, Slack, WhatsApp, WeChat (China), Google Meet, Skype, and Teams have dramatically enabled and enhanced virtual and remote working communications.

In times like these of geopolitical and socioeconomic turmoil, work and jobs are one stabilizing cornerstone of many workers' lives. Therefore, empathetic, encouraging, and enlightened leadership is a core requirement for assuring staff stability, focus, and motivation. In addition, there is a critical necessity for leaders to step into the newly created "digital gaps" in processes to provide the leadership direction and organizational "glue" to hold the fragmented company, its operations, and its teams together.

Remotely assigning tasks, work orders, sales calls, or supply chain orders as "ad hoc" transactional activities differs fundamentally from the more delicate and sensitive leadership soft skills. Effective leadership in this new remote context comprises motivating teams, recruiting and hiring staff, setting and monitoring objectives, delivering performance appraisals, resolving conflicts, and building remote teams.

Given the urgency, magnitude, and impact of the remote working transformation on industry, companies, and people, an urgent and holistic assessment of organizations, facilities, leadership, and staff is advisable. As I wrote this in 2021 and now edit in 2023, I am conscious of the passage of time relative to a future relegation of this coronavirus pandemic to history. Whether the pandemic officially ends in 2023 or beyond, it will eventually become an endemic-managed seasonal influenza-type disease. However, another lesson of history is that no one really knows what is around the corner.

If, however, as Bill Gates has advised and warned, other pandemics will occur, and with increasing frequency. Similarly, as discussed in the case study example of AlertNet, future preparedness is the fundamental key to an effective response. Thus, whether you are reading this at the tail end of the COVID-19 pandemic, in a hiatus before a future pandemic, or in the throes of a new one, the following learnings and lessons are material for future scenarios and strategies to cope with, survive and thrive against these threats.

From today's vantage point, let's look at the impact, benefits, challenges, enablers, and risks of remote working for the enterprise, the leadership, and employees.

Organizational Design for Remote Working

To prepare a robust response to the challenges of the changing landscape posed by the pandemic or to chart an optimized future strategy, management must take stock of the current situation versus likely future scenarios. The organization must assess its overall immediate, medium, and long-term strategies relative to organizational design, staffing, and facilities now and in the future. Key factors to consider are:

- Emerging Organizational Designs incorporating on-site, remote, and hybrid working structures
- Enhanced leadership and management approaches to remotely and asynchronously coaching and managing staff
- New collaborative operational procedures to accommodate and enable remote working processes
- The latest enabling communications, videoconference, collaboration, and document-sharing technologies

The sudden wholesale shifts from on-site to remote have forced companies to look at sustaining critical aspects of the company vision, corporate culture, and ethos in a remote environment. Conceivably, the corporate culture, as we currently know it, requires a fundamental reevaluation in the context of significant numbers of staff working remotely. What has changed, what is different, and how can we mitigate the challenges and leverage the opportunities? How can we constructively weave this into a vision and message that instills remote workers with a feeling of community and commitment? See Book 1, Chapter 1, "Vision Infused with Purpose." To be effective, a healthy corporate culture should be foundational and pervasive throughout the organization and creatively fostered and sustained by leaders, especially in the new remote or hybrid context.

An adaptable organizational design must consider the new style and degree of virtuality, whether fully remote, hybrid-flex, or on-site office-based. Recognize that one size does not fit all. Each company's culture, context, remote or virtual structure, and roles are unique. This requires customized solutions to ensure maximum efficiency and adaptability to your unique challenges and opportunities.

A full operational review of processes should be conducted with a clear and concise idea of the optimal organizational structure for your new hybrid or remote business. It is critical to link up and optimize newly created remote processes to mitigate impediments to process flows and efficient operations in the distributed remote environment. Ensure that the latest remote procedures bridge any prior physical handoffs, sign-offs, or other tasks that now need to be virtualized.

With an end-to-end process analysis, you can employ technologies such as workflow, flow-through processing, or supply chain tools to confirm that no digital gaps in the physical processes or inefficiencies cripple or break the new virtual processes or methodologies.

Consider what methods or processes require synchronous people support activities or asynchronous actions that lend themselves to remote digitally time-shifted procedures and operations. The organization, communications, and processes must be systematically re-networked in the remote distributed structure.

In analyzing the organizational design of the current team-based structures, you may need to realign and reorientate people in newly designed remote team arrangements, considering the following:

- Remote group development setup and design
- Membership alignment and skill balancing
- Redesign of responsibilities and new assignment of roles
- Management of task assignments and feedback mechanisms
- Ensure technical, physical, and communications resources

Leadership and management structures may need to be adapted as well. Given the challenges of a distributed workforce and time-shifted work-flows, leadership may need to flatten the organizational structure to foster greater empowerment and efficiencies, improve communications, and enable democratized decision-making. Depending on your company context and level of staff competence, you need to reassess issues and governance of centralization and control versus empowered decentralized decision-making.

The previously discussed situational leadership and competency models will help you decide if you can safely delegate and empower staff to take more responsibility or if temporary centralization of control is necessary to ensure rapid decision-making and implementation. The new organizational design should also consider remote staff autonomy, social relationships, and competence needs.

Benefits of Remote Working—For the Corporation

While the enforced move to remote working and working from home has created many urgent challenges, some potentially significant benefits exist for the company, leaders, teams, and employees. The most dramatic potential organizational benefit is future real estate and facilities savings. In the short term, during the successive COVID-19 pandemic lockdowns, brick-and-mortar facilities are a vast, underutilized drain on organizational balance sheets. As we come out the other side of the pandemic, we may return to some semblance of "normality." However, many virtual and remote working elements are probably with us to stay.

While most organizations are highly unlikely to jettison their headquarters altogether, it is clear that they will look to reduce the size, scale, footprint, and cost of headquarters facilities in the future. With many overbuilt headquarters facilities in major metropolitan areas around the globe, there is likely to be a shock to many companies and the commercial real estate market for perhaps the next decade.

From my vantage, the most likely scenario is that we will see smaller, high-tech, innovative showcase headquarters with distributed regional facilities for geographically clustered hybrid working. While the full financial impact and office space rightsizing will take years to play itself out fully, the remote working requirement due to the pandemic has transformed the staff landscape virtually overnight.

Each industry, company, and role is different and has diverse work requirements. Some functions require presence, and others are obvious candidates for work from home. For example, many knowledge workers, computer-based support and training roles, and service industries such as post offices, food service, and medical workers clearly require a workplace or physical presence. Further, collaboration, complex decision-making, performance calibration, and innovation are best done in person. Conversely, routine and repetitive tasks involving data management, transactions, administration, and reporting are suitable candidates for virtual work. Services like retail and banks will evolve further from face-to-face to a hybrid situation with continued substantial growth in virtual digital services.

However, as a high-level projection to begin the dialogue for companies, the following future staff working location requirement prediction may be helpful. One can easily envision a future scenario where a typical company, depending on its products, services, and activities, can anticipate the following staffing requirements:

- A reduced number of staff that are full-time office-based (25–30 percent in total)
- A majority of staff (50–60 percent) move to "flex" hybrid roles: work from home and come to the office two to three days a week for updates, team meetings, and customer meetings.
- Staff who will work permanently from home (15–20 percent)

Couple this with an associated reduction of a large number of employees, some of whom will be moved to contract or contingency roles, and the requirement for the large behemoth headquarters of today will be severely reduced. In addition, the rapid growth of staff in the tech sector over the past decade has already suffered a substantial adjustment and downsizing, further affecting the office space rightsizing.

It is worth noting that many companies, especially in major urban areas, have already embarked on and validated this trend pre-COVID-19 with "flex workspaces." The pandemic will only fuel and accelerate this movement. Considering the reduction of headquarters, creation of satellites, and reduced cost of remote employee BYOD (bring your own device) workstations, one can easily imagine and project a potential real estate and facilities cost-saving approaching 35–45 percent over today within a decade once current physical assets are "sweat" and reduced as much as feasible.

Calculating the low end of the estimate of 50 percent of the current staff working three days per week reduces staff workstation requirements by 20 percent overall. Then again, add the low estimate of 15 percent who will be permanently remote, and you have already identified a 35 percent potential workstation reduction. At the higher levels, with 60 percent hybrid workers working three days, yields an overall reduction of 24 percent, plus the higher end of 20 percent fully remote workers, you then see a total workstation requirement reduction of 44 percent. Even if you anticipate some staff growth for some successful companies, you can still see a dramatic impact, which requires significant ongoing analysis and replanning. A broad-based estimate, therefore, would be to anticipate a reduction of overall office workspace requirements by a third.

Benefits of Remote Working for Leaders

Benefits for leaders in the remote working world come as a clear advantage for some and a potential opportunity for others. With large teams of dispersed staff working from home, more "inspiring and influence management" types of leaders and communications skills are required than in traditional office-based leadership roles.

Interestingly, a nuance of remote working is that it highlights who is actually doing the work rather than appearing to do it through long hours or busy work sitting at the desk or hanging on the phone. An important consideration is that the experienced remote worker is often more autonomous and independent. This employee may require less tactical guidance than a more junior worker in a typical on-site command-and-control role with an ever-present leader providing regular real-time instruction and guidance. To ensure continued alignment and motivation, a leader should use active remote relationship-building to maintain the team-based bond and ensure continued loyalty and retention of high-value, capable workers.

As mentioned, a one-size approach does not fit all workers, especially in the case of remote worker management. I suggest you refer to the Hersey Blanchard Situational Leadership Maturity and Capability Model and Martin Broadwell's Four Stages of Competence discussed in Book 1. These are invaluable models for adapting your leadership style to your employee's maturity, capability, and motivation level.

A leader with strong leadership soft skills who has a motivated and capable team will be highly effective in setting the vision, guiding, coaching, and encouraging team members. In contrast, a leader who has not had the opportunity to develop their people skills sufficiently has the chance to mature and practice their skills to become a more effective and well-rounded leader. See "Servant Leadership" and "Leading with the Heart" in Book 1. Further, Book 1, chapter 4 provides a comprehensive overview of the most critical leadership characteristics leaders can use to identify their strengths and potential areas for further development. Regardless of experience or position, all leaders can and should continue to grow.

Benefits of Remote Working for Teams and Staff

Collective benefits for remote teams lie in opportunities for exploring, testing, and using creative new technologies and tools for electronic communications and collaboration.

There are many potential benefits for staff inherent in remote working. Top of the list is improved employee work/life balance compared to on-site roles. These improvements derive from the following:

- Improvements in work/life balance and a better quality of life

- Reduction in long working hours away from home
- Elimination of long commutes and lengthy business trips
- Repurposing of former commute time to avocational activities (e.g., hobbies)
- More time with family, spouse/partner, and children
- Ability to "time-shift" personal and professional activities (e.g., facilitating school, bank, and medical appointments)
- Potential for more nonlocal career opportunities
- In some cases (not all), a reduction in work-related stress

Challenges and Risks of Remote Working— For the Company

Along with the long-term financial savings realized from reduced head-quarters real estate, there are short-term challenges of excessive surplus real estate, facilities, and furnishings. As mentioned, this may take a decade to rectify itself with enforced real-estate rightsizing to adapt to a new hybrid workforce comprised of a significantly higher percentage of remote workers. In the short term, the prospect of lavish headquarters buildings sitting vacant of the thousands of former resident employees represents an extraordinarily underused asset expenditure.

Excess headquarters and office space challenges run alongside the above requirements to strategically replan the organizational and staff-ing design to adapt to the new future staff location landscape. A robust short- to long-term staffing requirements plan must be developed to model on-site, hybrid, and remote workers' levels over time. As many staff return to the office, new social distancing requirements must be reengineered for lobbies, elevators, workstations, toilets, and dining facilities. This will require a significant overhaul of the future office lay-out, as existing business-as-usual environments do not comply with the new office social distancing safety requirements. Beyond the near-term necessary health and safety adaptations, in the midterm, companies are already planning for more engaging environments, interactive social lob-bies, terraces, exercise, open spaces, and dining facilities to attract staff back to the office.

In consideration of these plans, human resources and manage-ment will need to adapt the associated recruitment, onboarding, and outplacement practices to manage the ebb and flow of staff efficiently and humanely through the associated organizational shock waves.

Another related company macro-level issue is maintaining a healthy corporate culture as people move off-site and no longer have the same pervasive on-site organizational presence, culture, and support systems. Perhaps an orthogonal analogy, but most are likely to relate to, were the traditional family holidays during 2020. Our feeble attempts to remotely maintain our customary family holiday traditions give you a sense of the challenge corporations will have in sustaining a healthy and motivating corporate culture for the work-from-home workforce.

Challenges and Risks of Remote Working for Leaders

As discussed briefly in our introduction to remote working, one of remote working's most significant challenges and opportunities is for the leaders who manage these dispersed teams. Remotely inspiring, motivating, coaching, guiding, and correcting employee (or contingent worker) behavior is very different from giving them an in-person spontaneous smile or thumbs-up, patting them on the shoulder, grabbing a quick coffee, or delicately correcting and reprimanding deficient behavior.

The requirement for supportive servant leadership and mature leadership people skills is at least equally, or perhaps even more, critical for managing staff you only see occasionally on a video chat or Zoom team meeting. Leading remotely highlights the demands for new dimensions of heightened leadership soft skills. Leaders must shift to more inspiring and influencing leadership behaviors to motivate and guide staff virtually. The emotionally intelligent leader must have increased sensitivity, deepened social intuitiveness, and exhibit genuine empathy for staff. Further, they must have excellent communication skills, be proactive and consistent with coaching and training, and encourage delegation and staff empowerment.

Most leaders are already using many of these same verbal, nonverbal, and written communication skills and behaviors; however, recognize that the context, timing, frequency, media, and tools have changed and increased for remote management. Thus, the adaptable leader must accentuate those skills and behaviors to compensate for the loss of team face time.

Leaders must also be confident, decisive, strong, and adaptable in problem-solving and decision-making. In other words, a remote leader must be effective in inspiring, motivating, and leading in the new virtual context and guiding, operating, and controlling to ensure core projects and processes progress efficiently despite these new remote challenges.

Further, the emotionally intelligent leader in this new hybrid world must be astute, intuitive, and adaptable to assess the organization's challenges, including the team's capabilities, to determine how to manage effectively the objectives and operations in person and remotely.

Tactical and transactional activities, such as setting objectives, assigning responsibilities, monitoring project progress, providing feedback, and reporting, can undoubtedly make the leap to the virtual world. An astute, involved, and attentive manager can provide effective virtual hands-on guidance, mentoring, and support.

However, the leader must also recognize the context and value of face-to-face collaboration and further understand when and where it is needed. Activities ideally best handled in person are team inspiration and culture building, recruitment, brainstorming and ideation, complex problem-solving and decision-making, empathetic mentoring, and coaching relative to staff emotional concerns.

In both contexts, on-site and remote, effective modern leadership depends on the interplay between the leader and the staff. The leader establishes trust, provides psychological safety for staff, and builds a coherent, motivated, high-performing team. Some of the critical issues to address in developing trust and safety within the team are:

Achieve alignment of values first
- Setting a vision and purpose
- Getting alignment and team building—setting common goals
- Agreement of goals is more important than a physical location
- Tacit coordination
- Repeated synchronous interaction
- Replace normal office social supports (lunches, breaks, etc.)
- Build confidence and trust with small gestures and wins
- Build reliance, anticipation, and predictability

Other significant new remote working challenges that require entirely new management approaches are recruitment, orientation, onboarding, and work assignment discussions for new staff. Hiring new staff is particularly challenging depending on the type of role, seniority, competence, and emotional profile of the employee. For example, an extroverted interview candidate who performs well in a video interview may be an excellent choice for a salesperson. However, don't inadvertently overlook a shy, introverted, or sensitive person who may be an exceptional graphic designer.

Staff recruitment and hiring raise several issues and challenges in the remote context. Again, this is not entirely new, as with global corporations; major companies have been increasingly interviewing, hiring, and managing staff globally since the 1980s. However, the scale and propensity needed to do this have just increased exponentially. Videoconferencing technologies help enormously; however, if, as postulated, 90 percent of communications are nonverbal, then the interviewer's (and interviewee's) job has just become that much more challenging.

An approach that can help and better inform the interviewer is to front-end the process through a more robust recruitment search methodology. First, recruiters should implement more comprehensive skills, competency evaluations, and psychometric assessments. These take time to develop and must be checked for ethical and legal acceptability. Still, once done, these tools can be scaled and leveraged across multiple hires throughout the organization. Secondarily, recruiters must concentrate on systematic references and referrals, which again must be checked by legal for ethical and legal equality purposes. However, the significant effort put into competently developing and vetting references and referrals will be rewarded many times over by efficient selection and successful hires. Some excellent recruitment tools are highlighted in Book 1, for example, Korn Ferry Leadership Assessment and Thomas International Personality Profile.

When orienting new staff and giving work assignments, be conscious of the confidence and competence level of the employee. Because of the limited bandwidth of electronic communications vis-à-vis face-to-face communications, you may need to be more directive initially, breaking down and modularizing activities. Provide more immediate and micro-support à la *One Minute Manager*[1] and supply vital mutual alignment, calibration, and confirmation activities.

Many of the issues above for leaders are also best practices, regardless of being on-site or off-site. Just be aware that with remote and dispersed staff, you will have to increase and heighten your leadership communications and people skills to compensate for the psychological challenges and technological limitations of remote digital communications. Fortunately, organizations are already upping their game relative to human resources and people operations, providing leaders with training and tools to evaluate and accentuate their communications and people skills. Depending on your leadership skills profile and personal development program, you may consider reviewing and applying some of the excellent leadership assessment tools referenced in Book 1, for example, Insights Discovery, Myers–Briggs Type Indicator, Korn Ferry Leadership Assessment, and Dunham and Pierce's Leadership Process Model.

Challenges and Risks of Remote Working for Teams

An immediate consequence of staff working at home is the impact on teams and associated projects. Team building and team management are unique situations that relate to the organization, the project or activity, and the individual members of the team. Once you take a long-term, colocated, and high-performing team and disperse them into work-at-home individuals, you disrupt the team's social alignment aspect: the collaborative working environment, the peer support aspect, and the immediacy of interactions. The team issues that can arise and to look out for are:

- Challenges in starting up remote teams and team building
- Disruption of team social interaction, including separation anxiety
- Reduced collaboration and calibration requires new alignment
- Reductions in peer coaching, support, and reviews
- Lack of spontaneous ad hoc, team-based support networks
- Reduction of tacit coordination based on shared knowledge
- Difficulties with remote multitasking on different projects
- Dispersed working can cause data and project misalignment

- Ensure a "single version of the truth" and data version control
- Challenges with balancing diverse team skill requirements
- Loss of face-to-face bonding and trust-building behaviors
- Team anxiety and conflict without ongoing communications
- Loss of spontaneous team-based brainstorming and ideation

All of these can destabilize existing teams and projects unless the leader and the team members all work together to overcome the new impediments to communications, calibration, and collaborative working.

Further, even a perfectly well-formed and operational colocated team can become dysfunctional when distributed remotely. Given the challenges of former colocated teams that are now scattered, the leader should take a fresh look at the team in the new remote context, as they may need to make some new adaptations to roles and responsibilities. These adjustments may be necessary because of the changes in availability and new clustering of knowledge, skills, and competencies. In addition, these adjustments must consider staff profiles of extroversion and introversion, confidence and risk, and natural leader/follower inclinations.

Effective teams require the collective effort of multiple people with diverse capabilities and roles. Teams that have been operational for lengthy periods will have developed ways of working and support systems that make these groups appear to operate virtually automatically with perpetual motion. As mentioned, those peer support systems can change or even be disrupted when dispersed. The leader will then be well served to identify the key roles that existed formerly, which may need to be reinforced, replaced, or re-formed virtually. For example, required team roles may use the Belbin Team Roles Model: Champion, Shaper, Coordinator, Resource-Investigator, Implementer, and Completer-Finisher.[2] Should specific roles be lacking or unavailable in the new remote team, the leader must ensure these roles are explicitly reassigned to provide the requisite skills necessary to function as effectively as previously.

Reviewing the team-based role assessment tools in addition to Belbin Team Roles, including Situational Leadership and Insights Discovery found in the Leadership Models chapter and Tuckman Stages of Group

Development in Chapter 2 will be helpful. These tools can help you remotely rebuild a competent, balanced, and self-sufficient team structure.

Challenges and Risks of Remote Working for Employees

Cal Newport, an associate professor of computer science at Georgetown University, wrote a fascinating article in the *New Yorker* discussing "What Hunter-Gatherers Can Teach Us About the Frustrations of Modern Work."[3] He cites fieldwork by James Woodburn into hunter-gatherer communities in the Rift Valley of East Africa. Woodburn found that in such societies, "People obtain a direct and immediate return from their labor."

This "immediate-return" economy is a far cry from work today, where our efforts rarely provide immediate rewards. The persistent demands of multiple projects with constant interruptions and distractions from emails, calls, and meetings force us to multitask aggressively, juggling numerous activities simultaneously.

Further, he insightfully states: "We spent most of our history in the immediate-return economy of the hunter-gatherer. So we shouldn't be surprised to find ourselves exhausted by the delayed and ambiguously rewarded hyper-parallelism that defines so much contemporary knowledge work." Additionally, the intensity and always-on nature of global remote working further fragment our efforts and rewards.

The net result of this is that the nature of our work and requirements for performing it fragment our activities and split and separate the self-satisfying personal rewards of "immediate returns" for our efforts.

He further argues that while remote work eliminates commutes and provides some measure of personal flexibility, the nature of remote work does not resolve the fundamental problems of the fragmentation of work and rewards. In fact, due to the physical separation, remote working exacerbates the personal rewards previously enjoyed by immediate and especially informal feedback from bosses and colleagues.

Along with the various team-based issues related to remote working, several personal and professional concerns arise with individuals based on new remote or work-at-home requirements and challenges.

Many individuals, particularly single staff, have become accustomed to the office workplace providing a social support environment in their lives. Thus, social interaction and isolation are genuine issues in WFH, especially during the waves of COVID-19 lockdowns and subsequent hybrid working situations. Therefore, the leader should identify staff members with high affiliation needs to support them and attempt to provide for work-based or related social activities to mitigate the impact of isolation with remote working.

Other sources of stress for remote working staff are the issues of job-based anxiety. This can be based on a change of role or responsibilities because of separation from the team and associated adjustments to work assignments. Further, an employment status might sometimes change from either side, resulting in changes from full-time to part-time, employment to contracting, or vice versa. Finally, due to the current economic crisis and the lack of regular management or peer reinforcement, some staff may have perceived or legitimate concerns about job security and even losing their jobs. Leadership awareness of these concerns, personal empathy, and continuous communication will help provide psychological safety and support for employees to maintain their confidence and motivation.

Difficulties with the transition to working from home can occur relative to the performance of job responsibilities. Some individuals struggle with change, lack of routine, reduced face time with peers and management, and diminished team bonding and collaboration. Leadership should increase guidance, coaching, and feedback, provide ongoing calibration regarding task requirements, and encourage the team to provide peer-to-peer reviews, mentoring, training, and support to maintain consistent quality and morale.

Leadership should be aware that their management, communications, and support are often vital and value-adding. However, also recognize and respect the remote worker's flextime context and work vs. home boundaries. In the past, walking up to an employee's desk for a quick chat was accessible and appropriate. Leaders should now be sensitive to employees' remote personal space and time shifts. Leaders of remote workers can no longer expect an employee's 100 percent dedicated availability from 9 a.m. to 5 p.m. Especially as the worker may be delicately juggling professional, family, and personal activities by employing flextime to work over a longer but less concentrated workday, say from 8 a.m. to 8 p.m.

Nevertheless, be cautious about the extended hours. For example, a call at 7 p.m. for a single person may be welcome and entirely acceptable; however, this may significantly disrupt the family evening routine for a worker with small children. Everyone has different needs; thus, an astute, sensitive leader will anticipate different workers' needs and proactively discuss the employees' desired approach to flexible working to ensure they are helping the employees and not invading or disrupting their personal domain.

Finally, be aware of employee externalities that may affect an individual's ability to work effectively. This could be the lack of a separate and appropriate workspace, inadequate internet, particularly in rural areas, and potential family distractions, such as young children. Be sensitive, aware, and flexible regarding supporting and assisting individuals in managing these issues. You may need to help them psychologically decouple their personal and professional activities to de-stress and optimize the situation. Help ensure that the employees can manage their time, responsibilities, and work hours to stay physically and emotionally healthy and avoid burnout.

One issue that is particularly challenging today with the prevalence of two or more adult workers (and students) in the home is the issue above of inadequate dedicated workspace. A previous spare bedroom, storage room, and office/study may suddenly be inadequate if both parents or partners work from home. How do you manage two simultaneous Zoom calls in one office? How do children handle video classes alongside parent meetings? The quick answer is that many awkward or unsatisfactory compromises will likely occur in the short term. So what can be done in the mid to long run?

It is easy to say but impractical to assume that people can simply uproot themselves and financially opt for a four-bedroom instead of a 2- or 3-bedroom apartment or home to accommodate the requirement for two offices. Something to explore in the future is the possibility of a financial work-from-home company stipend to supplement and offset the cost of a larger accommodation. This could potentially be funded from the aforementioned company savings from reductions in headquarters and regional offices and facilities. The challenge here is that the individuals are assuming a higher level of financial risk in the event of a termination, where a potential loss of the salary could be accompanied by an unmanageable higher rental or mortgage cost. Further, there may be a long-term opportunity for companies and employee advocacy groups to lobby governments to extend the tax deduction enjoyed by independent contractors for tax write-offs on the portion of accommodation used for home-working.

Enablers to Remote Working

Having discussed the challenges and risks of remote working extensively, let's finish with a list of enablers and opportunities to avoid or mitigate some of these risks.

As discussed, relative to the corporate facilities and organizational design, having a robust but adaptable plan for various potential future staffing and facilities scenarios is essential. This will help ensure you are prepared with efficient, flexible, and cost-appropriate facilities based on evolving requirements and trends for remote, virtual, and hybrid working. As stated, even post-pandemic, it is clear that a significant percentage of workers will continue to work at home, both from the employee preference perspective and also as a part of the corporate facilities' resizing plan.

However attractive future office space reduction and cost savings are, companies are seriously grappling with the prospect of overbuilt, underused office buildings today and will be for the foreseeable future. As a result, companies are confronted with too much office space, and simultaneously, employees are struggling with issues such as inappropriate home office space because of dual-income working couples.

Many companies and various roles will require on-site staff or still benefit from hybrid working in the future for a part of the workweek. Therefore, companies must mitigate the risk of a "brain drain" of employees exiting major metropolitan areas to relocate to more economical residential real estate markets. Therefore, companies must be creative with attractive ways to retain staff within reasonable commute distances from headquarters or regional offices.

It may not be viable for everyone, especially for families with children. But imagine the conversation with a young, upwardly mobile employee when offering them an upscale thirtieth-floor New York Hudson River,

San Francisco Bay, or London Thames view apartment at a 25 percent employee discount. With no commute, subsidized meal facilities, a gym, and daycare, it may be an attractive option, even as a taxable benefit.

There may be other alternatives, but what is clear is that the headquarters and commercial real estate market is broken due to the onset of the pandemic. Conversely, the flip side of the problem is that the work-from-home option is also broken for many people. Therefore, solutions must be found, and win/win ones that help both parties collaboratively look very appealing on our current threshold of the future.

The physical office previously provided a critical social support network for many in the past. Therefore, some will have separation anxiety by not regularly seeing their work colleagues. Individuals will all have different and varying levels of effectiveness in coping with the new remote, work-from-home ecosystem. Be aware of the difficulties for new and younger remote workers to bond and build relationships with existing teams and to be able to establish themselves, gain vital visibility, and advance within the organization.

This unique new context of extensive remote working places new demands on leadership. Given the scattered, autonomous, and independent nature of remote work, the leader must compensate and cultivate new behaviors and activities to sustain employee motivation and team effectiveness. These behaviors must be supported by intensified coaching and communication skills to adapt to and accommodate the unique needs of remote staff. In addition, leaders must significantly increase their verbal and written communication to overcome the lack of office-based peer communication. Ensure clear objectives, current updates, and sustained team motivation. These interactions are essential to maintaining morale and loyalty to realize what the political scientist Robert Putnam refers to as positive reciprocal "social capital" between the leader and team members.

However, make sure you select the right tool for the right task! In the past, people frequently complained about nonstop meetings all day long in the office. In the virtual workspace, don't make the opposite mistake and send an elaborate email when a collaborative meeting is what is required to get an agreement or build consensus. Conversely, don't book a Zoom call unnecessarily when a quick phone call might suffice, as booking a VC implies additional preparation and privacy. Just as too many meetings in the past were tiring and ineffective, be judicious and careful not to create "Zoom fatigue" by scheduling too many VC meetings. Finally, instead of sending an endless series of texts or a running WhatsApp commentary, why not just pick up the phone and have an actual dialogue? You might find it is faster and more efficient and allows you pleasant and appreciated collaborative interaction with a colleague. You may not be, but is your colleague isolated and lonely? Reach out . . .

In the past, when the office provided an element of peer support and on-the-job learning, leaders must now dedicate more time to team members and facilitate new linkages between team members. In addition, the effective remote leader in the digital environment must take special care and initiative to be particularly sensitive to colleagues' and team's comments, quips, contributions, and even poignant silences.

Some former leadership soft-skill enablers, such as social interactions like taking a staff member for a chat or a coffee or beer for a heart-to-heart, are very different. The quick compliment in the corridor or approving nod during a meeting must be replaced with conscious and intentional new remote actions and behaviors. Active encouragement and small comments may be necessary to draw people out, give reassurance and positive reinforcement, and gentle adjustments or redirection for flawed or disruptive actions. Even small, digital, or remote supportive gestures, like a "well-done" private chat during a team meeting and consistent regular communications, go a long way toward helping staff feel confident, safe, involved, and motivated.

This encouragement can also include supervisor virtual mentoring, formal and informal training activities, and additional informal VC discussion forums for brainstorming, innovation, or problem-solving. These new virtual forums can partly compensate for the lack of office-based face time and provide valuable forums for creative idea generation, problem solutioning, and team building. In addition, leaders should organize and "orchestrate" remote calls, conferences, and workshops to ensure equal contribution from all team members and participants. Depending on the team's size, the additional management overhead of these activities may also be delegated to personal assistants, office managers, or even new specialty employee well-being managers. These roles may be able to support the leader/manager with additional value-added employee social support activities and communications events.

The leader must be acutely aware that an extroverted employee may not perform as effectively in a socially constrained Zoom call as in a face-to-face client presentation. The creative introvert may also need extra encouragement and be provided new opportunities to contribute their ideas and recommendations remotely.

Numerous new technology enablers can support and partially mitigate the impact of dispersed and separated workers. Internet telephony, videoconferences, virtual collaboration, and whiteboard technologies can all assist in enabling electronic communications, collaborative working, and document sharing. Tools such as those mentioned earlier, Zoom, Slack, WhatsApp, WeChat (China), Google Meet, Skype, and Teams, go a long way toward overcoming remote working challenges. In addition, new applications for conferencing, messaging, calendars, document and data sharing, synchronization, and project management are being created virtually daily. Expect an explosion of new remote working applications in the coming months and years.

Another major concern that has arisen with remote working is anxiety about job security without the continuous reinforcement of office-based support systems. This can lead to significant employee stress and has manifested itself in various ways, including the employee putting in much longer working hours instead of the shorter hours many had anticipated when they began working from home. In addition, with extended work hours, especially for those with multiple time zone responsibilities, there is a tendency to be always on and on-call, with people struggling to switch off. As a result, work-life balance can suffer an increased risk of employee burnout.

Further, for you, your partner, and your family's mental health, ensure you set as regular a work finish time as possible. Otherwise, you may find yourself texting over dinner or emailing during a movie with the family and kids. Give your work your full attention when you are working, and give yourself and your family full attention when you are not. Being half in and half out of work for extended periods is a poor compromise for both your work and your family. Also, it sets unrealistic expectations for your boss and colleagues, who will become conditioned that they can contact you at any time, day or night, on weekdays and weekends. Long hours might be expedient for a short time when starting a new job or during a significant deliverable, but avoid making it a routine. Ensure you break the habit of being "always-on" relative to work, or your work creativity will decline, you risk burnout, and your quality of life or relationships may deteriorate.

Some people are implementing "virtual commutes," where they walk around the block to separate the time between waking up and working and at various intervals during the day. For me, a short time in the garden is refreshing and de-stressing. The same goes for lunch, coffee-time, teatime, and finishing work. Taking this time to collect your thoughts is essential, get some exercise, and create a psychological boundary between home and your WFH workstation.

The leader can help mitigate stressful situations and their impacts with regular communications and by organizing relaxing and motivating team-building catch-ups and necessary breaks. For example, organizing "Zoom-free" time when no meetings are scheduled can help staff focus on productive deep dives into research and projects or to catch up on administrative work.

Recognize that remote work has many clear benefits and some potential liabilities and functions differently for everyone. For example, substituting virtual conferences for in-person workshops and high-tech tools for low-tech social interaction will not be effective for everyone. Make it clear that you recognize the challenges remote working presents and that your "virtual door" is (almost) always open. Proactively plan catch-ups for hybrid workers and an occasional visit for work-from-home staff.

Further, ensure you are available for questions, training, and support on how each employee can cope better with the WFH environment and its emotional and productivity implications. Also, recognize that these lessons for maintaining motivation and reducing stress apply equally to your employees and yourself as a leader. For example, the hero syndrome of extremely long hours for leaders and managers carries the same risks of reduced quality of life, diminished creativity, and burnout as it does for staff.

You must be keenly aware, intuitive, and sensitive to realize when people are struggling, and you must be empathetic and creative in mentoring them to cope effectively. Use positive reinforcement, gratitude, and recognition to maintain communication and motivation. There are effective lessons you can draw on from the past, but there will also be new challenges leaders must recognize, embrace, and conquer as we enter, explore, and conquer this new uncharted territory.[4]

> *The best way to predict the future is to create it.*
> —*Peter Drucker—management consultant, author*[5]

Key Takeaways—Remote Working

- New digital applications such as Zoom, Slack, WhatsApp, WeChat, Google Meet, Skype, and Teams have dramatically enabled and enhanced remote working communications and collaboration.
- Recruitment raises challenges for remote hiring. Enablers to mitigate the lack of personal interviews are more robust skills and competency evaluations, psychometric assessments, plus referrals and references.
- Remote staff benefits are improved work/life balance, reduced time away from home due to no commutes or business trips, more personal time, and the ability to time-shift work and personal responsibilities.
- Remote staff challenges are lack of suitable workspaces, distractions, isolation, time-shifted but long work hours, reduced collaboration and calibration, job insecurity and anxiety, and reduced psychological safety.
- Due to a lack of staff facetime and reduced office peer social support, leaders must be more sensitive, empathetic, inspirational, and communicative to guide remotely, coach, support, and motivate staff.

CHAPTER 4

Organizational Design — Usability, Design Thinking, Virtual Teams

Usability and Design Thinking

In the high-octane, hyperefficient, high-technology business world we work in today in the mid-2020s, the interplay of new business models and technology are essential business partners and collaborators to compete in the marketplace to deliver new value to shareholders, staff, and customers.

Whether you are a C-suite executive or a middle-management leader, none of us operate in a vacuum or in isolation from our wider organization or even the industry ecosystem within which we operate. Therefore, we have both a responsibility and an opportunity to be a positive agent of change in our role to continuously improve our products and services, as well as to evolve and transform our organization to be successful in the future.

Therefore, it is incumbent upon us to consider and innovate within our areas of responsibility relative to the resources, capabilities, and organizational design of our department or company required to meet those challenges. This chapter on organizational design, design thinking, and virtual teams is designed to model learning and best practices in these areas. And further to provide an example of how a leader can take charge, raise their head above the parapet, and use the capabilities and tools at their disposal to change the game in a positive way for the future.

The following extensive two-part case study has multiple interlocking objectives. First, they represent radical innovation and business transformation in both product and organizational design. Second, the context of usability design and design thinking provides detailed learning for user-centricity and product design. Finally, the virtual team organizational design gives comprehensive practical guidance and tips that presage and reinforce the discussions we have just had on remote working and the work-from-home challenges, solutions, and best practices.

The context is the intense, mission-critical, high-stakes investment bank trading systems world. This comprises a detailed case study of the Reuters Group usability and design labs' development through the creation of the original virtual team concept. Both the usability design labs and the virtual teams were the leading examples of both at the time globally.

As training director for Reuters Asia based in Hong Kong and Singapore in the 1990s, my team was responsible for investment bank trading systems training across a territory stretching from Cyprus to New Zealand.

These were the heady days of globalization, and financial service products were proliferating rapidly and dramatically beyond the traditional foreign exchange, equities, and commodities markets. The investment banking derivatives market spawned an exotic array of new financial instruments: futures, options, and even options on futures. Accordingly, Reuters Trading Systems businesses surged with the explosive expansion of the global financial trading markets.

With the electronic automation of emerging global market exchanges and their associated instruments, the complexity of functionality necessary to deal with multiple international markets and new derivatives rapidly exceeded our ability to incorporate them seamlessly and elegantly into user-friendly and useable designs for our new trading terminals.

As a result, my team of more than forty trainers was utterly overwhelmed by launching complex new country-specific products in Japan one day, Hong Kong and Taiwan the next, and then on to Australia, NZ, India, the Middle East, etc. The faster we ran, the further behind we would fall. It soon became clear to me that there was no way that we could possibly keep up the pace of change through traditional workshop training. Thus, I began experimenting with computer-based training and online e-learning to scale rapidly and distribute the required training for these diverse products in distinct markets. This stopgap solution helped us cope for a while; however, designing the computerized training brought to light the poor usability and design inconsistencies of these early online trading systems.

I realized we were at the end of a long chain of activities that forced us to reactively develop computerized training to alleviate and compensate for the systems' unintuitive interfaces and poor usability. It was apparent that there had to be a better way if we could work our way upstream in the organization to arrive at the source of the issues within the core design and development groups.

With heightened awareness of the customer usability problems and the proven success of the innovative computerized training, I proposed a plan to reengineer the usability problems out of the systems at their origin within the global product design and development operations. Fortunately, I had the ear of the new global chief executive, Peter Job, who had hired me when we were both in Hong Kong. I submitted the usability and customer support team proposal to Peter and the Group Board, who agreed and asked me to move to London to lead it.

I arrived in London on New Year's Day 1993, full of excitement and anticipation for my mission to strike at the heart of the problem of conceiving, designing, and developing a new range of user-friendly Reuters Trading Systems.

I reported for duty to Peter Job, the CEO, with my approved business and resource plan in hand for the start-up of the twenty-four-person customer performance support department. Unfortunately, in the issuing months between the board approval and my arrival, increasing financial pressure on the company resulted in a global hiring freeze. Therefore, I was asked to start the department with two people and "See what happens"!

As one sometimes does in moments of total panic, with my family camped in a hotel and all our personal belongings on a freighter somewhere near the Cape of Good Hope, I had an inspiration. I thanked him for his confidence in me and advised him that I would, therefore, require a million-pound investment to externalize the project mobilization. He was relieved and instantly agreed with the suggestion, as his pressing issue was the company's rapid FTE growth. Moreover, he had personally imposed the hiring freeze and couldn't show exceptional bias toward one of his protégés. I left his office a bit rattled but energized, as I still had his support, and despite the staff setback, I now had the financial resources I needed. I just had to figure out a way to make it work!

But where to start? My initial mobilization plan was out the window, so I did a "hard reset" and began with the basics. The systems were incredibly "feature and function" rich, but as a result, they were extremely complex to learn and unintuitive to operate. Everyone knew there were problems, but where were they, why did they exist, and what did we need to do to fix them?

I started interviewing the headquarters' product and development people, many of whom were skeptical since I was an outsider and a protégé of the new chief executive, who was also from the Asian Operations. Further, not only was I from the Asia Operation, but worse, I was not British or even Canadian, but an American! No matter how humble or soft-spoken, in those days, Americans were automatically suspect and certainly not one of the British "old boys' club"!

Although initially, I didn't make the expected progress talking to the internal teams; they did, however, concede there were serious problems to be addressed. Thus, the next step was to talk directly to customers and users at a number of Investment Banks in the City of London. Conversely, they were enthusiastic about sharing their concerns. Several interviews and quite a few coffees, teas, beers, and ports were enough to appreciate there were critical glaring problems.

First of all, the "damnable" critical "Quote List Set-up" function was thoroughly counterintuitive. Disturbingly, this was the core portfolio functionality a currency trader used to set up the reference list of instruments they traded continually. Unfortunately, it was extremely complicated to learn and use and perplexingly had some vital hidden setup tricks that many people were frustratingly unaware of.

I now had an indication of at least one major issue that needed to be addressed urgently. But I needed more information, concrete evidence, and an estimate of sizing to understand how important and pervasive it was and then how to fix it.

Next, I conducted an analysis of UK consultancies that were best of class in help desk systems, ergonomics/human factors (UI/UX), and User Interface Design. With no one consultancy ticking all the boxes, the study resulted in a complex consultancy matrix of different specialists in multiple consultancies. The investigation revealed that the University of Loughborough had a strong ergonomics and human factors program. I visited the faculty there, who advised me that some of their best graduates had ended up in Admiral Computing, which had a strong help desk and ergonomics practice. LogicaCMG had a very mature user interface design team, and a boutique design firm, Bird Consulting, had some creative designers springing out of London Southbank College of Design and from Apple Computer in California.

I kicked off my project with the Chinese CTO I brought from Hong Kong and a British product manager I met during my internal interviews. I started by appointing Admiral Computing to analyze the customer calls from our bank trading system customer help desk.

First, we needed support from the customer call center management, who immediately bought into the idea of capturing, logging, categorizing, and analyzing the results. They were highly supportive, as they were suffering as much as we had been in training. Together, we built a call logging system for agents to track the calls, durations, level of criticality, and estimated support costs.

Within a month, we had a detailed report of over sixty priority issues and incidents, categorized, prioritized, and sized by impact. At the top of the list was the glaring issue of the Trader's Quote List Setup function. We calculated that single issue alone was costing over 450K Sterling annually in direct help desk support. This would be circa 1.4 million dollars in today's currency. This direct help desk cost savings did not even consider the financial impact of lost time for the high-flying financial traders. Let alone the opportunity losses they might suffer in the split-second world of international currency trading.

Next, we set up some user tests with key traders and videoed the customers' flailing attempts to create the Quote List. In addition to the specific quantitative results, we now had definitive qualitative evidence of major customer usability problems. This included the frequency of incidence, where the errors occurred, and emotive customer comments regarding the seriousness and potential impact on their trading activities.

We took the help desk report and customer usability videos and called in human factor consultants to analyze exactly where and why the failures occurred and to recommend how to resolve the workflow process issues. Within a few days, we knew exactly where and why the failures occurred and how to resolve them. We took the results to the product and development teams, and for approximately 35k Pounds Sterling, we prototyped an improved function that we delivered to the development teams. As a result, the problem was finally permanently resolved.

We were on our way! We had rapidly addressed the most significant usability problem with our Reuters terminal and realized a half-million annual resource savings in help desk support staff.

We developed and documented our usability plans and processes. This comprised interviewing customers, running continuous help desk analysis, and identifying the usability problem areas through analysis of the help desk reports. Next, we conducted formal ergonomic and human factors usability tests. We prototyped solutions and validated them with usability lab tests. Finally, we delivered the results to the product teams for validation and specified and agreed on designs to be presented to the development group for enhancement and release.

With indisputable qualitative and quantitative evidence on the table, including customer video testimonials regarding usability concerns and some substantial quick wins, we had unequivocal confirmation and validation for our product usability reengineering proposals.

This gave us the necessary momentum and political support to mobilize properly despite the development teams' continued reticence. The developers still resented an outsider coming in to tell them the obvious fact that they had problems. Further, frankly, as they had built the systems in the first place, they would have rather resolved the issues themselves; thank you very much!

From a standing start with the help desk analysis, the usability assessment, and the quote list setup quick fix, we mobilized a usability team of circa sixty consultants from four consultancies over the next six months. Within a year, we would peak at nearly a hundred consultants from six different consultancies employed either full- or part-time. We accelerated fast, as the market was impatient, and the company was restless, with Dow Jones Telerate and Bloomberg beginning to nip at our heels from New York.

We matured and institutionalized the help desk tracking and reporting systems, giving us ongoing product functionality, usability metrics, and cost analysis. Next, we constructed two formal state-of-the-art usability labs with one-way mirrors and sophisticated video recording systems. Following that, we built systems for conducting, monitoring, and measuring user actions during customer usability tests. We would eventually set up another full lab in New York and Milan and a remote Singapore satellite with full synchronous video lab testing between sites. This allowed us to test our systems with local customers globally using the specialist usability technicians in the London labs.

In addition to our quick win with the help desk reporting systems, we designed, documented, and published formal usability testing technologies and procedures. Then, we set up user interface style guides and libraries and reusability code object libraries for use across the company.

The final piece of the puzzle came when the development labs finally capitulated, acknowledging the issue with the product designs and usability problems. They stated, "Yes, now we know we have problems and where they are, but what do we do about it? Help us fix the problems." With our interface and graphic design teams in place, we embarked on developing our "design lab." We combined the resources of Logica, Edwards Churcher, Bird Consulting, and a graphic designer from Apple Computer in Cupertino.

The design labs were ultimately the critical secret sauce in the whole transformation. We knew where the problems were, the magnitude of the impact, the priorities, why they occurred, and how to fix them. The only thing remaining was ensuring that the designs were intuitive, consistent, and compelling across the product suites. To help achieve that, we studied linguistics, logographic Asian languages, and iconography.

We even dabbled briefly in hieroglyphics to understand the most intuitive and useable approach to user interface icon design.

The challenge was that we could fix the usability problems, but we needed to do it in a consistent, extensible, and standardized way. Today, this sounds straightforward, but to what standard? This was the mid-1990s with the early days of Microsoft Windows, and we were an early beta tester of Windows. There were no consistent menu bars at the time. With Microsoft as a core partner in the usability group and Excel as a core component of the Reuters Terminal, we decided that standardizing on Microsoft was a more practical and sustainable solution than creating, promoting, and permanently maintaining our own global interface standards.

Thus, we began by analyzing the Microsoft interfaces. To our dismay, Windows Word, Excel, and PowerPoint had completely different interfaces, icons, menu structures, and locations at that time. We decided to document all of Microsoft and our products to create "usage cluster maps" of functionality and interface tools. After a period of intense analysis with internal staff, Reuters customers, and my son Matt's Boy Scout group and son Chris's Cub Scout group, we had a very robust analytical and quantitative taxonomy analysis of functionality. This included functionality usage, incidence, commonality, and discrepancies. Common functions were file, open, close, save, edit, insert, delete, copy, paste, font type, size, margins, colors, etc. This complex cluster map demonstrated high usage correlations across all Microsoft, third-party, and Reuters Products. Although each application was different, despite the inconsistent layouts, the basic navigation tasks were highly consistent. Thus, we clustered and aligned navigation icons and file structures according to usage frequency. Perhaps it is obvious now, but it was not the standard or best practice then. We then grouped all "like" functionality under header categories of File, Edit, Font, Print, etc., with drop-down menus, including all the associated options. The design logic was validated by testing, and the new navigation layout was enormously simplified, systematized, and optimized. Then we knew we were on to something important!

With two of my directors, Victor and Peter, we flew off to Microsoft in Redmond, Washington, to meet with Tandy Trower, the head of

Microsoft's advanced interface team. We presented our research and the proposal for creating a clustered "parent menu" with associated drop-down menus and icons to Tandy and his team. They were immensely interested, and after an hour, he said he would clear his schedule in two weeks and fly to London to spend a week at our labs.

We spent that week running through the research, playing back the usability tapes of finance traders, normal users, professional users, Boy Scouts, and Cub Scouts. We gave Tandy the detailed analysis, and perhaps nine months later, we were delighted to receive a nice note from Tandy along with a beautiful shrink-wrapped copy of the original Office 95.

At the time and even to this day, we don't know the full value of our contribution. All we know is what had happened, but we had no visibility of what occurred on Microsoft's side. However, within the year, Microsoft Office had a parent and child menu structure following almost precisely the same concepts and approach we had proposed. This comprised virtually the same icon and menu clustering we had researched, identified, and presented to the Microsoft head of advanced interface design. However, in our compulsive focus on fixing the Reuters Terminal and competing with Bloomberg, we did not see the broader value of what we were doing. We didn't envision the subsequent explosion of Microsoft Office in the marketplace. We were just trying to solve our own problems of creating the best, most intuitive, recognizable, and usable interface for the Reuters terminals.

That is what happened. Unfortunately, Victor has passed on, but our team, particularly Peter and I, remember this well. We make no official, commercial, IP, financial, or even egotistical claims, as all that would be fruitless. Still, despite no financial or patent benefits from any developments at Microsoft, we take solace in the belief that we may have had a material role in the design of one of the most successful software applications in history.

Reflecting on this now, twenty years later, the next epiphany occurred over the Christmas holiday that same year when I "saw the light." As an IT innovation specialist, I could no longer ignore the force of the internet. I decided to reinvent the usability and design labs and myself into the internet age. After the holiday break, I entered the labs on the morning of the 2nd of January, greeted the staff, and announced in a booming voice with as much drama as I could muster, "tools down!" With a room full of astonished, expectant, anxious eyes upon me, I decreed, "All projects are now canceled. From this point forward, every project, every design, proof of concept, prototype, and task will now be internet-based." No new project would be approved or started that did not have the internet as its core objective and technology.

After a brief period of confusion, challenge, and alignment, the team accelerated again and began a new internet-based transformation period.

That was 1996, the time frame when, as discussed in the chapter on Clayton Christensen's *Innovator's Dilemma*, we developed the internet-based financial trading system— Enterprise—in the Reuters usability and design labs. As mentioned, this groundbreaking new internet trading system was well before its time and, therefore, unfortunately, was not progressed by the group board. Looking back and trying to second-guess what might have happened is futile; however, at the time, we had the most advanced internet-based financial trading system operational in our labs.

In summary, during the mid-90s, this was undoubtedly the most advanced global usability lab network. With IT technicians and white lab-coated ergonomics experts, we ran five to six formal usability tests daily in multiple geographies on any of a dozen core systems targeted for usability enhancement. Eventually, online usability monitoring and testing overtook these technologies, but they were cutting-edge and hugely valuable at the time.

This is a detailed case study of "what" we were doing in the Reuters usability and design labs. Let's now look in-depth at "how" we were working through the development of the virtual team concept.

Virtual Teaming

To deliver the required Reuters product and business transformation just discussed and to create a new generation of user-friendly and usable products, we needed to move fast, faster than traditional recruitment of specialist resources could provide, and that required a radically new operational approach.

Because of the urgent competitive challenges ahead, starting and swiftly building the Reuters usability group from scratch meant breaking free of traditional management strategies, breaking free of conventional operations, and, in short, breaking free of corporate inertia.

I didn't have the time, the staff, or the energy to build a skills base from ground zero, but what I did have was money. Desperation is often the parent of invention! Looking back, initially, I didn't think I was starting anything unique, just another day-to-day example of outsourcing, but this was the first step toward creating a virtual team.

Regarding the setup of the Usability Group, our initial analysis gave us the information we needed to prioritize our activities, size our tasks, and start drawing up a shopping list of the skills we needed. And what an eclectic and esoteric list it was.

- Human factors and ergonomists
- Cognitive psychologists
- Graphic designers
- User interface prototypes
- Usability lab testers
- Artificial intelligence experts

And that was just the start. Looking at the challenge and fast pace of change, we began to feel that the focused innovation and creativity we were looking for would only happen by building a unique team.

We called in a recruitment consultant. We asked them to research and nominate the best in every field we wanted, with the proviso they couldn't suggest themselves. We found that no organization of any size could supply all those skills and competencies.

It began to look increasingly like we would somehow have to get the different consultancies to work as a team. But it still looked daunting, as, at the time, there weren't any role models for this.

So, we started small, with the sure bets in the UK, Microsoft, Admiral, and Logica, known names, reliable resources, and people we knew could deliver on isolated projects. They concentrated on two areas. On the market side, the usability and user interface, and on the technical side, prototyping and tool-building. The consultancies made significant progress toward improved usability and were working well individually.

But we needed more—complete and total flexibility, both in scale and task. And we needed even more specialized skills. We needed hyper-growth, taking on more and more interconnected projects. That hyper-growth would only happen if people from diverse backgrounds, disciplines, and organizations worked side by side on the same projects. After six months, with scores of resources on-site, after an initial buzz of successes and enthusiasm, it became clear we were fragmented into professional but siloed consultancy work streams.

Admiral Computing was responsible for the ergonomics and usability analysis, Logica for user interface design, and Bird Consulting for the look and feel. Microsoft was responsible for emerging Microsoft standards and technologies. SEMA (Atos Origin) for coding and development, plus some boutique consultants and independent contractors.

As discussed in the Usability chapter, we had tremendous intellectual capital cloistered and concentrated in lab facilities just off Fleet Street in the City of London. However, Admiral's ergonomics and human factors specialists overlapped with Logica's UI design. Further, Logica's UI design was intertwined with the UI look and feel that Edwards Churcher and Bird Consulting were creating.

Despite the strong leadership and financial support from the Reuters board, I could not justify any duplication of effort or, worse, competitive friction arising between the consultancies. It became apparent that the consultancy-based, stovepipe functional project structure was not optimal. Whether in a moment of inspiration or frustration, I decided to reorganize the rigid consultancy-based structure.

I called an off-site conference for all staff, consultants, and contractors and asked the consultancies to bring their commercial and legal people to the meeting. We held the conference around the corner at Hamilton

House Conference Center alongside the Temple Gardens, the gathering place for the Knights Templar for the twelfth-century crusade, just adjacent to the Temple Church. This venerable and beautiful Victorian building would be the site of several career- and life-changing events for me, the first of which was this conference.

I convened the consultancy meeting for a heart-to-heart "hard reset." After an impassioned speech about what we were trying to accomplish for our investment bank trading systems reengineering, I reviewed what we had already achieved and where we intended to go in the future. Together, we had created the finest ergonomics, human factors, and user interface design team in Europe by the mid-1990s. However, the structure was suboptimal and unsupportable going forward. Separate fiefdoms of consultancies, all working secretly alongside each other in the same collocated offices, were no longer desirable or acceptable.

I decided to reorganize and restructure the organization into cross-disciplinary functional teams. The consultancy structure could not be sustained or supported in this new design. Instead, we would create a "virtual team" of individual consultants merged into functional project teams, all collaborating, sharing, and working toward a common goal. I introduced each of the consultancies, explained the good work they were all doing, and painted a vision of how we would all work in the future with a common objective of building the finest usability labs anywhere. Each consultancy was invited to participate, but the rules were clear and nonnegotiable. We would work in merged cross-consultancy teams according to the business's functional needs, not based on any separate corporate or consultancy commercial structure.

We needed to draw in people from disparate companies, cultures, and countries. Bring them in instantly, apply them directly to the heart of a problem, tackle it, and move on. As a result, we would operate in an ever-evolving, organic way, mixing and matching skills, adding and subtracting skills, and creating and dissolving project teams on virtually a daily basis.

But we faced one last hurdle before we could truly become a virtual team. Who would own the intellectual property rights? I had to be firm on this. When you've got four different consultancies working on a project, there can't be any lack of clarity about intellectual property;

therefore, we would own them. The intellectual capital would be owned entirely by Reuters, but the learnings would be shared freely among the consultancies. However, they would only be able to buy into that if they all signed nondisclosure agreements with Reuters and each other.

This had the potential to be a deal-breaker for the consultancies, particularly the larger multinationals. I knew they would only sign if I could convince them that every consultancy had more to benefit by staying on the team and learning from it. In my view, no individual or company had more expertise than the collective knowledge of the group. So I ventured to the assembled group that each of the consultancies, including Microsoft, had more to gain from this technologically advanced, multi-million-pound venture than they could possibly lose in intellectual capital leakage to their competitors.

I then called a coffee break and instructed them to break into separate consultancy meeting rooms to confidently discuss and debate the new model. Further, I stated that any company or entity uncomfortable with the new business model, unhappy with the IP contract arrangement, or dissatisfied with signing mutual NDAs should not be present when we return after the break.

I returned in thirty minutes to find everyone, including all consultancies, present in the main conference room. Contracts and NDAs were distributed and signed, and the legal and commercial staff were thanked and dismissed. The usability and design team experts remained to design, build, and operate the usability and design labs unencumbered by the strictures and structures of the consultancy bureaucracies back at their headquarters.

With the IP issues resolved and cross NDAs signed, the staff returned to the office to reorganize around projects rather than the consultancy stovepipe functions. The structure was simple and straightforward: market research, usability testing, support systems, user-centered design teams, user interface, etc. We assigned each consultant to their functional project teams, restructured the office layout and seating as a workflow process, and assigned team leads to the different groups. Each cross-consultancy project team was led by its most experienced member, regardless of whom they worked for. Fortunately, there was a fair spread of senior consultant leads from each consultancy across the six teams, so there was no perception of commercial preferential treatment. Following is an example of the group structure from an article about our virtual team written by Tom Peters:

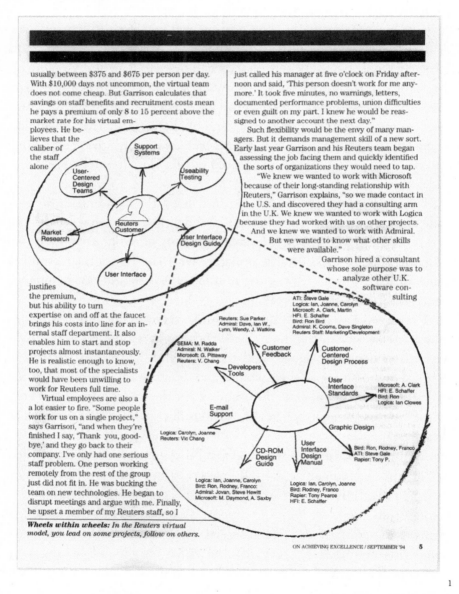

usually between $375 and $675 per person per day. With $10,000 days not uncommon, the virtual team does not come cheap. But Garrison calculates that savings on staff benefits and recruitment costs mean he pays a premium of only 8 to 15 percent above the market rate for his virtual employees. He believes that the caliber of the staff alone justifies the premium, but his ability to turn expertise on and off at the faucet brings his costs into line for an internal staff department. It also enables him to start and stop projects almost instantaneously. He is realistic enough to know, too, that most of the specialists would have been unwilling to work for Reuters full time.

Virtual employees are also a a lot easier to fire. "Some people work for us on a single project," says Garrison, "and when they're finished I say, 'Thank you, good-bye,' and they go back to their company. I've only had one serious staff problem. One person working remotely from the rest of the group just did not fit in. He was bucking the team on new technologies. He began to disrupt meetings and argue with me. Finally, he upset a member of my Reuters staff, so I just called his manager at five o'clock on Friday afternoon and said, 'This person doesn't work for me anymore.' It took five minutes, no warnings, letters, documented performance problems, union difficulties or even guilt on my part. I knew he would be reassigned to another account the next day."

Such flexibility would be the envy of many managers. But it demands management skill of a new sort. Early last year Garrison and his Reuters team began assessing the job facing them and quickly identified the sorts of organizations they would need to tap.

"We knew we wanted to work with Microsoft because of their long-standing relationship with Reuters," Garrison explains, "so we made contact in the U.S. and discovered they had a consulting arm in the U.K. We knew we wanted to work with Logica because they had worked with us on other projects. And we knew we wanted to work with Admiral. But we wanted to know what other skills were available."

Garrison hired a consultant whose sole purpose was to analyze other U.K. software consulting

Wheels within wheels: In the Reuters virtual model, you lead on some projects, follow on others.

ON ACHIEVING EXCELLENCE / SEPTEMBER '94   5

At this point, we began to see the virtual team concept not as an abstract model but as the best and optimal solution for our needs.

The new structure was far more logical and efficient than having artificial, overlapping, suboptimal organizational boundaries between the companies. Since the reorganization was eminently rational and team leaders' and members' assignments were logical to everyone involved, the transformation and change took root almost instantaneously. The transition to the new structure took less than a week until everyone in the new project teams was fully operational.

One member might lead in one area and follow in another, all with no prejudice, jealousy, or competition, as everyone wanted to learn, share, and grow. The team spirit was exciting, energizing, and fun. We grew rapidly and were flooded with CVs and résumés of people who wanted to be a part of the usability group and the virtual team. On any day, we might have had up to seventy or eighty members of the team working from our center in London.

Moreover, we had the best of all worlds. When you recruit an individual consultant, that's just the tip of the iceberg. That individual will pull in all the help and support they need from their companies to do their job. They were getting all the advice, equipment, and technical assistance required to keep them functioning. Given the practical support team members received daily from their parent organizations, it was like running a virtual team of hundreds of specialists. It also meant that we benefited from those organizations' advances, for example, access to Microsoft's latest tools.

Within a surprisingly short time, the entire organization shifted into overdrive, where everything started to work faster and more efficiently. The strategy and structure made sense to everyone, and the communications and processes were free, open, and fluid. Consequently, everyone began to work and feel more efficient and effective. Motivation increased noticeably, as did the activity, conversations, excitement, and overall general noise level!

The teams gelled virtually overnight, the workflow pace between the groups became obvious, more explicit, and defined, and the productivity accelerated dramatically. The energy, excitement, productivity, and fun were palpable. The teams bonded, and cross-functional teams began collaborating, e.g., the help desk analysts and the usability testers got very focused on the problems at hand. Next, the usability testers and the functional and UI design teams began to work together to solve usability-related issues. People got to know each other without the emotional impediment of their companies' situation as competitors in the outside world. We worked together, had coffee and lunch; some partied, and others even dated. Something extraordinary had begun. We had natural predators, competitors, and customers working side by side on our team, sharing creative challenges, creating, and enjoying it.

We were no longer a ragtag group of independent "multisourced" project teams. Suddenly, we ceased to be Reuters, Microsoft, Logica, Admiral, SEMA, and Bird Consultancies. It was no longer them and us. Instead, we were the "usability group—virtual team," which we all realized was a "REAL TEAM."

As such, we danced to a different drummer, to our own beat, and we needed to create our own virtual team-based modus operandi, which was a blend of the best practices from everyone that, when merged and agreed upon, worked effectively for the collective benefit of all.

As a minor but practical example, each company had different travel and expense policies. We consciously harmonized all these policies to ensure there were no inequities when mixed groups of Reuters staff and different consultancies traveled together. As we would pay for it, we set the policy; therefore, everyone traveled in economy. We collaborated on holidays and shared coverage with different team members, leading or following on various activities.

Again, we had no model to work to. I realized that if I didn't set up and agree on new policies and procedures for the virtual team, I'd have to cope with ten different styles of time sheets, purchase requisitions, and payroll plans, you name it. So, I said we would create a virtual way of working, and we negotiated and published a joint agreement on policies and procedures with all the member companies. Naturally, every consultancy had its own internal systems that were interfaced but suppressed behind the virtual team processes and systems. Subsequently, when a new team member joined, they knew from day one how we operated.

Based on our experience, how would you set about creating a virtual team? What steps would you need to take, and what would you get from it? First of all, you need to win support for the idea and be clear about what you're aiming for and the benefits you expect to achieve. For starters, here are some critical advantages of the virtual team.

The most significant advantage of running a department like this is that we achieved a tremendous amount in a very short period of time. If you tried to build a team like this with all the specialists, recruiting your own staff would take a very long time. I would estimate that looking at what we accomplished, it would probably have taken us about two to three years, if at all, whereas we have got there in just over six months. So that's a measure of what you try to do when you gear up like this.

In a virtual team, every consultancy was recruited, deployed, and played to its strengths. Any weakness was covered by others who were stronger in that area. The team was designed, out of necessity, to have a complementary set of skills and to work together collaboratively as a team.

To recap, what are the key benefits that will help win support for a virtual team? You don't need to grow the skills or build the infrastructure; you just do it. Conventional outsourcing would've been too narrow—we needed the consultants to pool their talents to have competitors working together. In our case, it was the best solution because no one organization had all the answers. In hindsight, we had undoubtedly pulled together the highest percentage of human factors and ergonomics experts anywhere at that time.

Further, you don't spend time and money on recruitment. You benefit from the personnel functions of the consultancy home office. It means that you can build a skilled workforce with zero bureaucracy. We couldn't have hired this caliber and variety of people on the open market, and even if we could, we wouldn't have needed many of these highly esoteric and specialized skills as ongoing, full-time posts. We needed to be able to turn the skills switch on and off.

The virtual team allows you to combine rare and specific skills flexibly, creating a just-in-time skills pool. Plus, the group had total flexibility; you could start and stop projects instantly, without pain, guilt, or hassle, being nimble enough to turn on a dime. As in the case of the shift of all projects to the internet, which happened virtually overnight! In fact, we went through a total reinvention at least once a year based on evolving requirements and our continually developing skills.

Those are some benefits; what about the costs? How do you make the business case for a virtual team? At first glance, it looks like we paid a premium of between 8 percent and 15 percent over the fully loaded cost of standard employment. But not when considering the real TCO costs of employing specialist people of this caliber. You only pay for actual creative work: no downtime, no holidays, and no additional costs like pensions, transport, benefits, or recruitment and redundancy costs. You can win the financial argument in the long term by demonstrating that you have the proper project management, legal, and financial controls in place. That makes management feel much more secure.

But remember, it's not only your organization you have to sell the idea to. You must also prepare the way carefully for the partner companies and your new team members as well. After decades of adversarial business relationships, competing consultancies are understandably wary about working together. This was more than partnering or subcontracting; it implied completely virtual collaborative working within teams. Consequently, you've got to remove these artificial boundaries, overcome distrust, and create win/win partnerships. You must explain how the virtual team works, clarify accountabilities, and set the absolute ground rules. There are no Chinese walls, and there is total cooperation between consultancies working together with fluid and unfiltered communications.

That will only happen if you create an atmosphere of personal responsibility and set up a creative environment. The creative spark will die if you treat a virtual team in a pedestrian or bureaucratic way. You need to set up and manage creative tensions and carefully mix individuals with distinct personalities and approaches. Mix multitaskers and specialists. Mix people from diverse business cultures and backgrounds. And observe what happens.

Once you've prepared the way and convinced people it's a creative, highly skilled, and practical way to work, you need to think about how to get the results you need and the attitude and alignment you want from people you don't actually employ. So, how do you motivate members of the virtual team?

The management style you can use in a virtual team can be one where you encourage, applaud, nurture, and gently steer rather than command

and control. In part, it's recognizing that rewards are often intangible. You're not their direct employer, so your reward to them is really on a personal level. In short, it's an adult-to-adult relationship, and you're appealing to their sense of personal responsibility, growth, and worth.

One added benefit of the mix of consultancies and independents was that everyone took pride in their work and company. While everyone worked together collaboratively toward the same objectives, each individual and team did their best to deliver a great result and represent themselves and their organizations in the best possible way.

So, with the team in place and on board with your ideas, it's time to give them the freedom to use their skills and empower them to deliver the desired results. One of the strengths of working in a virtual team is the leverage you get from different companies with different skills and strengths. Still, in a true, aligned virtual team, everybody works toward the same goal, and it doesn't really matter who you work for. However, individuals in the teams all benefited and learned from the knowledge, skills, and experience of members from the other consultancies and teams. Everyone gained something from everyone else.

Working in a virtual team demands significant flexibility from team members. Not only did they typically hop between five to six project teams in a day, but their role also often changed from one project to another. For example, one member might lead one team and be a participant in another, and vice versa. This resulted in mutual respect, additional skill development, and a unique opportunity for various individuals to enhance their leadership skills. In addition, by observing and demonstrating best-practice leadership, mentoring, and technical expertise in a nonthreatening environment, everyone gained skills that would not have been possible in a traditional organization.

Running a virtual team demands new skills and presents unique challenges as well. You need to monitor carefully. As with all project planning, the key is hitting the right level of detail. With so much activity and so many people in so many projects and locations, your costs can run away with you if you're not conscientiously keeping on top of things and up to date.

Even with the most robust project management feedback systems, there's no substitute for walking around, watching, and talking. You must touch base, pick up on concerns, check out what's happening, make timely decisions, and take rapid action.

It's advantageous that the virtual team members are in the office for a significant amount of time, if possible, to get to know and develop relationships with all team members. With this very positive experience, I strongly advocate for colocated projects where possible.

While many of the Reuters virtual team worked remotely worldwide, it was vital to provide a place for the core team to work together in our London center. If, as it has been theorized, 92 percent of communication is nonverbal, people interpret far more than you can squeeze down the line, even fiber, with today's technology. There's still no communication device that can match the creative interplay that happens face-to-face in the meeting room, at lunch, or around the coffee machine. Working on different projects and with all the interconnections helps establish good working relationships. With mutually vested interests, including shared objectives and new knowledge acquisition, there was a great deal of collaborative camaraderie in the office.

For example, even in the mid-1990s, through videoconferencing, we could show developers how customers across the world actually used their products, giving them a ringside seat for usability tests. But at the end of the day, relationship-building is central to the virtual team, and that still takes regular personal contact. Psychologically, groups benefit from a home base, a place where they belong.

But it wasn't just physical support. We had to ensure that individual consultants could work within the team and across Reuters as a whole. An essential management function was recruiting the staff and managing the relationship between them and the rest of the host organization, opening doors for externals and steering them in the right direction.

We were looking for a pretty exceptional mix of skills and behaviors. We needed to employ consultants who had the right skills and personality profiles and could fit into our unique team and culture. We interviewed excellent specialists who had the right competencies and skills mix but whose personalities and behaviors didn't fit with the team. No matter how good someone is, you can't afford to let them undermine the team spirit. It's not easy. It takes an open, secure, and flexible person to fit in. We needed to maintain that delicate balance of creativity and push the envelope without creating tension or letting our egos get in the way of progress. It was a high-ly-skilled, creative, and intense but collaborative atmosphere.

To ensure people join and hit the ground running, you must induct them, introduce them, and show the work you do, the products you make, and the team-specific policies and procedures you work to. Also, attempt to team up new people with a buddy for support, another like-minded individual, ideally someone from a different organization.

It's in the nature of a virtual team like this that you start and stop projects almost instantly, but that doesn't mean it's not sad when people depart. Even with contingent workers or contractors, teams may be working together for many months or even years. Try to manage this carefully on a social level and even have a virtual alumni organization. These people have been part of something special, and you want to keep the relationship ticking over; after all, you may need to tap their skills again. As I mentioned, I brought one team member with me to three successive organizations.

In managing the team, you've also got to retain what you could call the team's tribal knowledge and folklore, the lessons and experience the group has learned together. In part, that comes through the people, as many team members, especially virtual members who are with you for significant periods of time, are steeped in what you do and how you work.

Given the challenge of leading over eighty people, some of whom you only see occasionally, what leadership style really seems to work? In my experience, you need to make people feel empowered. Lay out the guide-lines of what you expect, and let them sort out how they will do it. Your job as the leader is to boost their confidence and nurture them. After all, they're working in what is a unique environment for some people. To lead a virtual team, you will be operating with a high degree of indepen-dence but also interdependence. Therefore, you're asking everybody else to trust, be open, and be honest, and you've got to set that example and culture from the outset.

And as a leader, you need to take a genuine interest in your virtual team as people. Further, you have a real obligation and responsibility for their development. It's to your benefit and theirs that they take advantage of training and personal growth opportunities. But the real advantage is that with the diverse mix of skills in the virtual team, it's impossible not to learn. Think back to the Medici Effect example we discussed early on, which was a completely different time and context but precisely the same concept, process, and effect.

The Reuters Virtual Team was a learning experience for all of us. Let me share some additional final, personal leadership, and team learnings.

One of the key lessons we learned was hitting a comfortable ratio between the number of host company (in this case, Reuters) staff and consultants. At one point, our managers were overwhelmed. There were just too many activities to set up and too many relationships to manage. We concluded that the ideal maximum ratio was at least one Reuters manager for every ten consultants.

Success also depends on tight cost monitoring and excellent central project management. For example, if your consultants start breeding like voracious rabbits, you've got to be on top of the situation to see if it's justified.

Equally, keep an eye on the creative tensions you've set up to ensure the relationships are not getting too tense. It's vital to manage creative people carefully, monitoring and reining them back from falling in love with the technology, ensuring that they're focused on applied research that will be of actual practical benefit to customers. With several deep scientists and PhDs on the team, there was a tendency for other experts to want to initiate fascinating, but irrelevant for our purposes, digressions. Don't stifle creativity, but stay focused.

Communications are vital to such a diverse and dispersed team, and it needs to be regular, proactively planned, and carefully managed, or it could happen in a random, sporadic way.

We needed to break free of the past and move forward into the future. By late 1996, the "skunk works" project had achieved as much as possible as a separate initiative. Usable design and the usability labs had become part of the organizational culture and ethos. I began to recognize to complete the final step of the organizational transformation, it was time to embed the concepts, tools, systems, processes, and designs into the permanent fabric of the core organization. Therefore, we concluded that the most appropriate solution was to split up the usability project into the core components and embed them into relevant, appropriate existing internal departments. The help desk tools would go to the help desk. The usability labs moved into sales and marketing, the standards and tools to the CTO, and the design lab to the development groups.

The job was done by the end of March 1997, and the transformation and transition into the core businesses were completed. For almost five terrific years, our large dedicated "virtual team" of employees, consultants, and contractors had worked together, laughed, and cried together, and achieved amazing things.

During the closure luncheon, after all the prizes and speeches, there was a bittersweet moment; Ken Chakahwata, our guru financial quant, stood up and said: "Greg and all, I just wanted to say that despite all the press and accolades about the usability group and the virtual team, I just wanted you to know that this is not just a virtual team, this is a REAL TEAM!"

As a final message and image regarding this five-year transformation, here is a fun caricature of the Reuters usability group/virtual team created by one of the team's graphic designers.

Key Takeaways—Design Thinking & Virtual Teams

- Use design thinking not only for product development but as a tool and methodology to design your organization to be "fit for purpose" in the future according to the evolving needs of the market.
- Ensure everything you do and build considers high quality and customer centricity to achieve usable designs and product reliability.
- To realize hyper-growth, employ people from diverse backgrounds, disciplines, and organizations working side by side on the same projects within a virtual organization.
- For effective collaborative multisourcing, virtual teaming provides a model for cross-disciplinary functional teams to collaborate, share, and work toward a common goal.
- The most significant advantage of a virtual team is that you can achieve a tremendous amount in a very short period. To recruit your own staff of specialists would take a very long time.
- The virtual team permits combining skills flexibly, creating a Just-in-Time skills pool. It enables flexibility to start and stop projects instantly, being nimble enough to turn on a dime.

CHAPTER 5

Leading External Teams: Radical Alignment: Beyond the Boundaries

In the past, leaders in traditional organizations managed internal projects and teams with internal staff resources and occasionally in conjunction with outsourced functions. However, that outdated model is no longer skill-wise, operationally, or financially optimal in the work world we operate in today. There are many reasons: globalization, outsourcing, complex partnership ecosystems, open innovation, contracting, and multisourcing. Whatever the reason, a leader must now manage and orchestrate a diverse landscape of internal and external staff and partners collaboratively and efficiently to achieve maximum efficiency and operational throughput.

With the blindingly swift pace of business change, particularly with new business models and technological advances, knowledge, skills, and tools are evolving rapidly and simultaneously obsoleting just as promptly. Thus, many unique new technical skills are in high demand but often initially represent only infrequent and occasional, but not permanent, core competency requirements for organizations. Consequently, companies increasingly require external specialty support teams to implement new systems and solutions, carry out transformational changes, or provide low-cost commodity services. This support may be in the form of contractors, consultants, or professional service firms delivering these requirements or managed services.

Working with Contractors and Externals

Most organizations today, especially in this "gig economy," must ensure that contractors and consultants working in medium- or long-term roles within or alongside the internal teams must be incorporated, inculcated, and aligned with the internal team's agenda and culture. There are multiple reasons, but in principle, these colleagues need the same or often even more motivational attention than the internal staff. They don't enjoy the continuity of employment or strong internal collegial relationships; therefore, they require extra care and consideration to earn their genuine allegiance beyond just being a contract day laborer. Also, you need to ensure that the externals are collaboratively allied with your internal team to avoid unhealthy competition or conflict. As people are people, this team alignment is usually relatively easy as long as you treat the externals as vital extensions of and an integral part of your existing team. Moreover, as they are less familiar with your organization, you must carefully indoctrinate them, communicate the team's vision and objectives, respect them, involve them, and share the team's successes and challenges with them.

An important nuance to this relationship working with externals is to be clear about who the boss is and who is in charge. However, you must also win their respect and, hopefully, their hearts and minds. You need to strive for full alignment across your entire team, including your internal staff, contractors, and consultants. Externals must understand that you respect and honor them and their employer's governance and control but that they work for you on a day-to-day basis. At the end of the day, you, the client, are calling the shots, not their boss back in their home office. As a result, they must be guided by your leadership, the company's project governance, departmental policies, and your team's work assignments and deliverables.

Sometimes, the contractor or consultant can get caught between the proverbial rock and a hard place with schedules, contracts, deliverables, and payments. This is the time to be very transparent with the contractor or consultant and their employer about your requirements, that you are in control, and that they are working for you. The effectiveness and quality of relationships and the externals' productivity and output depend explicitly on the success of the commercial relationship you maintain with the workers' employers.

It's essential to be sensitive to and recognize the commercial pressure the worker and their relationship manager have to generate work, win work, deliver work, make a margin, and on-sell additional services. Despite that, simply being transparent and open about your requirements and the supplier's responsibilities goes a long way toward establishing and confirming a collaborative working relationship, taking the pressure off your contractors. This allows them to focus on the actual work without being distracted or conflicted by uncertainty, conflict, or lack of alignment between themselves, their management, and you, their customer.

Treat a consultant as a consultant or contractor, and they will function as a consultant or contractor. Treat them as an essential member of your team, and more often than not, they will act as such and become an integral and active part of your team and extended organization.

Contractors or consultants, by nature or nurture, are often highly adaptable from one situation or engagement to the next. Although their employer is still valued as their "rice bowl" or "bread and butter," a unique bonding can occur in medium- to long-term contracts of more than a couple of months. This is where, on a daily basis, that individual is much more a part of your team than their employer's. This is particularly true of long-term contractors or consultants who are primarily fully billed out and spend more time with their clients than their actual employer. I once had a consultant, Neil, who worked for me for five years, but interestingly, he had never been to his own employer's head office! We are still in contact after twenty years.

Occasionally, you will find a contractor or consultant who may have had regrettable prior experiences with clients who have been inconsiderate, disrespectful, and even abusive. They may have been treated as high-priced hired hands, continually overloaded and run into the ground. This is often because of the clients' urgent demands and the perception that consultants and contractors can be treated almost as indentured labor and overworked due to their high billable rates.

Unfortunately, managing external workers tactically and demandingly is an all-too-common error managers make. Because of extreme time pressures and high costs, managers tend to think they must drive externals harder and faster than their own employees. Some managers feel they must justify the contractor's higher cost by unrealistic, higher productivity. I have often witnessed managers pressuring consultants and managing them callously and sternly in this manner. This is neither sensitive nor sensible.

However, if you scratch beneath the surface of the external contractors, you often find that despite consultants' high billable rates, they are not compensated at a level much different from your people, and often even less. In addition, their working conditions of extreme hours, lengthy absences from home, family disruption, and feelings of estrangement from your internal teams can lead to dysfunctional extended team relationships.

Therefore, excessive or abusive demands and pressure on the contractor or consultant are exceedingly unfair to them. In this case, they will only work for you out of necessity and may secretly harbor resentment against you for those unreasonable demands. Heavy-handed management erodes the relationships between the client, contractor, and supplier and is likely to harm the team spirit and working relations between the external and internal teams.

Extensive research and continuous experience attest to the fact that low-level micromanaging, aggressive task mastering, reign of terror, or tyrannical management create fear, defensiveness, and dysfunction. This shortsighted management approach can cause consultant or contractor resentment and potential burnout in long-term projects.

This can create a greater risk than any associated productivity benefit. You could lose valuable team members to burnout or illness or even have the consultant request their management to remove them from the account. In that eventuality, you lose critical time and waste the vital knowledge acquisition and team bonding you have invested in.

An additional flaw in this type of behavior is that tactical and directive management behaviors are typically only effective with junior workers, who are not self-directed and may need guidance or support on what and how to do their work. Conversely, senior staff with high-level skills and specialist knowledge must be managed carefully with relationship skills to bond, motivate, and bring out the best in them. In fact, because of the unique nature of some engagements, these highly skilled specialist experts may have a better idea of how to deliver the unique work than you do and should be valued accordingly.

Consequently, experience and evidence have proven that building relationships, motivating, and involving these staff is a far more productive approach than being a tactical slave master. Staff will work harder, longer, and with higher creativity of their own will and volition than by your goading and being a taskmaster. Therefore, we must overcome the naive and immature perception that we must drive the external staff harder to be more productive to compensate for the higher cost and achieve the project's demands or program.

It's also interesting and important that you do a TCO—total cost of ownership—analysis of the external resource cost against a full-time internal staffer. Recognize that you pay only for work conducted; there are no further costs, including bonuses, vacation time, redundancy, or related personal costs. Given the short-term and incremental use of these resources, you will likely find that an external resource may be more cost-effective than a full-time internal resource for specialty activities and projects.

External staff, contractors, and consultants are people like everyone else who naturally desire and will thrive in a benevolent and nurturing environment. Therefore, treat them honestly and fairly, with respect and understanding. As a result, you will build trust, create a bond, and develop a degree of loyalty while building a high-quality, high-performance team. This also assists and accelerates internal and external team bonding. External team allegiance and loyalty can sometimes be earned rapidly, as the interpersonal relationship is less threatening and has less baggage than actual employment. In addition to your staff, I have found that some of these relationships and bonds can be highly collaborative, productive, and value-creating, and they can last for decades, even if you or they move companies.

Once this bonding has been achieved, for all practical purposes, operationally, you can treat contractors and consultants virtually the same as internal team members. They will appreciate this acceptance and participation and feel a part of something important along with the permanent employees. Finally, your acceptance of the externals will model behavior and foster their acceptance by the internal team.

Following are some personal experiences vividly validating these leadership principles for external consultants and contractors, evidenced by the resulting level of highly motivated and self-actualized team members.

Working with Outsourced Functions and Organizations

Much of the previous motivational and alignment discussion applies equally to internal staff as external staff in outsourced functions. However, there are some crucial nuances and lessons to be addressed relative to effective value-creating management, administration, and motivation of people in outsourced operations.

Beyond these motivational issues and the obvious: "we are all human beings that need to be managed and motivated honestly and with respect," you need to understand what drives your supplier's commercial management that sits behind your outsourced service delivery teams. They operate to entirely different commercial and financial metrics than the teams on the ground. So again, the simple answer is to find a win/win relationship with them, but achieving that is not quite so simple, as there are numerous typical pitfalls and hidden landmines one should attempt to avoid at all costs.

My direct experience in this area stems initially from when I was at PwC—PricewaterhouseCoopers. I spent some years working with corporate finance outsourcing specialists, then subsequently in outsourced secondments, and finally managing major external contracts as a line manager in CIO/CTO roles. These varied outsourcing experiences, from both sides of the equation, formed my findings and positively validated these approaches.

The most dramatic of these experiences was working with client companies to salvage and realign three separate billion pound/euro IT outsourcing contracts. In each of these large contracts that were drifting or failing, when digging deep to identify the "root cause" of problems, it almost always came down to a contract misalignment, with some fundamental flaws in the original service contract negotiation. These critical misalignments of objectives, commercials, and outcomes drove the wrong behaviors right from the start and directly from the home offices down through middle management to the service delivery people on the ground.

In many major outsourcing contracts, the client typically identifies non-core tasks or services to their corporate core proposition of skills and capabilities. Peter Drucker, the management guru who pioneered what eventually became known as outsourcing, stressed, "Do what you do best and outsource the rest." He advised companies to engage only in customer-facing activities that are essential to building the company's core products and services.

In simplistic terms, which is adequate for our leadership discussion here, once you've identified the non-core activities, the client then decides to externalize or outsource these activities to a professional outsourcer. This is often a professional services consulting firm specializing in a specific domain or area that can provide a commodity, high volume, and cost-effective services.

This approach is often presented and sold on the proposition that an external expert with in-depth knowledge, extensive experience, and specialty tools can leverage high volumes, systematize processes, and automate these services in a highly efficient and cost-effective way. Therefore, the client business case is built on the premise of improved timeliness, consistency, higher quality, and significant cost savings. Fair enough, but be very careful; the devil in the details in the execution raises some stumbling blocks or potential fallacies to these basic assumptions.

When constructing the outsourcing business case, the internal sponsor must promote and sell the outsourcing concept and program to their senior management. The challenge here is that the initial outsourcing implementation project often carries a very high cost compared to the current amortized internal staff cost. Significant operational benefits and cost savings can be realized, but predominantly in the context of a long-term contract. However, to get the service proposal approved and passed through, the sponsors will struggle to make the project costs in the initial implementation year attractive enough to the senior business and financial management to convince them and get the proposal across the line. Therefore, before you've even started, you may have to identify significant cost savings that will be challenging (or impossible) to realize in the short term, especially within the current fiscal year. Major outsourcing is always a long-term play.

In order to proceed, these long-term significant cost savings often get translated into potentially attractive or exaggerated synergies and benefits that must be recognized and "banked" in the eyes of finance and senior management. Next, you have to go to procurement and build an attractive request for proposal (RFP) case. Despite the unreasonably high promised cost savings, you need to develop a strong enough case to make the RFP appealing enough to attract vital high-quality suppliers to bid on the proposal.

Next, you issue a comprehensive and robust RFP to all the usual outsourcing suspects who are specialists in this field. This will include the top global professional services firms, a few local in-country regional experts, and perhaps a couple of boutique outsourcing specialists. Once you have done a credible job of developing the RFP, all the suppliers will rub their hands in glee with the prospect of a multimillion-dollar, -euro, or -pound contract. From the supplier's perspective, the contract would build their business capabilities and credentials, deliver a long-term annuity contract, and, at the same time, help them achieve their targets, secure their bonus, or preserve their jobs.

As a result, the supplier will spend the next month, including evenings and weekends, alongside their business-as-usual activities, selling this "terrific" opportunity to management and investing extensive time and resources in building an unbeatable proposition to win the RFP contract. As a consultancy lead, I frequently spent weeks on these.

The problem is that, with so much at stake professionally for the firm, financially because of the high cost of developing the RFP response, and personally for the sales engagement team, then they cannot afford to lose. Even if they are a multinational firm, as we all know, you are only as good as your last sale.

Then, during the RFP process, with all the great and good of your industry pitted against each other, in the fierce dog-eat-dog RFP process and final "beauty parade" competition, the supplier engagement teams will do almost anything to win. Then there is no other choice; you have to "promise the world." You are competing with the big boys on cost, the regionals on local knowledge and cultural alignment, and the boutiques on high-quality specialist services. You have to guarantee you can deliver improvements in time, cost, and quality, which collectively are virtually impossible and, therefore, unrealistic. Many of you will have heard the old story: for your objectives and KPIs, your choices are time, cost, and quality . . . choose two! Given the delivery challenges and these three diametrically opposed criteria, realistically, you can only ever achieve any two of the three! Time or cost or quality.

After all the sugar coating and the promises of bells and whistles during the final RFP round, it eventually all comes down to price. Unfortunately, now it becomes a fierce winner-take-all battle for the finish line. Your competitors, who may sense they are behind in the race, will become increasingly anxious and start cutting costs to, or even below, the bare break-even cost minimum. This dramatically increases the commercial and financial pressure on you.

Finally, if you are fortunate enough to win the contest, the next stage, the procurement negotiation, will be even more painful! You are then handed over to the clients' professional negotiators and procurement people. You will be forced to trim your cost and, therefore, the margin down even further, if not to a loss-leading status, at minimum to an unattractive margin. The result could be that you might not be able to afford to deliver the quality of services that you promised or have been pressured to agree upon.

Painful as it is, you have now come too far, worked too hard, invested too much, and promised too much to your management that you cannot afford to lose or walk away. Now the die is cast, you are committed, and your only choice appears to be to continue down this path to agree to the unattractive or fundamentally flawed contract. You may now hope that by some miracle, you will be either recruited, promoted, and moved or win enough additional business to cover the losses. If not, you may need to reckon with realigning the services at some point before the "crows come home to roost" in eighteen months to two years when margins are collapsing, service is failing, the client is complaining, and your management is criticizing. Let's analyze this further to understand where it all goes wrong.

Having taken part in these three separate billion-dollar contract realignment/renegotiation reviews, the service contract assessment ultimately identified the same root cause of these major IT and BPO outsourcing failures. In each case, the origin and underlying cause of the misalignment were again, as mentioned before, a flawed contract negotiation that put the supplier in a disproportionately disadvantaged position vis-à-vis the customer. The customer, the competition, internal procurement, and the RFP process itself have all pressured and squeezed the supplier too hard to reap maximum cost savings from the contract and transformation. Subsequently, this leaves the supplier struggling to make a profit margin within the contract-enforced service level agreements (SLAs).

Eventually, the supplier simply cannot make a satisfactory margin and simultaneously provide high-quality services. Remember time, cost, or quality! Let's analyze the additional challenges of implementing the flawed service contract. The supplier resorts to increasingly desperate measures to maintain a profitable margin. The only remedy for the beleaguered supplier, whose commercial management pressure will become increasingly impatient and intense, will be to begin to trim costs out of the contract.

The provider will gradually rotate high-quality, expensive staff off the engagement, replacing these senior star staff with lesser quality, more junior, and cheaper resources in a hazardous attempt to cut costs and raise the margin. The high-quality staff will then be redeployed to higher-value clients or be used to win new contracts. Besides cutting quality and services, the supplier may reduce or eliminate trips to the client site, which conspire to reduce understanding, service, project quality, morale, oversight, and outcomes.

As a result, the client will inevitably suffer complaints of inferior quality, lack of knowledge, and reduced responsiveness on the supplier's part. Even worse, there may be service failures due to lack of attention or expertise, with losses of hundreds of thousands of dollars/pounds/euros resulting in comparatively trivial tens of thousands of dollars in SLA penalties. These SLA-driven penalties hardly compensate for the service outage disruption, revenue loss, and damaged customer reputation.

Then, perhaps 1.5 years later, at the halfway point in a three-year contract, when all is said and done, the situation may be dire, and the relationship is potentially irretrievably broken. The client may have transferred their original mission-critical internal staff over to the supplier, lost essential internal intellectual capital and product/service knowledge, and eventually made the client overly dependent on the supplier. The supplier may have been forced to sell on the senior staff to more profitable clients and "dumb down" the service team to cut costs and make a margin. At this point, the contract, account, and relationship have seriously deteriorated. Typically, a major client-supplier assessment is kicked off. Often, a renegotiation occurs, a new transformation is started, or the contract is canceled or ends up in a tedious, painful, and costly lawsuit.

Critically, ultimately, both parties suffer. The supplier loses margin and potentially credibility. The customer realizes a poor result due to reduced service quality, dissatisfaction, complaints, and even against expected savings. The long-view total cost of ownership analysis will determine that the outsourcing activity may have resulted in an abysmal return on investment when factoring in the cost savings versus service and reputational damage. All of this is undesirable and, ultimately, unnecessary.

I will mention one caveat to this story relative to a short-term opportunity that can address part of this dilemma. In recent years, new robotic process automation (RPA) technologies have been developed to create high-performance automated procedural "AI robots" to perform standardized, repetitive tasks economically. This is now a burgeoning opportunity to use these AI automation tools to achieve dramatic efficiency and cost savings improvements.

Once the provision of these automation processes becomes ubiquitous in time and the competitive playing field is leveled again, there will be little margin remaining for a price advantage. Another risk is that if applied incorrectly, these automation robots might be deployed to take over tasks best handled by knowledge workers. Consequently, customer service levels and quality may decline yet again. Also, client knowledge brain drain and internal skill deterioration may occur.

Therefore, what is the alternative?

Avoid outsourcing in the first place? In the situation above, yes, indeed. Interestingly, while at Accenture, I saw them wisely walk away from a couple of $100 million contract-value bidding battles they realized would only result in unacceptable margins and, ultimately, client dissatisfaction. This was an astute and correct decision on their part. But unfortunately, both parties lost out on what could have been a valuable partnership.

There is a better way to proceed successfully and avoid these pitfalls. The importance and nuance of the term "partnership" cannot be overstated. The vital key to the success of outsourcing and contracting is an honest, transparent, long-term, mutually beneficial, win/win collaborative partnership.

How is this achieved? It is not rocket science, but it is a delicate process. It starts with staying true to your principles and integrity and creating a clear strategy with realistic pragmatic expectations. First of all, creating a relationship based on honesty and trust, plus an associated contract of "equals," is an essential starting point. You must recognize and accept that this is a long-term "marriage," not a thoughtless temporary fling or a one-time, walk-away sales deal.

Much has been written about win/win partnerships, including in game theory research and discussions of "principled negotiation." In addition, there is an interesting body of study on "non-adversarial negotiations" conducted by the Harvard Negotiation Project, which spawned the bestseller *Getting To Yes*[1] by Roger Fisher and William Ury. Further, in addition to an honest, respectful relationship, there is a basic premise that any unequal win/lose or lose/win negotiation or relationship eventually always deteriorates into a mutual lose/lose endgame. The reason is simple: both parties need to realize an appropriate "value exchange" during a long-term service contract.

The agreement does not necessarily have to be "exactly equal," but must be value-creating for both parties. If the contract or subsequent service turns out to be too unequal or one-sided, there will be resentment and eventually some form of retribution or required recompense to correct the discrepancy. Or it may even result in some form of commercial, service, or financial retaliation. Otherwise, service will deteriorate, and both parties will eventually suffer.

Therefore, if you are going to work constructively and successfully for a number of years and receive exemplary service and value for money, you must clearly communicate, understand, and carefully respect and balance each other's requirements, expectations, and objectives.

The client needs reliable, long-term, value-enabling services. The supplier wants a constructive, long-term business and a credential-building service contract that allows them to make an "honest buck." In other words, they have to make a profit and enough of a profit that encourages them to invest in the service quality and the relationship throughout the life of the contract. The client, who ostensibly initially holds all the cards, must play those cards fairly and to the benefit of the "relationship" such that a fair game is played, or invariably, it will come back to haunt them.

Next, you both need to understand your mutual needs and objectives. The process of drafting the SLAs and contract will guide this understanding to a certain point. Also, carefully examine the RFP and the response from both sides to understand what is critical and superfluous, what can assuredly be delivered, and what is smoke and mirrors. Further, the principle of going the second mile or paying it forward will provide a benevolent climate for client negotiation and subsequent management.

The process is simple and basic: What are your counterparty's drivers and pressures, and what do they need to sell or justify to their bosses, commercial stakeholders, or legal or purchasing partners? Remember, you are not just negotiating with the person in front of you. You are negotiating through them to procurement, their boss, finance manager, compliance officer, and the board.

Finally, after a lengthy, costly, and draining RFP process in which both parties have invested a great deal of time and effort, pressure will build back at both home offices. The client will have lost more time than expected and just want to get on with it. The supplier will want solid guarantees to sew up the contract. The next major hurdle will be the complex and protracted contract negotiation process. The supplier will want or require commercial coverage to be in place before investing in teams and tools to mobilize the services. Long delays can ensue with the lawyers, and right off the bat, frustration and tempers can flair unnecessarily before the service delivery even begins. Anticipating this from the outset and planning for a bridging contract with an initial start-up/contract signing fee to start the mobilization process will take significant pressure off both sides. This allows the procurement and legal teams to do their jobs cautiously and calmly without disrupting the delicate initial mobilization and team-building process.

Perhaps the best way to explain how to build a win-win partnership is by virtue of a true-to-life example where the client and the supplier both built trust and respect, conducted equitable negotiations, invested in each other, operated as one team, went the second mile and both played the long game. Read on.

Takeaways:

Ensure that contractors and consultants working in long-term roles alongside the internal teams must be incorporated, inculcated, and aligned with the internal team's agenda and culture.

Make sure externals are collaboratively allied with your internal team to avoid unhealthy competition or conflict.

Treat a contractor or consultant as an external hired hand, and they will act as such. Embrace them as a valued member of the team, and they will become one.

In major projects and outsourcing contracts, many fundamental operational problems harken back to misalignments in the original contracts.

- In negotiations, any win/lose or lose/win outcome deteriorates over time to a lose/lose.
- Strive for genuine win/win partnerships where both parties are invested in success.

Project "Drive" Case Study

One of the critical qualitative measures of a successful business partnership is each party's desire, both client and supplier, to continue, extend, and grow the relationship.

Project Scope

As promised, here is a detailed case study for a major project I've referred to during diplomacy, team building, and project management discussions. It is a particularly good case study as it was of substantial size, approximately a year, circa $12 million in total cost, and employed over one hundred people. It involved managing a three-company carve-out, creating eighty new offices and 220 new legal entities, and building and launching thirty-eight new IT systems in forty-five countries. Ultimately, it was delivered on time, within budget, and with zero defects. Let's explore how and why it was successful.

Partnership

This project is an example of a successful partnership. A testament to its success is that the client, TUI Group, and the prime contractor Accenture agreed at the end of the project that it was one of the most successful IT projects for both companies in recent memory. However, this notable success does not imply that this project was a "walk in the park." It was complex and challenging, had significant hurdles and risks, and had no definitive guarantee of success.

Let's look at some key project success factors, learnings, and leadership principles that we can derive from this case study and which can be applied to your partnerships and projects in the future.

Building on some of the previously discussed learnings regarding managing outsourcing projects and running RFPs, here I'll reinforce some of the critical principles of win/win contract resolutions I mentioned regarding leadership diplomacy in Book 1.

Mobilization

After the lengthy proposals and the in-principle awarding of the project to the preferred supplier, we both enthusiastically began plans to mobilize the project. However, there was one remaining legal technicality (indirect damages, a frequent sticking point in large contracts) with the supplier lawyers holding up the project launch. Consequently, despite the internal team having already been mobilized, the crack team the supplier had reserved was still on hold. Further, we had a critically tight deadline with almost no margin for error to deliver the project in eleven months' time.

Anticipating a rapid project start-up, we had previously agreed on a 10 percent signing bonus to mobilize sixty consultants immediately. However, to break the legal deadlock and jump-start the project, I proposed we advance the supplier a 5 percent unsolicited "Bridging Contract Signature" payment. This unexpected half-a-million-euro advance payment surprised and motivated the supplier management, who promptly reciprocated by resolving the contract dispute and immediately mobilized the initial team.

Retrospectively, I'm reminded of our discussion on building trust, where one partner offers a type of "olive branch" as a catalyst for building trust and initiating a reciprocal "value exchange" transaction. One can argue this offer represented a risk, as the contract was still in negotiation and, therefore, required a significant leap of faith. However, in a case such as this, where there was close to zero chance of us changing suppliers, it was a reasonable calculated risk based on the criticality of the rapid mobilization. This is another case where your greatest risk is not taking enough risk. So, again, make sure you are playing the long game.

This bridging contract payment gesture transformed the relationship chemistry literally overnight from the supplier boardroom, through the client engagement partners, down to their delivery team on the ground. The supplier responded extremely positively, which began a mutually constructive relationship. This set the stage and platform for a highly successful long-term partnership, which assisted significantly in successfully delivering this challenging project.

Modus Operandi

As we began to mobilize the team and finalize our fixed price contract, we soon detected that some of the required team members were not traveling to be on-site as expected. In discussions with the supplier's project management, they advised us that not all the team resources were always essential. We protested that we were building a collaborative, colocated, high-performance team and required them to be on site. However, when the supplier began to question each individual's regular presence, we decided to "cut the Gordian knot"[2] and change the equation. The issue was that upon examination, the contract had a fixed percentage of contract travel allocation.

As the final contract was still under negotiation, I advised the supplier to cut the fixed 400,000€ projected travel costs out of the contract. Then, as the client, we would accept, jointly manage, and separately pay the actual travel costs incurred for the project duration. The project quality and success were vital for us, and we perceived the consultants' active presence to be essential to building a cohesive team. Therefore, we communicated (insisted) to the supplier that we enthusiastically required their constant presence and were happy to pay the additional premium for high-quality, dedicated, and colocated consultants for the project's duration. Had we left it to the supplier's project commercial managers, team participation would have been sporadic and less immediate, and we could not have built the strong team spirit we wanted. The supplier agreed, and subsequently, the team alignment was successful, and the joint team's motivation, collaboration, and spirit were exceptional.

One Team

Next, we implemented a virtual team concept that we will explore in greater detail in the next section. This virtual team was structured with a "One Team" organizational philosophy, comprising ourselves, the client, a major international professional service company, a major global infrastructure and networks firm, and some contractors. Thus, virtually everyone was colocated within the primary or directly adjacent project rooms. We outlined the project vision carefully, identified and introduced teams and skills, and clearly articulated and carefully delineated responsibilities. The commitment and investment in these structures and processes resulted in robust project clarity, rapid mobilization, and efficient operations.

The initial core message and culture we endeavored to create and instill in the team was: "We are one team; it is by pure luck, a happy accident, or just coincidence that you work for the client firm, the professional services firm, or the infrastructure provider. This is what we set out to accomplish within this time frame, etc. You are all experts in your own area, each essential to the project and each other's success. There will be no finger-pointing, no complaining, only joint commitment to the goal and each other. We cannot achieve a project of this magnitude alone without each other, so you are all stakeholders in 'Project Drive' and the project's mutual success or failure. You will work hard, play hard, learn, and grow together, and either this success will be one of the creative and successful milestones of your career, or you will think back on this with painful memories. The bottom line is that we will be successful, we will win, you will give it your all, and we will make this the pinnacle of our careers up until now. So let's make a commitment to ourselves, each other, and to the project."

The Team

Highly fortuitously, I found kindred spirits in Accenture's commercial lead Mercedes Oblanca, and Prime Contractor Program lead Juan Carlos Garcia. They firmly echoed and reinforced the "one team" concept and the culture of mutual commitment across their organization and the subcontractors under their watch. Together, we carefully established and socialized the vision and mission, getting everyone excited and on board with the project and the one-team way of working. As a result, the motivation was high, and cross-organizational team bonding flourished.

However, starting well is one thing; sustaining the mission, motivation, and execution is another challenge. The devil is always in the details. After carefully selecting the internal and external team members after a couple of months, the project grew rapidly, and the number of subprojects and controls began mushrooming. There was excellent progress in many areas, yet some subprojects were running better than others, potentially putting the overall program at risk. So, we began joint internal and external analysis and some "soul searching."

The internal project manager was making excellent progress in some critical areas, but there were additional cross-functional work streams that needed synchronization. It became clear that he excelled in various mission-critical and domain-specific areas; however, we needed to build alliances and consensus across all cross-functional subprojects of the entire program. With analysis, we realized this excellent resource was a relatively recent hire to the company when what was needed was a long-timer in the company who knew the people and had relationships across all the project's functional domains.

As it turned out, another team leader, a twenty-year company veteran, was being requested in almost all areas and seemed to be everywhere at once, touching this and tweaking that. This employee, with extensive long-term internal connections and networks, provided the glue necessary to pull together all the pieces of the project and the cross-functional teams. Both colleagues were essential, but their skills and experience were better suited to different roles.

I had made the initial organization structure, so I also had to acknowledge that a reorganization was necessary. After some fretting about maintaining the critical motivation of all team leads, we reorganized. I appointed the veteran team member as the Program Lead and assigned the former Program Manager to lead the most critical work stream. Fortunately, the former program manager had high personal awareness and emotional intelligence and saw the wisdom of the move. Consequently, he was fully on board with handing over the project coordination lead to the other team member with critical long-term connections within the internal company. No disruption or delays occurred, and the team and project immediately shifted into turbo drive.

The newly empowered internal program manager Salvador and the exceptional external program manager Joaquim recognized each other's importance and value and leveraged each other's strengths, compensating and covering for each other from parallel vantage points. Thus, the whole program took form and accelerated rapidly.

The leadership tripartite comprised my setting the strategy, managing the internal stakeholders, and motivating and mentoring the team. Next, the internal program lead marshaled all the internal resources and coordinated multiple work streams. Finally, the external program lead headed up all the external teams as the prime contractor. As a result, the three of us formed a strong, cohesive, and effective leadership team. Vitally extensive stakeholder alignment also led to a strong team of work stream leads who took full responsibility for their individual work streams and critical coordination between them.

Critical Success Factors

Some of the critical success factors for the program were selecting the right partners, picking the right teams, setting a clear vision and objectives, and ensuring everyone was in the proper role, regardless of their title or previous responsibilities. Then, managing in real time, tracking the critical path at the micro and macro levels, and ensuring every issue, eventuality, or risk was addressed, both at the moment and against the overall critical path. This guaranteed that no issue impacted or compromised the endgame and time frame.

Challenges and Contingency Planning

This is not to say there were no problems, as we had some huge issues, including some fundamental architectural and systems changes. This included some existential threats to the project, which could have not only derailed the project but potentially could have ultimately caused a total systems failure. Tensions and risks were high, with each partner having some shared responsibility for the potential systems design failure. This required serious but delicate leadership from each of the partnership's perspectives. By firmly but sensitively reminding the partners and individuals in the teams that we would all sink or swim based on our collaboration and cooperation, eventually, we found a resolution. We had to make some tough decisions and invest in new solutions, and together, we made it work.

Risks

Our project required a launch in late November. Any delay due to the legal and fiscal implications, including year-end reporting, meant that if we missed that launch window because of the year-end fiscal closure, the next launch window would be at the end of February. The impact of that risk was enormous. With sixty-eight external consulting specialists deployed full-time on the project, a delay would mean we would need to retain the whole external team for the entire delay period. Otherwise, putting them on hold for more than three months with every likelihood of the consultancy firms reassigning key individuals to another client engagement was a severe risk. Furthermore, retaining the essential team would mean an additional 2.7 million euros of unbudgeted contingency spend. An eleven-month project would swell to over a year and collapse our plan and budget.

Therefore, with each hurdle we encountered, we needed to manage it as a critical dependency against the full project delay. First, the plan was to avoid any delay. Second, mitigate any impact. Third, ensure the entire project did not move to the right by picking up the slack elsewhere. Finally, replan to ensure we could still hit the launch date. The external project manager astutely micromanaged each task within a 3.8k task project plan. The internal program lead and I managed the macro program, each of us making sure that no activity could impact the overall schedule to the extent that it would cause a delay.

Determination and Collaboration

The team leadership created a compulsive determination to maintain the critical path through multiple challenges, any of which could have caused problematic slippage. In addition, we employed continuous contingency planning to adapt and protect the detailed project plan to ensure we could accommodate any delays and maintain the critical path.

Besides being flexible with the initial contract signing payments, we also worked collaboratively with the consultancies based on scope changes, change requests, and issues that arose on both sides of the project. In some cases, the scope increased; in others, it was streamlined. Thus, we netted off the changes to ensure that the overall impact was not too onerous for either party. We managed payment milestones flexibility, recognizing the commercial pressure on the suppliers and adapting contract milestones to accommodate scope and timing changes. This flexibility helped immeasurably to keep the consultancy commercial and financial management satisfied or at least placated.

Organizational Design

One particularly valuable nuance to the project and the transition to business-as-usual was the awareness and idea that the consultancy team developing and launching the technical solution would assimilate a tremendous amount of knowledge about our systems and products. Therefore, we wanted to leverage the project knowledge into the future BaU delivery structure. Thus, one of the project's operational strategies was that the external technical delivery team would evolve to become the company's future software development factory post–go live.

Therefore, we drew up a three-year contract for fifteen identified, trained, and already indoctrinated external staff. They already knew our company and products, as they had worked with our internal teams during the implementation project for the previous eleven months. Consequently, a seamless transition occurred without affecting the internal or external teams. We would transition seamlessly, literally overnight, from project delivery and launch to software factory support with no hitch or delay.

The Launch

The launch day arrived; we had approximately 110 people on-site, with perhaps another fifty resources off-site in the data center and the software factory. We worked systematically through the launch plan with seven on-site work streams synchronized: finance, business processes, back office, core systems, infrastructure, and management, executing 782 discrete tasks over 30 hours. After eleven months with multiple functional work streams, the work of hundreds of people, 80 new offices, 220 new legal entities created, and 38 new systems, we launched within 45 minutes of the projected launch window set almost a year earlier. We worked through the nearly 800 deployment tasks and launched the 38 systems one by one. Finally, at 6:45 p.m. on the 21st of November 2015, we completed all the tasks, including the required tests. Everything was running with no faults or failures. We looked at each other, and I said: "Very well done, team! Let's go for drinks and dinner!" We launched on time, on budget, and with zero defects!

The Result

This exceptional result resulted from the high trust, openness, collaboration, and mutual commitment to creating value for each other through the win/win partnership. Further, each company shared the risk, contributed to the relationship, worked through and collaborated on the challenges, and reaped the rewards. This was a client/supplier relationship at its best, where each party intrinsically felt and understood the benefits of investing in the mutual partnership relationship. Key outcomes were:

Project Drive Key Metrics

- The critical success factors identified were leadership, trust, positive attitude, "one team" collaboration, communications, determination, contingency planning, and constant adaptability.
- The 11-month program included a core IT Team of 60–65 members with over 100 specialist IT staff.
- The program comprised a Plan of 3,898 tasks with multiple internal teams, three separate IT Teams, plus two primary and eight smaller contractors.
- The requirement was to clone, prune, develop, and test 38 IT Systems to deliver a completely new IT landscape across 45 countries.
- The IT Team collaborated with cross-functional teams to plan the Financial and Legal split of the TUI business into three business units in 16 countries.
- A new data center was created with 156 terabytes of data in 128 servers.
- A team of 107 Inc. 78 IT staff executed 782 tasks successfully with no defects during the launch.
- The IT separation was delivered on time, according to plan, on budget, and launched with no delays, no failures, or significant defects.

A formal project debrief was conducted with the joint TUI, Accenture, and Telefonica project teams to document lessons learned for both organizations to share the challenges and successes of Project Drive. Following are the formal lessons learned from this successful project and launch:

Project Drive—Lessons Learned

- A culture of trust and the "One Team" approach was established and built upon as a project ethos. This fostered the continuous sharing of mutual needs and resolution of problems on both sides, resulting in a "win/win" relationship with strong cooperation and alignment.
- Leadership and management were respected but also fluid and flexible. Leaders and managers ebbed and flowed according to project challenges. Leaders sometimes led their own work streams and, at other times, were participants in other teams.
- Leadership created a "compulsive" determination to maintain the "critical path" through multiple challenges. We employed continuous contingency planning to adapt the project plan to ensure we accommodated any slippage to maintain the critical path.
- The key to effective major outsourcing is win/win partnering. Critical success factors were: A clear, communicated long-term vision. Establishing an honest, respectful, and trustful relationship. Ensuring transparent and immediate bilateral communications. Constructive and collaborative objectives and governance. Honoring and involving all internal and external staff.

CHAPTER 6

Conclusion—The Thousandth Time

In *LEAD!* Book 1, we examined the foundational personal character and intrinsic attributes of exceptional leaders. Throughout *LEAD!* Book 2, we explored the extrinsic behaviors, strategies, and actionable methodologies designed to guide you in enhancing and executing your leadership skills and practice. Whether you are an experienced or aspiring leader, your time and effort analyzing and practicing these techniques, tools, examples, and case studies will help you further develop, mature, and master your leadership knowledge and skills.

In addition, a review of leadership best practices, case studies, and valuable external resources will give you positive challenges, goals, and opportunities for personal and career leadership development.

Once you've read and studied these methods and tools, in the future, during your leadership adventures, return and refer to *LEAD!* as a reference and refresher of leadership tips, hints, and best practices.

I leave you with one last story. This occurrence is perhaps the principal reason for how I've found the will and courage to persevere despite setbacks, disappointments, and stumbles. In addition to my parents, my most "significant other" figure was my grandfather, Harry Hudson. He was a wiry old guy with a quick wit, strong opinions, infectious humor, and an acute sense of ironic banter. When growing up, I always looked forward to Friday nights when he'd arrive like a whirlwind despite his awkward, determined gait striding up the driveway toward us on two ancient, in those days, actual, wooden legs. Nothing was going to stop Harry. Certainly not the train accident that cost a colleague's life and both his legs.

Harry, at age twenty, had just left a date with my to-be grandmother, catching the last train home. Unfortunately, the driver fell asleep, and a terrible train accident ensued. Harry lost both his legs and half his blood and was not expected to live. However, he most certainly did, and subsequently married his girlfriend and had seven children, including my mother. Harry endured incredible physical, emotional, and financial hardships, raising his family as a disabled person during the Great Depression. There are many family stories of how he overcame severe obstacles through his indefatigable courage and determination. These included the loss of a daughter to scarlet fever and his wife, my grandmother. However, none of this broke his spirit, will, or humor; it only steeled him with resolve and gave him yet another hurdle to leap with his drive to survive, overcome life's obstacles, and thrive.

All of us have obstacles and challenges, and I've had my fair share and a bit. But, in part, because of Harry as a role model, I gained an extra dose of tolerance for risk and resolute stamina. Throughout my own trials and tribulations, Harry's example and inspiration never let me give up or lament any bad luck or lack of opportunity. Whenever I was down or down on luck, the memory of Harry's contagious spark and joie de vivre would flash back to me to humble, inspire, and encourage me to pick myself up and start again.

Once, in fact, more than once, when I was a teenager, he would tell me with deep personal knowledge and conviction: "Greg, they can knock you down 999 times, but he who gets up the thousandth time can never be defeated." With his experience, strength of character, persistent positive attitude, and courage, I believed him.

Following the familial line, my father also provided much encouragement against adversity. He would often repeat his version of the Nietzsche aphorism with great emphasis and a sense of some eternal wisdom: "What doth not kill thee strengthen thee!" That always seemed to fit alongside my image of Harry's life and message.

My final counsel, I leave with you. You never know what life is going to throw at you, but rest assured, life is constantly in flux, and consequently, there will always be some trial just around the corner. Expect and anticipate it; be brave, be bold, and have courage; this too will pass. Use each challenge to prove you are alive and willing to embrace life, come what may.

Just make sure to get up, even until the thousandth time!

LEAD! Book 2—Key Takeaways

- Creativity and Innovation are inextricably connected. Creativity is the inventive process, and innovation is the implementation and commercialization of that invention.
- Innovator's Dilemma: Traditional companies perpetuate historically successful behaviors that may be inappropriate for new emerging and disruptive products in new markets, which may lead to their demise.
- Open Innovation: No one has a monopoly on knowledge and can depend solely upon their organization for innovation ideas. Therefore, they should broaden their approach to include other external organizations.
- A leader is strategic and focused on the big picture; a manager is operational and tactical; however, an experienced leader/manager must shift naturally and fluidly between modes based on the team's needs.
- Hiring the Team: After a careful recruitment capability assessment, look for 'hidden treasures" within your organization first. Then, to re-invent, source new blood for specialist or emerging roles.
- Decision-Making: Know when and why to make rapid, sound decisions based on prior knowledge and experience. And when to use careful analysis and reasoned judgment in new or complex situations.
- Remote staff challenges are lack of suitable workspaces, distractions, isolation, time-shifted but long work hours, reduced collaboration and calibration, job insecurity and anxiety, and reduced psychological safety.

- Remote staff benefits are improved work/life balance, reduced time away from home due to no commutes or business trips, more personal time, and the ability to time-shift work and personal responsibilities.
- The Virtual Team allows flexibly combining specific skills, creating a Just in Time skills pool. Virtual teaming provides complete flexibility to start and stop projects instantly, being nimble enough to turn on a dime.
- Misalignment of objectives, commercials, and outcomes with suppliers drives the wrong behaviors from the start and directly from the home offices through middle management to service people on the ground.
- A successful value-creating multi-year service contract is fostered by a long-term win/win partnership that recognizes and respects each other's commercial and financial requirements and objectives.

Appendix

Innovation Processes and Road Maps

Building on the innovation information in the first chapter, the following procedural and operational detail will be helpful for anyone with the desire or need to set up and run an innovation initiative or lab.

When producing proof of concepts, prototypes, and projects, ensure your innovation process is formally project-planned and road-mapped. This will help the project team and the organization efficiently track projects from concept through development to completion, implementation, and eventually, benefits realization. All this is invaluable in maintaining credibility and confidence with senior management.

Following are sample innovation road maps from my innovation labs for tracking innovation projects throughout execution and implementation.

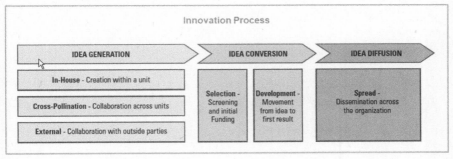

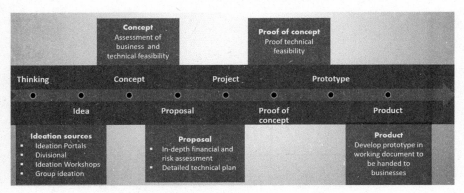

Innovation Portal Ideation Process

Innovation portals are a formal and systematic way to generate and manage ideas. There are a number of effective commercial ideation portals in the market, and most multinationals have the technical expertise to develop these tools internally as well.

These tools comprise web-based systems for launching ideation campaigns for internal staff and stakeholders. Campaigns can be targeted at specific internal opportunities or concerns and used for general ideation and idea generation. A further benefit of these formal tools is the ability to capture idea submissions, rate and rank, and vote on ideas submitted through peer review collaboration with the staff and stakeholders.

I created the following infographic to depict the generic use of an ideation portal and innovation campaign.

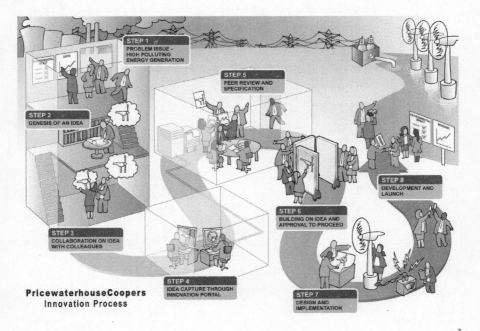

PricewaterhouseCoopers
Innovation Process

3

Step 1   Identify a major challenge or intractable problem with your business partners. Next create and socialize a "problem statement."

Step 2   Through ideation workshops, use ideation processes, brainstorming techniques, and idea-generation tools to produce a long list of possible ideas to explore.

Step 3   Collaborate with the innovation team, knowledgeable internal subject matter experts, and business stakeholders regarding candidate ideas.

Step 4   Prepare an ideation campaign, identify an appropriate community of participants, and launch the idea-capture process through an innovation portal.

Step 5   Agree on the evaluation process and voting criteria, submit idea candidates to an internal expert peer review process, and create a shortlist of promising solutions.

Step 6   Submit the candidate solutions to the business for elaboration and validation, present for solution approval, and prepare the formal business case.

Step 7   Create and develop a proof-of-concept design, test and validate the solution, secure agreement, and proceed to a minimum viable product development and implementation.

Step 8   Develop the final solution and launch. Validate the solution and document benefit realization.

Innovation and Business Collaborative Working

Finally, to ensure your innovation initiative is a full partner with the business, you must map the innovation road map processes against current business improvement activities. In this manner, the innovation team generates ideas that directly relate to business initiatives that can eventually be handed off to the business. Conversely, complex game-changing innovation ideas generated by the business can be reassigned to the innovation team to research, analyze, test, and develop proof of concepts.

The Innovation Lab role is to catalyse ideas and develop Proof of Concepts to be transferred to the Business Units

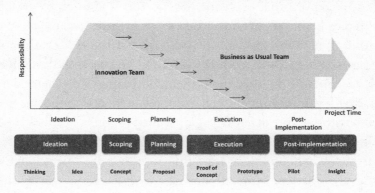

4

These handoff processes ensure the business is not distracted by more speculative or longer-range trials. Also, the innovation team focuses on longer-term game changers rather than "business as usual" issues. The following complex-looking but logical process model simultaneously shows the innovation, business road maps, and mutual handoff mechanisms. The milestones and checkpoints include the final handover processes from the innovation team to the business for implementation and launch.

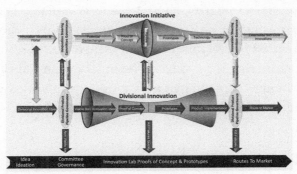

5

As we survey this graphic depicting the interfaces and potential synergies between an innovation initiative and the business, recognize that carefully managed, the relations between the organizations can be collaborative and value-creating. This structure permits the business to focus on its mission-critical delivery responsibilities and shifts uncertain long-term research and speculative developments to a dedicated team of innovation specialists.

However, herein also lie several potential pitfalls and risks to watch out for, avoid, or manage.

First, recognize that everyone has a career and a job to protect and wants to be a hero. Further, most people are creative and enjoy inventing and building new things. Thus, there is always the risk that the people in the business itself, who own the products and services and have more knowledge and information about them, will want to do their own innovation; thank you very much! The major risk here is that the business side will be territorial and defensive against innovation specialists meddling in their domain.

Further, when products are aging or there are operational issues, handing over matters from the business to innovation carries an air of criticism, deficiency, or fault on the part of the business. In this case, it is natural that the business would like to resolve its own issues rather than have some highfliers swoop in to solve their problems.

Similarly, but perhaps to a lesser extent, there is also a tendency within innovation to want to hold on to new ideas, prototypes, and proof of concepts for too long. People "love their babies" and, therefore, are reluctant to hand over promising new initiatives to the business, who will implement and deploy them, ultimately getting the credit.

Therefore, the boundaries, handoffs, and governance must be carefully managed to create a climate of "esprit de corps" where everyone has a vested interest in everyone else, and there is shared recognition and reward. Recognize that the symbiotic boundary conditions between the business and innovation represent a great opportunity, as well as a grave risk, to an innovation initiative's viability and success.

Innovation Organization and Governance

Once you have identifiable successes during the innovation journey and your champions, partnerships, and steering committee governance are in place, you are ready to build innovation objectives into staff objectives, team targets and metrics, business cases, and budgets.

Finally, it will be beneficial to agree on an initial organizational innovation structure, potentially virtually, to start and then formally within your organization. Here is one such model:

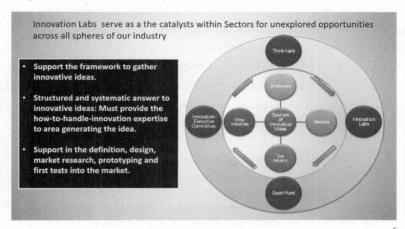

6

Initially, I'd recommend a practical, lightweight innovation portfolio governance during the mobilization ramp-up until some quick-win innovation projects are mature. Then, projects can be transferred to the existing business side, project portfolio planning, and governance mechanisms.

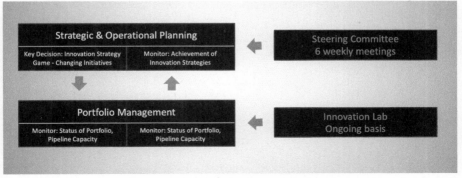

7

Innovation Metrics

A critical project governance activity, essential for any innovation initiative, is to plan for and identify "business benefits realization" metrics and results. New initiatives in any organization are always vulnerable to economic downturns. Consequently, innovation candidates and activities are particularly exposed, particularly game changers, which often have benefits that occur well beyond the current annual targets and fiscal year. Therefore, identifying, agreeing, and tracking appropriate innovation and business benefits realization metrics is critical to demonstrating ongoing value and maintaining commitment.

It's easy to get bogged down with unnecessary complexity regarding innovation metrics and business benefits realization. Keep metrics as high-level and straightforward as possible to avoid confusion and reduce debate. Following is a simple but practical list of innovation metrics we prepared with one of my innovation teams:

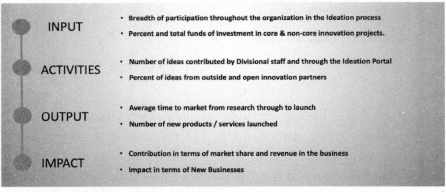

INPUT
- Breadth of participation throughout the organization in the Ideation process
- Percent and total funds of investment in core & non-core innovation projects.

ACTIVITIES
- Number of ideas contributed by Divisional staff and through the Ideation Portal
- Percent of ideas from outside and open innovation partners

OUTPUT
- Average time to market from research through to launch
- Number of new products / services launched

IMPACT
- Contribution in terms of market share and revenue in the business
- Impact in terms of New Businesses

8

Acknowledgments

A special greeting and thank you to my former colleagues at Accenture Consulting Europe, TUI Group, Hotelbeds, PricewaterhouseCoopers London, Worldsport Networks, AOL Europe, Reuters Usability Labs (London), Reuters Asia Training (Hong Kong and Singapore), and American Express Travel USA, who gave me their friendship, encouragement, and support over the years. There are too many friends to name, but I cherish all our memories. Thank you! Greg

Endnotes

Chapter 1

1   Brown, Joel. 2013 Success Advice—Words Of Advice From The Founder Of
    Sony "Akio Morita." 12 April. Accessed April 24, 2021. https://addicted2success.
    com/success-advice/words-of-advice-from-the-founder-of-sony-akio-morita/.
2   De Bono, Edward. 1999. *Six Thinking Hats*. New York: Back Bay Books.
3   Vigen, Tyler. 2015. *Spurious Correlations*. New York: Hachette Books.
4   Vigen, Tyler, Spurious Correlations—Attribution 4.0 International (CC BY 4.0).
    Accessed November 13, 2021. https://tylervigen.com/spurious-correlations.
5   Garrison, Greg/Hotelbeds 2021 Innovation Strategy. Palma Mallorca, Spain:
    Graphic developed by Greg Garrison within the framework of his employment
    relationship at Hotelbeds. All rights reserved.
6   Lang, Tillmann. 2021. Our "Efficient Frontier" Investment Theory. Accessed
    November 13, 2021. https://inyova.ch/en/expertise/efficient-frontier-investment
    -theory/
7   Cleaver, Eldridge. 2013. Philosiblog. 11 December. Accessed January 02, 2021.
    https://philosiblog.com/2013/12/11/if-youre-not-part-of-the-solution-youre-part-of
    -the-problem/.
8   Thomson Reuters. 2020. Thomson Reuters Foundation. 27 December. Accessed
    December 27, 2020. http://www.trust.org/.
9   AlertNet 2000 "Millennium Products Archive." Design Council. Archived from
    original (PDF) on 19/07/2011, p.109. Accessed May 05, 2022. http://www.design
    council.org.uk/Documents/Documents/About%20us/Millennium_Products.pdf.
10 Leahy, Terry. 2013. *Management in Ten Words*. New York: Random House
    Business.
11 Butler-Bowdon, Tom. 2018. "50 Business Classics." Terry Leahy, p. 185. London:
    Nicholas Brealey Publishing.
12 Einstein, Albert, and Komik, Oleg. 2016. Albert Einstein Imagination. 08
    January. Accessed January 03, 2021. https://economicsociology.org/2016/01/08
    /albert-einstein-on-the-power-of-ideas-and-imagination-in-science/.

13 Jobs, Steve. 1981. Chapter 3 Building the Innovative Organization. Accessed December 31, 2020. https://www.oreilly.com/library/view/managing-innovation -6th/9781119379454/c03.xhtml.

14 Johansson, Frans. 2020. The Medici Group. 31 December. Accessed December 31, 2020. https://www.themedicigroup.com/books.

15 Johansson, Frans. 2004. *The Medici Effect: Breakthrough Insights at the Intersection of Ideas, Concepts, and Cultures*. Boston: Harvard Business Review Press.

16 Johansson, Frans. 2015. "Frans Johansson Medici Effect" http://www.fransjohansson .com/. 26 June. Accessed May 6, 2021. https://commons.wikimedia.org/w/index .php?curid=41215916.

17 Johansson, Frans. 2004. *The Medici Effect: Breakthrough Insights at the Intersection of Ideas, Concepts, and Cultures*. Boston, MA: Harvard Business Review Press.

18 Smith, Frederick W. 2020. Here's an Idea. 31 December. Accessed Dec.31,2020. https://www.fastcompany.com/39461/heres-idea.

19 Cunha, Frank. 2018. I Love My Architect. 18 March. Accessed June 18, 2021. https://ilovemyarchitect.com/tag/medici-effect/.

20 Jacobson, Clayton. 2020 31 December. Accessed December 31, 2020. https: //en.wikipedia.org/wiki/Clayton_Jacobson_II.

21 Hassabis, Demis. 2020. DeepMind cofounder: Gaming inspired AI breakthrough. 02 December. Accessed December 02, 2020. https://www.bbc.com/news/technology -55157940.

22 Allan, Dave, Kingdon, Matt, Murrin, Kris, Rudkin, Daz. 2021. "Sticky Wisdom: Welcome to the Revolution." Usage Approval—Dave Allan whatifinnovation. 19 July. Accessed June 18, 2021. https://manualzilla.com/doc/5958348/sticky -wisdom-welcome-to-the-revolution.

23 Christensen, Clayton M. 2020. *Profit Magazine*—Business Thought—Clayton Christensen. December. Accessed April 24, 2021. http://profitmagazin.com/editions /number_080–081.620.html.

24 Steinegger, Remy, and World Economic Forum 2013. "Clayton Christensen World Economic Forum 2013." WikiMedia Commons. 23 January. Accessed May 6, 2021. https://commons.wikimedia.org/wiki/File:Clayton_Christensen_World _Economic_Forum_2013.jpg.

25 Christensen, Clayton M. 2011. *The Innovator's Dilemma: When New Technologies Cause Great Firms to Fail* (Management of Innovation and Change) New York: Harper Business.

26 Christensen, Clayton M. 2011. *The Innovator's Dilemma: When New Technologies Cause Great Firms to Fail* (Management of Innovation and Change). New York: Harper Business.

27 Hinchcliffe, Dion, and Christensen, Clayton. 2005. Disruptive Forces in Web 2.0 Business Models. 20 October. Accessed May 09, 2021. https://www.flickr.com /photos/dionh/54287036.

28 Christensen, Clayton M., and Overdorf, Michael D. 2000. "Harnessing the Principles of Disruptive Innovation." *The Innovator's Dilemma*, Boston: Harvard Business School Press.

29 Altshuller, Genrich, and Starovoytova Madara, Diana. 2015. "Theory of inventive problem solving (TRIZ): his-story." https://www.researchgate.net/. 7 July. Accessed December 31.

30 Tartarari. 2020. "Genrich Saulovich Altshuller.jpg." Creativecommons.org 15 August. Accessed May 6, 2021. https://search.creativecommons.org/photos/b2fa11e1-bd6a -4ab2–95cf-b8d64629b69b.

31 Lerner, Leonid. 1991. "Genrich Altshuller. Father of TRIZ." *Russian Magazine Ogonek*. Accessed June 18, 2021. https://www.researchgate.net/profile/Frank-Voehl /publication/269815611_The_Directed_Evolution_methodology_A_collection_of _tools_software_and_methods_for_creating_systemic_change/links/54c230d40cf 2911c7a46ba9e/.

32 Barry, Katie, Domb, Ellen, Slocum, Michael. 2006–2010. TRIZ—What is TRIZ. Accessed June 18, 2021. https://triz-journal.com/what-is-triz/.

33 Oxford Creativity. 2015. "WikiMedia Commons." Prism of TRIZ Oxford Creativity.png. 21 May. Accessed May 10, 2021. https://commons.wikimedia.org /wiki/File:Prism_of_TRIZ_Oxford_Creativity.png.

34 Business Collaborative Innovation. 2021. Accessed June 18, 2021. https://digital sparkmarketing.com/business-collaborative-innovation/.

35 Garrison, Greg / Hotelbeds. 2021. Innovation Strategy. Palma Mallorca, Spain: Graphic developed by Greg Garrison within the framework of his employment relationship at Hotelbeds. All rights reserved.

36 Chesbrough, Henry. 2020. Open Innovation Community. 31 Dec. Accessed December 31, 2020. http://openinnovation.net/about-2/open-innovation-definition/.

37 Chesbrough, Henry. 2003. *Open Innovation: The New Imperative for Creating and Profiting from Technology*. Brighton, MA: Harvard Business Review Press.

38 Chesbrough, Henry. 2021. "Open Innovation." Courtesy of Henry Chesbrough. 12 July.

39 Chesbrough, Henry. 2021. "Open Innovation." Courtesy of Henry Chesbrough. 12 July.

40 Ringel, Michael. 2015. The Most Innovative Companies. 02 Dec. The Most Innovative Companies 2015—Greg Garrison Graphic. Accessed Dec. 31, 2020. https://www .bcg.com/publications/2015/growth-lean-manufacturing-innovation-in-2015.

41 Garrison, Greg / Hotelbeds. 2021. Innovation Strategy. Palma Mallorca, Spain: Graphic developed by Greg Garrison within the framework of his employment relationship at Hotelbeds. All rights reserved.

42 Garrison, Greg / Hotelbeds. 2021. Innovation Strategy. Palma Mallorca, Spain: Graphic developed by Greg Garrison within the framework of his employment relationship at Hotelbeds. All rights reserved.

43 Garrison, Greg / Hotelbeds. 2021. Innovation Strategy. Palma Mallorca, Spain: Graphic developed by Greg Garrison within the framework of his employment relationship at Hotelbeds. All rights reserved.

44 Toyota. 2021. Toyota Production System. Accessed June 20, 2021. https://global .toyota/en/company/vision-and-philosophy/production-system/.

45 Straker, David. 2020. "Creating Minds, How to Create Anything." 21 April. Accessed April 18, 2020. http://creatingminds.org/.

46 Straker, David. 2020. "Creating Minds, How to Create Anything." 21 April. Accessed April 18, 2020. http://creatingminds.org/.

47 Garrison, Greg / Hotelbeds. 2021. Innovation Strategy. Palma Mallorca, Spain: Graphic developed by Greg Garrison within the framework of his employment relationship at Hotelbeds. All rights reserved.

48 Garrison, Greg / Hotelbeds. 2021. Innovation Strategy. Palma Mallorca, Spain: Graphic developed by Greg Garrison within the framework of his employment relationship at Hotelbeds. All rights reserved.

49 Kim, W. Chan, and Mauborgne, Renee A. 2015. Blue Ocean Strategy. Brighton, MA: Harvard Business Review Press.

50 Garrison, Greg / Hotelbeds. 2021. Innovation Strategy. Palma Mallorca, Spain: Graphic developed by Greg Garrison within the framework of his employment relationship at Hotelbeds. All rights reserved.

51 Garrison, Greg / Hotelbeds. 2021. Innovation Strategy. Palma Mallorca, Spain: Graphic developed by Greg Garrison within the framework of his employment relationship at Hotelbeds. All rights reserved.

52 Edison, Thomas, and Daum, Kevin. 2016 11 February. Accessed January 4, 2021. https://www.inc.com/kevin-daum/37-quotes-from-thomas-edison-that-will-bring-out-your-best.html.

Chapter 2

1   Handy, Charles. 2009. *Gods of Management*. London, UK: Souvenir Press.

2   The Harris Poll. 2021. May 13, 2021. Accessed February 22, 2022. https://theharrispoll.com/axios-harris-poll-100-release-2021/.

3   Moultrie, James. 2016. Design Management—Belbin's team roles. Accessed June 20, 2021. https://www.ifm.eng.cam.ac.uk/research/dmg/toolsandtechniques/belbins-team-roles/.

4   Bohm, David. 2021. "Difficult Dialogues—What is dialogue?" Clark University. Accessed October 03, 2021. http://www2.clarku.edu/difficultdialogues/learn/index.cfm.

5   Senge, Peter M. 2006. *The Fifth Discipline: The Art & Practice of the Learning Organization*. New York: Doubleday.

6   Butler-Bowdon, Tom. 2018. "50 Business Classics." Robert Townsend, page 349. London, UK: Nicholas Brealey Publishing.

7   Matuson, Roberta. 2017. You're Kidding, Right? 50% of New Hires Fail. 14 April. Accessed December 11, 2021. https://www.linkedin.com/pulse/youre-kidding-right-50-new-hires-fail-roberta-chinsky-matuson/.

8   Doran, George. 1981. "There's a S.M.A.R.T. Way to Write Management's Goals and Objectives." *Management Review* 70, Edition 11, pp 35–36.

9   Lakein, Alan. 1996. *How to Get Control of Your Time and Your Life*. Kolkata, India: Signet.

10 Blanchard, Ken, and Johnson, Spencer. 1982. *The One Minute Manager*. New York: William Morrow & Co, Inc.

11 Guardian. 2000. "People were walking out with i-Macs under their arms." 17 July. Accessed December 12, 2021. https://www.theguardian.com/media/2000/jul/17 /newmedia.mondaymediasection4.

12 Badaracco, Joseph. 2002. *Leading Quietly*. Boston: Harvard Business Review Press.

13 Lakein, Alan. 1996. *How to Get Control of Your Time and Your Life*. Kolkata, India: Signet.

14 Butler-Bowdon, Tom. 2018. "50 Business Classics." Robert Townsend, Page 348. London, UK: Nicholas Brealey Publishing.

15 Covey, Stephen. 2004. *7 Habits of Highly Effective People*. New York: Simon & Schuster.

16 Garrison, Greg. 2010. Time and Activity Prioritization. Presentation, London, Palma: Hudson-Garrison.

17 Garrison, Greg. 2010. Time and Activity Prioritization. Presentation, London, Palma: Hudson-Garrison.

18 Garrison, Greg. 2010. Time and Activity Prioritization. Presentation, London, Palma: Hudson-Garrison.

19 Garrison, Greg. 2010. Time and Activity Prioritization. Presentation, London, Palma: Hudson-Garrison.

20 Garrison, Greg. 2010. Time and Activity Prioritization. Presentation, London, Palma: Hudson-Garrison.

21 Garrison, Greg. 2010. Time and Activity Prioritization. Presentation, London, Palma: Hudson-Garrison.

22 Garrison, Greg. 2010. Time and Activity Prioritization. Presentation, London, Palma: Hudson-Garrison.

23 Garrison, Greg. 2010. Time and Activity Prioritization. Presentation, London, Palma: Hudson-Garrison.

24 McKay, Brett, and McKay, Kate. 2013. The Eisenhower Decision Matrix: How to Distinguish Between Urgent and Important Tasks. 23 October. Accessed June 20, 2021.https://www.artofmanliness.com/articles/eisenhower-decision-matrix/.

25 Oshin, Mayo. 2018. The Eisenhower matrix: How to decide on what's important and urgent. 4 June. Accessed June 20, 2021. https://www.theladders.com /career-advice/the-eisenhower-matrix-how-to-decide-on-whats-important-and -urgent-without-a-to-do-list.

26 Pareto, Vilfredo. 2021. Vilfredo_Pareto. 29 July. Accessed August 22, 2021. https://en.wikipedia.org/wiki/Vilfredo_Pareto.

27 Kruse, Kevin. 2016. The 80/20 Rule And How It Can Change Your Life. 7 March. Accessed August 22, 2021. https://www.forbes.com/sites/kevinkruse /2016/03/07/80–20-rule/?sh=213fa863814b.

28 Klatt, Bruce—original Maslow, Abraham H. 1999, 1968. *Toward a Psychology of Being*. New York: D. Van Nostrand Company.

29 Crosby, Philip B. 1979. *Quality Is Free*. New York: McGraw-Hill.

30 Imai, Masaaki. 1986. Kaizen (Ky'zen), the key to Japan's competitive success. New York: Random House Business Division. Accessed December 27, 2020. https: //en.wikipedia.org/wiki/Kaizen.

31 Imai, Masaaki. 1986. Kaizen (Ky'zen), the key to Japan's competitive success. New York: Random House Business Division. Accessed December 27, 2020. https://en.wikipedia.org/wiki/Kaizen.

32 Garrison, Greg. 2008. "Kaizen vs Continuous Improvement." London, January.

33 Ohno, Taiichi. 1988. Toyota Production System: Beyond Large-Scale Production. New York: Productivity Press. Accessed December 27, 2020. https://en.wikipedia.org/wiki/Kanban_(development).

34 iSixSigma-Editorial. 2021. WHAT IS SIX SIGMA? Access May 24, 2021. https://www.isixsigma.com/new-to-six-sigma/getting-started/what-six-sigma/#:~:text=Six%20Sigma%20is%20a%20disciplined,and%20from%20product%20to%20service.

35 Kepner, Charles H., and Tregoe, Benjamin B. 1981. *The New Rational Manager: An Abbreviated Use of Problem Analysis*, 64–67. Princeton Research Press, Princeton N.J. Accessed Dec. 12, 2021. https://www.kepner-tregoe.fr/linkservid/1BA87498-AD75–4EA4-A7403BAFE518296C/showMeta/0/.

36 Kepner, Charles H., and Tregoe, Benjamin B. 2020. Kepner Tregoe Problem Solving and Decision Making. Accessed December 31. https://www.kepner-tregoe.com/training-workshops/our-workshops/problem-solving-decision-making/.

37 Kepner-Tregoe. 2014. Problem Solving & Decision Making Processes. Accessed June 20, 2021. http://www.kepnertregoe.com/default/assets/File/PSDM_Tech_Broch_Final%202014.pdf.

38 Kepner-Tregoe. 2021. "KT Troubleshooting Methodology." Kepner-Tregoe.com. 23 December 2021. Courtesy Phillip A. Thompson. Kepner-Tregoe Inc.

39 Drucker, Peter. British Library—Peter Drucker. Accessed August 25, 2021. https://www.bl.uk/people/peter-drucker.

40 Solheim, Eirik. 2009. Daniel Kahneman WikiMedia Commons. 27 January. Accessed May 6, 2021.https://commons.wikimedia.org/wiki/File:Daniel_Kahneman_(3283955327)_(cropped).jpg.

41 Kahneman, Daniel. 1994. *Thinking, Fast and Slow*. New York: Farrar Straus & Giroux.

42 Gladwell, Malcolm. 2011. *Outliers: The Story of Success*. New York: Back Bay Books.

43 Rand Corporation—Objective Analysis—Effective Solutions. 2020. Accessed December 31, 2020. https://www.rand.org/topics/delphi-method.html.

44 Lencioni, Patrick. 2002. The Five Dysfunctions of a Team. 18 April. Accessed August 22, 2021. https://highlights.sawyerh.com/highlights/wHGYXdyRYkB23i phRpT5.

Chapter 3

1 Blanchard, Ken, and Johnson, Spencer. 1982. *One Minute Manager*. New York: William Morrow & Co, Inc.

2 Belbin, Meredith. 2020. "The Nine Belbin Team Roles." 30 December. Accessed December 30, 2020. https://www.belbin.com/about/belbin-team-roles/.

3   Newport, Cal. 2022. "What Hunter-Gatherers Can Teach Us About the Frustrations of Modern Work." *New Yorker*. 02 November. Accessed November 07, 2022. https://www.newyorker.com/culture/office-space/lessons-from-the-deep-history-of-work.

4   Mortensen, Mark. 2020. The Three Main Challenges of Remote Working." 27 March. Accessed Jan. 19, 2021. https://knowledge.insead.edu/leadership-organisations/the-three-main-challenges-of-remote-working-13651.

5   Maciariello, Joe. Joe's Journal: On Creating the Future. 2011, 24 March. ed March 30, 2023. https://www.drucker.institute/thedx/joes-journal-on-creating-the-future/.

Chapter 4

1   Peters, Tom. 1994. "Virtual Teams: Here Today, Gone Tomorrow." *On Achieving Excellence* 1–7.

2   Garrison, Greg. 1997. "The Usability Group Virtual Team." Caricature.

Chapter 5

1   Fisher, Roger, and Ury, William. 1981. *Getting to Yes*. New York: Penguin Group.

2   Gordian Knot. 2021 February. Accessed March 24, 2021. https://en.wikipedia.org/wiki/Gordian_Knot.

Appendix

1   Garrison, Greg / Hotelbeds. 2021. Innovation Strategy. Palma Mallorca, Spain: Graphic developed by Greg Garrison within the framework of his employment relationship at Hotelbeds. All rights reserved.

2   Garrison, Greg / Hotelbeds. 2021. Innovation Strategy. Palma Mallorca, Spain: Graphic developed by Greg Garrison within the framework of his employment relationship at Hotelbeds. All rights reserved.

3   Garrison, Greg / Hotelbeds. 2021. Innovation Strategy. Palma Mallorca, Spain: Graphic developed by Greg Garrison within the framework of his employment relationship at Hotelbeds. All rights reserved.

4   Garrison, Greg / Hotelbeds. 2021. Innovation Strategy. Palma Mallorca, Spain: Graphic developed by Greg Garrison within the framework of his employment relationship at Hotelbeds. All rights reserved.

5   Garrison, Greg / Hotelbeds. 2021. Innovation Strategy. Palma Mallorca, Spain: Graphic developed by Greg Garrison within the framework of his employment relationship at Hotelbeds. All rights reserved.

6   Garrison, Greg / Hotelbeds. 2021. Innovation Strategy. Palma Mallorca, Spain: Graphic developed by Greg Garrison within the framework of his employment relationship at Hotelbeds. All rights reserved.

7   Garrison, Greg / Hotelbeds. 2021. Innovation Strategy. Palma Mallorca, Spain: Graphic developed by Greg Garrison within the framework of his employment relationship at Hotelbeds. All rights reserved.

8   Garrison, Greg / Hotelbeds. 2021. Innovation Strategy. Palma Mallorca, Spain: Graphic developed by Greg Garrison within the framework of his employment relationship at Hotelbeds. All rights reserved.

Index